FORTY YEARS IN THE MORMON CHURCH

WHY I LEFT IT!

BY
BISHOP R. C. EVANS
TORONTO, CANADA

Copyright 1976

By Lambert Book House, Inc.

LAMBERT BOOK HOUSE, INC.
Box 4007
Shreveport, Louisiana 71104

ISBN 0-89315-054-1

R. C. Evans

Introduction

JAMES D. BALES

The vast majority of books which have been written on Mormonism deal with the Church of Jesus Christ of Latter-Day Saints which has its headquarters in Salt Lake City. R. C. Evans' book is unique in that he was at one time one of the highest officials in the Reorganized Church and his book furnishes us with more information on the Reorganized Church than do most books. As far as I know, he is the highest official in that Church to have left it and to have written a book which deals with some of his experiences in that Church.

This valuable book has long been out of print and I have been unable to locate any more copies.

One understands the strong language which Mr. Evans sometimes uses when one realizes that he devoted decades of his life to that which turned out to be a fraud, and that the Reorganized Church involved him in a lawsuit after he left that Church. It is my conviction that in dealing with Mormons, one should not start with an attack on the character of Joseph Smith, Jr. They consider him to be one of the greatest, if not the greatest, of the prophets of God. Some of them have viewed Joseph Smith, Jr. as being next to Jesus Christ Himself in importance. An attack on Smith's character immediately raises barriers. Furthermore, they point out that David did wrong. Although one can show that the life, teaching, and deeds of Joseph Smith, Jr. show that he was not a true prophet of God, one can show that Mormonism is not of God without dealing with the character of Joseph Smith, Jr. When I have shown from various lines of argument and evidences that Mormonism is false, I can then discuss the character of Joseph Smith, Jr. and show that he founded a religion which satisfied, in so far as such desires can be satisfied, his lusts for power, money, and women. When dealing with others we must take their feelings into consideration and avoid, in so far as it is possible, unnecessarily antagonizing them.

When R. C. Evans left the Reorganized Church, he established, in cooperation with others, The Church of the Christian Brotherhood. In a pamphlet published by R. C. Evans after he left Mormonism, called "Mormonism or Latter Day Saintism", there is a picture of the church building and it is there called the "Church of Jesus Christ". Although Evans repudiated Mormonism, he still believed in modern revelations. However, his book gives evidence against Mormonism, which does not depend on modern "revelations" for its validity.

In the fall of 1942 in Berkeley, California a member of the Reorganized Church told me that R. C. Evans recanted on his death bed and returned to the Reorganized Church. He had not done so. I am reproducing the letters which were written to me by R. C. Evans' son, and by another member of Evans' church.

I purchased most of the books on Mormonism which R. C. Evans had in his library. Included in these was volume one of *The True Latter Day Saints' Herald.*

I have included material which shows that after he left Mormonism, and some time after he wrote his *Defence,* Oliver Cowdery associated himself with the Methodist Church.

Additional Material

James D. Bales, *The Book Of Mormon?* It is my hope that this book will be republished soon.

Brodie Crouch, *The Myth of Mormon Inspiration,* Shreveport, Louisiana 71104, Lambert Book House, P. O. Box 4007.

Jack Free, *Mormonism and Inspiration,* Concord, California: Pacific Publishing Co., 1962.

Modern Microfilm Co., Box 1884, Salt Lake City, Utah, 84110. Jerald and Sandra Tanner have republished many of the old and rare books published by Mormons during the first decades of the existence of the Church of Jesus Christ of Latter Day Saints. They have also written extensively on the subject as well as published some new discoveries made by them and by other researchers in the field of Mormonism. Write them for a list of their publications and for their newsletter.

David Whitmer, *An Address To All Believers In Christ.* I have reprinted this important document from a copy of the original edition which was published in 1887. Although I reprinted the book by photo-offset, I wrote a Preface to it and made an index to some of the important subjects in the book.

For my discussion of the fulfillment of the prophecy of Daniel in the establishment of the kingdom of Christ, see James D. Bales, *The Kingdom: Prophesied and Established.* Evans' discussion is found on pp. 163-167 of his book.

James D. Bales, Searcy, Arkansas 72143. November 16, 1975.

CONTENTS

CHAPTER I.

MORMONISM—ITS EARLY HISTORY

	Page
My Childish Faith	5
My First Doubt	6
History of the Book of Mormon	7
Willard Chase	9
Isaac Hale	9
William Stafford	10
Z. H. Gurley	10
The Gold Plates	12
Translation Perfect	13
Copied from the Bible	15
Early History of America	17
Spaulding Manuscript	18
The Witnesses Leave the Church	24

CHAPTER II.

WAS JOSEPH SMITH A POLYGAMIST?

Brief History of Joseph Smith	27
Churches All Wrong	27
Book of Abraham	28
Smith Vile, Yet Prophet of God	29
Was Joseph Smith Immoral?	31
Polygamy	32
Testimony of His Wife, Son and Others	34
Three Witnesses	37
Polygamy, Revelation of 1843	46
The Last Straw	55
The Doctrine of Many Gods	56

CHAPTER III

MORMONISM AGAINST THE WORLD

There are but Two Churches	61
God and Christ Visit Smith	62
Reorganized Church Deny God and Christ Appeared	62
John the Baptist Ordained Smith	63
Peter, James and John Ordain	63
Cowdery on Angelic Ordination	64
Holy Ghost before Confirmation	64
Smith and Cowdery Baptize Each Other	65
Smith and Cowdery Ordain Each Other	65
Cowdery, Pratt and Smith on Ordination	65
Young Joseph Denies Peter, James and John Ordination	66
Called by Revelation	66
Not Called by God	66
Apostles Led Church into Sin	67

CHAPTER IV.

HISTORY OF REORGANIZED CHURCH

J. W. Briggs, Polygamy, Apostasy	68
William Marks, Polygamy, Ordination	69
Z. H. Gurley, Polygamy, Digging for Lead	70
W. W. Blair, Baptism, Ordination, Polygamy	71
Samuel Powers, Ordination	72
Joseph Smith the Second	73
Joseph Not Appointed by Revelation	74
Joseph, No Evidence for Fifteen Years	75
Joseph, Head of Mormon Church	75
Joseph, Right of Lineage	76
F. M. Smith's Call	77
Reorganized Apostles Deny Revelations	80
Bishop McGuire's Call	80

CHAPTER V.

PROPER NAME OF CHURCH

Are They Mormons?	82
Baptism for Dead	85
Three Witnesses—Character	89
Sidney Rigdon on Smith	91
William Law	91
Lyman E. Johnson	92
Orson Hyde	92
William Smith	92
J. C. Bennett	92
Warren Parrish	93
Bishop Corril	93
Missouri Army	93
Nauvoo House	94
Christ Coming	94
Slavery Advocated by Smith	94
Prophecy on Rebellion	95
Temperance	96

CONTENTS

CHAPTER VI.
BOOK OF ABRAHAM
	Page
Plurality of Gods	98
Danites	101
Blood Atonement	105
All Churches Corrupt	107
No Salvation Outside Book of Mormon	109
Holy Scriptures Translated by Smith	110

CHAPTER VII.
UNITED STATES VS. MORMON CHURCH
Smith Organized a Kingdom—Destroy All Nations...114
United States to be Destroyed...119
Missouri Sink to Hell...120
Smith Ordained King...120
Printing Press Destroyed...121
Smith Arrested for Treason...122
Smith Like Christ...123
Smith Called for Pipe, Tobacco and Wine...123
Smith Killed Two Men—Last Act...123

CHAPTER VIII.
BOOK OF COMMANDMENTS
Book Complete, and Sold...126
Revelations Changed...128
Cowdery—Gift of the Rod...128
Smith's First and Greatest Revelation Not Published in B.C. or D.C...129
Book of Doctrine and Covenants...130
Revelations Added to...130
Revelations—How Received...131
Revelations—Smith Only One to Receive...131
God Wrote Preface of Book...132
Peter, James, John Ordained...134
Re-Organized Prophet's Revelation...135
Young Joseph Not Trusted with Money...136
Revelation on R. C. Evans and Fred. Smith...137
Luff to be Apostle and Doctor...138
Luff Not to be Apostle and Doctor...138
Fred's False Revelation Regarding Bishop...139
False Revelation, Rejected and Corrected...141
Leading Men Denounce Revelation...143
Leading Men Left the Church...144

CHAPTER IX.
ORDER OF ENOCH
	Page
History and Demands of the Order	145
Deed All Property	145
Order of Enoch Organized	146
Order of Enoch Described	146
Secret Names given	146
All Must Join the Order	147
No Salvation Out of Order	147
Young Joseph Not Trusted by the Lord	147
Revelation Shows Church Robbed the People	149
The Questionaire	149
Robs Man of His Liberty	150

CHAPTER X.
ALLEGED PROOFS THAT BOOK OF MORMON IS OF DIVINE AUTHENTICITY.
Claims to Come From God...151
Claims to Contain Fullness of Gospel...151
Claims to Convince Jew and Gentile Jesus is Christ...151
The Witnesses Examined...152
Claims to be History of Ancient America...153
Bible Prophets Examined...153
Smith, Harris, vs. Authon and Mitchell...154

CHAPTER XI.
PRIESTHOOD
No Salvation Outside of Mormon Priesthood...158
John Baptist Ordains Smith an Aaronic Priest...159
The Work of the Aaronic Priest...160
Aaronic Priesthood Abolished in Christ...161

CHAPTER XII.
NEBUCHADNEZZAR'S DREAM— DANIEL'S VISION
Deception of Mormonism in Days and Years...164
Evans Dragged Into Court...167
The Law-Suit...168
Bishop Evans' Challenge to President Smith...170

PREFACE

"FORTY YEARS IN THE MORMON CHURCH."

My reasons for presenting this little volume to the public are:—

First, that because my sermons have gone over the world for many years, millions of them have been published by the Canadian and American press, and the church has constantly advertised them, the consciousness that the world has the right to know from me, why I have left the church, advises me to present the facts.

Second, many books have been published by those who knew nothing of the inner workings of Mormonism. I have endeavored to give the true history of Mormonism, quoting very largely from their own works, and bringing into prominence the teaching of the Prophets, Seers and Revelators and other leading ministers.

Third, having been ordained to seven different offices in the Mormon Priesthood, from Priest to the Presidency of the church, standing next to Joseph Smith himself in the Highest Council of the church, the world will be interested to read the facts from one who has escaped from the Mormon thraldom.

Fourth, notwithstanding the cruel treatment that has been inflicted upon me by the leaders of the church from the moment they knew that I had determined to warn the world, I have tried to keep my heart from bitterness, but have, in this little volume, endeavored to show that Mormonism is the lying wonder of the Latter Days, with the hope that the honest in heart, now under the yoke of bondage will, like tens of thousands before them, make their escape and find peace and joy in the gospel of Christ as revealed in the Bible.

My earnest prayer for the many honest people of the church is, that they will abandon Joseph Smith, the Book of Mormon, the Book of Abraham, the Book of Doctrine and Covenants, the Book of Commandments, and all the other fraudulent works of Mormonism and embrace Christ and the gospel as presented in the Word of God.

MORMONISM—ITS EARLY HISTORY

The Reorganized "Mormon Church" does not teach or practice polygamy. Their great sin is in denying that Joseph Smith, their prophet, seer and revelator, received revelations commanding the church to enter into that God dishonoring and woman debasing doctrine under pain of eternal damnation, in denying that he taught, practiced and advocated it, privately, while he denied it publicly.

If human evidence is to be relied upon, then this book proves that the leading presidents, apostles, bishops, high priests, including the celebrated "Three Witnesses," as also many of Smith's own relatives declare that he had revelations commanding the church to enter into the practice of polygamy, and tens of thousands certify that they had many wives in consequence of his example and commandments.

When these testimonies were confirmed unto me, then I could no longer believe that God and Christ visited and conversed with Smith, that John the Baptist and Peter, James and John ordained him to the priesthood and that many other heavenly personages visited him, and I finally, under the blessing of God, came out to tell the world the facts.

Yours sincerely,

R. C. Evans

Toronto, Ontario,
Feb. 12th, 1920.

CHAPTER I,

Mormonism---Its Early History

My Childhood Faith

I first heard the Mormons or Latter Day Saints preach in the City of London, Canada, when but a child. My parents joined the church, I was baptized and from that hour became an earnest worker in the Sunday school and church, I was sincere, though very ignorant, having never mastered the multiplication tables in school, and could read and write with difficulty, but studied hard and was soon ushered into the Priesthood of the church, being ordained a Priest in 1882, Elder in 1884, Seventy in 1886, Apostle in 1897, a High Priest in 1897, in 1902 I was ordained Counselor to the Prophet Joseph Smith, thus holding the highest honor ever conferred on any man in the church under the prophet. I tendered my resignation from this position in 1907, but the Prophet declined to accept it and I remained in that position until 1909, when the Prophet said the Lord revealed to him that I should be released from that office, showing clearly that it was because of my continued petitions for release and saying in so many words **"He has been earnest and faithful in service and his reward is sure."** D. C. 129, 1.

The conference accepted this commendation as from the lips of the Lord, whereupon the Prophet stated that the Lord had shown him that I should be ordained a Bishop, the Presiding Bishop stated that he had seen me in a blaze of glory acting as Bishop of the church. I believed all this and was the same hour ordained a Bishop and placed in charge of the work in Canada.

I have been careful to make the above statements for two reasons: First, to show that I was in earnest and that the people so regarded me, and that I have been honored with seven different ordinations, going from the lower to the higher rungs of the ladder of Priesthood, an honor that no other man living in Mormonism ever enjoyed, if it is an honor; and second, to show that in all those years I was considered by them, fit for such positions, and if there is any faith left in them concerning their prophet and his revelations, this fact must be admitted by them and thus is disproved the maliciousness and cruelty of their base slanders against me, both from the pulpit and the press, since I left their church and denounced their corruption and superstition, as a fraud.

Receiving Mormonism in my childish ignorance, I followed on with a zeal that was admired by them all, every prominence possible was accorded me and my faith was such for many years that I sacrificed everything in life at the shrine of that monstrous deception, when books and papers were placed in my hands against the church, I was so completely grounded in the faith that while I read, it was only to fit myself to fight anything that was presented against it, so the years drifted away, I preaching in most every province of the Dominion of Canada, many parts of the United States, and the leading cities of the British Isles.

My First Doubt

The time came in the mercy of God, that evidence was presented to me that gave my faith a shock, it is not the first drop of water that drowns a person, nor the first straw that breaks the camel's back, but drop by drop, the water came upon me, until I found myself overwhelmed by the waves of truth and the last straw broke down my last effort of resistance, and I became convinced that the man Joseph Smith, whom I almost worshipped as God's prophet, seer, revelator, translator, mouthpiece and chief representative on earth, was an adulterer, liar, imposter, deceiver, false prophet and polygamist. This conclusion arrived at, my faith in his revelations found in the Book of Mormon, the Book of Abraham, the Doctrine and Covenants was shaken, and I began to investigate, until I found all to be a delusion and a snare, his inspired translation of the sacred scriptures I found to be a mess of infidelity, largely borrowed from the criticisms made upon the sacred book by such men as Thomas Pain and others who have wasted talent in finding fault with the Bible, the fruits of Joseph Smith's deception is found in the intrigue, deception and false revelations of the re-organization, and in the concubinage and polygamy of Brigamism, Strangeisms, and other branches of the Mormon church which is a withering blight to the morality of the world, to say nothing of the ethical teaching of pure christianity.

Joseph Smith was born of superstitious, lazy, shiftless parents, if there is any credence to be placed on human testimony, were I to submit the sworn affidavits of their neighbors as printed in many books, they were just such parents as would produce such a rascal as the combined history of the times and his own works represent him to have been.

Born in 1805, he professed to have been converted in his fifteenth year and when offering his first vocal prayer, under a tree, he tells us that God came from heaven, introduced Christ to him and that Christ told him, "Not to join any church, for the churches were all wrong. The creeds all an abomination and the professors were all corrupt, they who professed to worship in those churches were drawing near God with their lips, while their hearts were far from Him." Ch. His. Vol. 1, page 10.

In a word, Joseph's information from Christ was to the effect that the world of Christianity was a conglomerated mass of deception and hypocrisy from the priest and parson in the pulpit, to the mother, who in the dimming twilight and evening shadows, called her children to her side to teach them "Gentle Jesus meek and mild," was one huge system of hypocrisy.

His own history shows that this vision did not make any moral change in his life, for while his neighbors charge him with most every sin, he is frank to confess that he "displayed the corruption of human nature which led him into divers temptations to the gratification of many appetites." Ch. His. Vol. 1, page 12.

History of The Book of Mormon.

We are asked to believe that, notwithstanding all this, God sent an angel to him, and repeated his visit three times in one night, and that under instructions of this angel he went to a hill and dug up a "Golden Bible" (for that was the name they gave the book of Mormon), with it the Urim and Thummim, to interpret it with, and some other things. This Golden Bible, or Book of Mormon, is the foundation of the Mormon church. Smith said it was "the keystone of our religion." This book claims to be a history of two distinct peoples who lived upon the continent of America, the Jaredites and Nephites, it covers a period of about twenty-six centuries, the Jaredites came from the Tower of Babel, the Nephites from Jerusalem, the first people became a mighty people and finally fought among themselves until they were destroyed all but one man who was found by the other folk. The second colony became very numerous and they fought till their prophets hid their records (made on gold or brass plates) in a Hill in the State of New York, then this prophet tells us, all the good people are killed and he is alone and he buries the plates and the angel delivers them to Joseph Smith in 1827.

Joseph Smith and his people have contradicted themselves and each other as to the finding and translating this golden Bible, that it is safe to say that no two writers agree regarding the matter. We could fill a volume but will content ourselves by pointing a few of the hundreds of contradictions regarding the book.

We are requested to believe that God raised up these people to write on those metallic plates, beginning long before Abraham was born, and that the plates were made and filled with their history and they traveled from the Plains of Shinar over the ocean and all over America with their plates, then the other colony found them. The second colony start out with Nephi killing Labanm stealing a bundle of metallic plates that gave the history of the world as contained in the five books of Moses and of the books of the prophets down to Jeremiah, this young fellow Nephi kills Laban, steals the plates, steals Laban's clothes, steals his great sword and his breast-plate and makes a prisoner of Laban's servant, then escapes out of Jerusalem and joins his parents and brethren and they travel through the wilderness and not only drag along with all these brass plates, but in the wilderness they make more plates and engrave upon them their history.

Thus the book of Mormon starts out with lying, deception, robbery, murder and slavery, and the fellow who did all this was but a lad, from time to time for many hundreds of years they travel on until they become great nations and fill America with people, they make plates galore until we have tons of plates and finally one named Mormon makes an abridgement of all these plates, and hides them up and then his boy Moroni has a few plates and he writes seventy-seven pages on plates and hides them up in 420 A. D. in a hill in New York State, and in about fifteen hundred years after, he makes the acquaintance of Joseph Smith and shows him the plates and breast plate of Laban, and the Urim and Thummim and Joseph gets to work to translate them for the salvation of the world, and calls it THE BOOK OF MORMON.

Now let us read the conflicting testimonies concerning the manner of the translation of the plates:

"The Book of Mormon tells us that the interpreters, or Urim and Thummim, were prepared by God for the purpose of translating the book. They are described as being two stones in silver bows and these stones fastened to a breast-plate was the Urim and Thummim. See Book of Mormon, page 29, and Ch. His. Vol. 1, page 13. Others describe them as a large pair of spects. The Book of Mormon shows that Jared had them 2230 B. C., then we are told Moses and Aaron had them 1606 B.C., Lehi had them 600 B.C., Moroni had them 420 A.D. and Abraham had them to study the stars. So states the Book of Mormon, and the Book of Abraham, Mill. Star, Vol. 6."

Now while Joseph claims he received these wonderful spectacles for the express purpose of translating the language found on the plates into the English of the Book of Mormon, yet many of his own people show that he had a peep stone which he used in place of the Urim and Thummim. Thus God prepared these stones and preserved them for thousands of years to translate the plates with, and Joseph found a better way.

"Joseph Smith would put the seer stone into his hat and put his face in the hat drawing it closely around his face to exclude the light, and in the darkness the spiritual light would shine, a piece of something resembling parchment would appear and on that would appear the writing. One character at a time would appear and under it was the interpretation in English. Joseph would read off the English to Oliver—when it was written down and repeated to Joseph to see if it was correct, when it would disappear and another character would appear, thus the Book of Mormon was translated by the power of God." Whitmer address. p. 30.

"After the translation of the Book of Mormon was finished early in the spring of 1830 Joseph gave the stone to Oliver and told me, as well as others, that he was through with it, and he did not use the stone any more." Whitmer address, p. 32

"Martin Harris said: "That the Prophet possessed a seer stone which he was able to translate with as well as from the Urim and Thummim, and for convenience he then used the seer stone,—by the aid of the seer stone sentences would appear and were read by the prophet and written by Martin Harris, and when finished he would say "Written" and if correctly written that sentence would disappear and another appear in its place, but if not correctly written it remained until corrected, so that the translation was just as it was engraven on the plates, precisely in the language then used 'Myth' of Manuscript Found, p. 91."

Emma Smith testifies: "In writing for your father, I frequently wrote day after day, often sitting at the table close by him, he sitting with his face buried in his hat with the stone in it, and dictating hour after hour with nothing between us—he had neither manuscript or book to read from—the plates often lay on the table without any attempt at concealment, wrapped in a small linen table cloth which I had given him to fold them in." Tulledge, p. 793.

Joseph and others claim that when he had finished the translation he gave the plates and the Urim and Thummim to the angel who kindly called for them, but this story is contradicted by himself when he claimed to have them in 1835 to translate the Book of Arbaham with, see his mother's history, p. 149, Tulledge, p. 30, Mill Star, Vol. 3, p. 49. Now, let us expose all these contradicting and silly fasehoods.

Affidavit of Willard Chase.

"In the year of 1822, I was engaged in digging a well, I employed Alvin and Joseph Smith to assist me, after digging about twenty feet below the surface of the earth we discovered a singularly appearing stone. I brought it to the top of the well, and as we examined it, Joseph put it in his hat and then hid his face in his hat—the next morning he came to me and wished to obtain the stone he said he could see things through it. I told him I did not wish to part with it, but would lend it to him. He had the stone for about two years. He published that he could see things through it. I ordered him to return it and he did so, but some time after Hyrum came and borrowed it and promised to return it. In 1827, after Joseph had obtained the plates he told me that if it had not been for that stone (which he acknowledged belonged to me) he would not have obtained the plates. In April, 1830, I asked Hyrum for the stone, he told me I could not have it as Joseph used it to translate his Bible with. Harris and him abused me and I never received the stone." Sworn before Fred Smith, J. P., Dec. 11th, 1833, origin of Book of Mormons, by Shook, p. 22-28.

Affidavit of Isaac Hale, Father-in-law of Smith.

"I first became acquainted with Joseph Smith in Nov., 1825, he was at that time in the employ of some men who were called money diggers, and his occupation was of seeing or pretending to see by means of a stone, placed in his hat over his face, in this way he pretended to discover minerals and hidden treasures. Smith and his father and some other men, all money diggers, boarded at my house. Smith gave the diggers much encouragement but they left and never paid their board bill—while I was absent from home Smith ran off with my daughter Emma and married her. Smith stated to me that he had given up what he called glass looking and was now willing to work hard for a living. I took Emma and Joseph in to board with us. While there, he started to translate the plates—the manner in which he pretended to read and interpret **was done the same as when he looked for the money diggers with the stone in his hat and his hat over his face,** while the book of plates were at the same time hid in the woods." Affirmed before me, March 20th, 1834, C. Dimon, J. P., Ibid, p. 31-32.

Affidavit of William Stafford.

"I became acquainted with Joseph Smith and his family in the year 1820. They lived in Palmyra about one mile and a half from my house. A great part of their time was devoted to digging for money, I have heard them tell marvellous tales respecting the discovery of money—for instance, that at such a place on a certain man's farm there was deposited kegs, barrels and hogsheads of coined silver and gold, bars of gold and golden images, kettles filled with gold and silver, gold candlesticks and swords. Joseph said he could see by **placing a stone** of singular appearance **in his hat** in such a manner as to exclude all the light at which time he **pretended that he could see things within and under the earth.** Joseph came to me one night, told me that his son Joseph had been looking in his glass and had seen not many rods from his home, two or three kegs of gold and silver, some feet under the surface of the earth, and that none other than Joseph Sr. and myself could get them. We dug and Joseph went to the house to enquire the cause of our disappointment. He returned and said that Joseph had remained all the time in the house looking in the stone and watching the movements of the evil spirits—that he saw the spirits come up to the ring that we had dug, and they caused the money to sink—he said that we had made a mistake and that was the reason that the spirits were permitted to sink the money so we could not get it." Given under oath before Judge Th. P. Baldwin, Dec., 1833, Ibid. 28-31.

Z. H. Gurley.

We have learned that Joseph Smith secured the Peep Stone, found in the Chase well, with which he went about claiming to find gold and silver by looking through the stone placed in his hat, and with the stone he claims to have discovered the plates, as stated by Chase, and that by the Stone he claims to have translated the Gold plates of the Book of Mormon, and to show you that looking for hidden treasure did not stop when the Book of Mormon was published, it is clearly announced in the church papers and elsewhere that Smith led a party to Salem, Mass., in the year 1836 (long after the church was organized), to hunt for hidden treasures. They failed, but nothing daunted, Joseph had a revelation promising that "all the gold and silver under Salem would be found by them." For full history of this deception read Mill Star, Vol. 51, p. 822; Z. H. Gurley Tract, p. 3.

And to show that the reorganization is hypocritical in writing history, be it known that the same revelation that came through Julia Gurley stating that young Joseph was the legal successor to his father as president of the church, also directed her father and others to dig for lead ore in Wisconsin. "In the name of God it is here." But it was not there. Then they were commanded to dig "three feet to the north." They failed. Then the word of the Lord came again, "dig fifteen feet to the north." Many of their revelations were on finding lead in Wisconsin, all failed, yet the reorganization published part of these false revelations that had ruined the Gurley and Newkirk and other families, just because along with the digging, came the statement that Joseph was to lead the church. They knew when they published the part concerning Joseph, that the other part was not from God, but contained the old spirit of Mormonism, looking for gold and silver until Joseph found the Plates of Gold and made the Book of Mormon out of them.

Apostle Gurley shows clearly how his father was deceived by Joseph Smith and reorganized Mormonism, and while he became an Apostle and one of the most prominent men in the reorganized church, he with his brother and sisters and mother all left the reorganized church at the time that President Jason W. Briggs left and denounced it, with other leading men. Herald, Vol. 1, p. 23. See Apostle Z. H. Gurley Tract, Hist., of Reor. Ch. pp. 1-4.

Now all this twaddle is so foolish that many will be slow to believe it, but, dear reader, it is admitted by the leading people of the Smith church that **he had that stone** and that he not only used it to translate the book of Mormon with, but that before he was twenty years of age, he hired out to Mr. Stoal to hunt for gold and silver mines, and that Stoal came many miles for him, having heard his marvelous fame abroad. See Hist. of Joseph by his mother, p. 96-97, published by the Reorganized church.

Joseph called the Urim and Thummin a key, just as Mr. Stoal called it and his mother says Joseph kept the Urim and Thummim about his person by which he could in a moment tell whether the plates were in danger—he looked in the Urim and Thummim and saw the plates were safe. Ibid 107-110.

Now this was not the only stone that was doing wonders. I quote this silly rot from their own books. Hyrum Page, a brother of an Apostle, got a stone through which he received revelations, many of the leading men of the church believed in this stone of Page, including Oliver Cowdery and David Whitmer and the Whitmer family, so Joseph had a revelation regarding this Page stone and his revelations, and God told him they were all of the devil and so the Whitmers were re-converted to Joseph's stone, for proof read Reorganized ch. hist., Vol. 1, pages 111-119.

Just think, this same Cowdery and Whitmer are the chaps who tell us they saw the breast plate, the Urim and Thummim and plates, and an angel came from heaven and showed them and God spoke from heaven commanding them to bear testimony of the divine translation of the plates. See their testimony on the fly-leaf of every book of Mormon. Yet the Page stone could deceive them and they were led by the devilish revelations that came through it, these men we will see were strong witnesses for Joseph. Then it just seems that the devil with his seer stones were hot after Joseph and his seer stone, a girl by the name of Chase got a green stone or glass, and she would direct the mob to where Joseph had the plates secreted, and time after time Joseph just got there in time to save the plates. See Mother Smith's Hist., p. 115.

The Gold Plates

Now we desire to call the reader's attention to another foolish yarn. We are requested to believe that God inspired the Prophets and seers for thousands of years to write these plates so that the people of this generation could be saved by "the words of the Book" and while he had protected them by mighty miracles all along the lapse of centuries and at last had kept them "hid up" from 420 A. D. till 1827, then he sends an angel for Joseph to translate them by use of Urim and Thummim. Yet, listen to Joseph, his mother and others tell how Joseph had the time of his life to keep them, this is one of the stories of Mormonism that beats the Arabian Knights to a frazzle.

The angel is reported to have said to Joseph, "While the plates were in my hands they were safe, but now I give them to you, beware how you look after them." After Joseph took them from the stone box, in the side of a hill, he had much trouble to keep them. He first cut the bark off a log, took his knife and cut the center of the tree out, placed the great breast plate, spectacles and plates therein and turned back the bark to cover it over with brush. Then he took them and hid them in a chest. Then he hid them under his bed so he could feel them through the night, then he buried them under the fire place, then he hid them in a cooper shop, then he hid them in a red morocco box. Once he was traveling with them and had them stowed away in a barrel of beans, then the Lord lent him a hand at another time he was making a trip, and he just handed them to an angel. The day was hot and they saw a poor old fellow tramping along and they offered him a ride, this tramp turned out to be the angel Moroni, who at the end of the hot day's tramp, handed over the plates to Joseph. See Mother Smith's history, pp. 110-149.

Query, why could not the Lord have taken care of these plates a little longer, and save Joseph all this fighting with the devil's seer stones, that were bound to destroy them, but there is one time that the devil beat both Joseph and his helpers. Just think, God had preserved these plates so that their contents would come forth in this generation, but the Devil fooled them badly in that. After God had inspired Joseph to translate 116 pages (this was a large part of the book), and God had inspired Martin Harris to write the translation, the devil put it in the heart of Harris to ask Joseph for the 116 pages and he gave them to him. Mrs. Harris knew that her husband was being duped out of his money (for it was he that put up the money to get the fraud published) and she took the sacred 116 pages (preserved by the Almighty for a thousand centuries) and BURNED THEM, and they never were able to secure the sacred truths revealed but like the druggist, God gave Joseph a "Just as Good," and so the Lord gave Harris a good setting out and then he was accepted and permitted to spend his money to print the book.

It is said that Joseph, just a lad, got the plates and when taking them home, he ran three miles, knocked down three men who tried to get the plates, knocked his thumb out of joint, and he made this run of three miles, whipped these three men, while he had a big breast plate that Mrs. Smith said was worth more than five hundred dollars, all the gold plates and the sacred Urim and Thummim and the sword of Laban under his arm. He could carry hundreds of pounds of gold plates and breast plates and all the other stuff. To believe that is to believe some story. Mother Smith's history, p. 111. Can you beat it?

One writer speaking of the size and weight of the plates, to say nothing of the breast plate, says "It would require 2,000 pages of foolscap to contain it, one page of plates to one page of foolscap—that would be a pile of plates over four feet high, if we reduce it by half it would be a pile over two feet high. If gold it would weigh seven hunderd and fifty pounds, if brass about two hundred and fifty pounds. Joseph and others say they were of gold, the book itself says in many places, brass, but just think from 750 to 250 pounds weight, to have a fellow hit you with a gun and then you knock him and two others down and run three miles with all this under your arm. surely Mormonism is a marvelous work and a wonder.

Translation Perfect.

We call the reader's attention to another point regarding the Book of Mormon that will bury it by its own weight. The preface of the book says "The interpretation of the book is by the gift of God." If God inspired Smith to interpret the book by the sacred instruments provided by the Almighty, as stated several times over in the book, then there can be no mistakes in the book. The testimony of the three witnesses, found in the front of every Book of Mormon, says, speaking of the translation of the plates, "And we also know that they have been translated by the gift and power of God, for **His voice hath declared it unto us."** Here again it is shown that God inspired the interpretation.

We have already shown by the testimony of David Whitmer, Martin Harris, Emma Smith and others, that Joseph Smith would put the God appointed interpreters into his hat, close out all light, save the divine effulgence, and there the words would appear by a miracle, and if the writer made any mistake, God was there to correct it by refusing to take the words from the stone till the correction was made. There were no difficulties as to the human work, the translation appeared on the Urim and Thummim, or the Seer stone, or parchment, sentence by sentence and as soon as one was correctly transcribed the next would appear, and so every word was given by the direct power of the Almighty, and for one to say "if there are mistakes, they are the mistakes of men" is simply to deny the divine authenticity of the translation. God was the translator directly and to deny that is to deny every claim made by the book itself. This being true, what shall we say when it is admitted by the leaders of every faction of the Mormon church, that there are several thousand mistakes in the book, and that the translation given to the world in 1830 was corrected in thousands of places in the next edition in 1837, and so the corrections continued until one writer points out two thousand changes in the Book and when later corrections are counted up, there is found to be many thousands more.

From the statements made by God, the Angel, Smith, Cowdery, Harris, Whitmer and others, **if true,** God gave every part of the translation. If that be true, then there should be no mistakes in spelling, grammar, punctuation. If such mistakes appear by the thousands, then we are requested to believe that God was responsible for the mistakes, for we are repeatedly informed by Smith and the others that every word was placed on the seer stone by inspiration. The everlasting argument made in favor of the Book of Mormon as against the Bible is that the Bible has been translated by uninspired men and they have taken out much that God inspired the prophets and apostles to put in and that these wicked sons of an apostate church have put in many things that the Lord did not inspire the true servants to write. Mormon literature is full of that kind of talk. If then, God gave every sentence, every word by a direct revelation on the seer stone, we remark **His work would be perfect,** but when we turn to the Book of Mormon and find thousands of mistakes in spelling, punctuation and grammar, we are forced to the conclusion that God is not the author of this literary monstrosity, and therefore we must look to Smith, Rigdon or some one else upon whom must be placed the blame.

In this short paper we will content ourselves with representing a few points of interest regarding punctuations, spelling, grammar and ask the reader for an honest verdict as to whether the Book of Mormon is the product of Divinity or the miserable production of Imposter Joseph Smith and his confederates in a monstrous deception.

Maj. J. H. Gilbert, who printed the first edition of the Book of Mormon, makes the following statement: "There was not a punctuation mark of any kind from beginning to end of manuscript, sentences were not commenced with capitals. We were not allowed to correct any grammatical errors." This gentleman lived to be a very old man and all through life he bore this same testimony. I quote his statement from a letter written by him under date of Feb. 27, 1884, B. K. Debate, p. 382.

He further states in the same letter:

"If Mr. Whitmer claims that he has the manuscript that I used in setting up the Mormon Bible, and that it is punctuated, and the sentences begin with capitals, I say it has been altered since it left my hands, or that he has not got the original."

We may perhaps clear the way here by stating that the church history shows that Oliver Cowdery wrote a second copy of the manuscript and perhaps the one copy has punctuations and capitals, but not the original, and we may easily see why the printer was not permitted to make any changes, as the claim then and now is, that the whole Book was the direct production of Divine inspiration. It was written by miracle, preserved by miracle, revealed to Smith by miracle, translated by miracle. Smith or Cowdery's mental peculiarities and style could not appear in the Book of Mormon, they had no more to do with the words, style, truth, literary characters of the Book of Mormon than a speaking trumpet or phonograph have with what man utters through them. The only opportunity there is for a human error in the Book of

Mormon, is in typographical errors, but there can be none of these for it was proof read by inspired men, and those men testify that the voice of God declared to them that the translation was accomplished by the power of God and that the work is true, with these matters fairly presented it now devolves upon the reader to decide that all important question, is the Book of Mormon of divine authenticity?" The new covenant "given by the direct inspiration of God for the salvation of a ruined world." Or is it the production of Joseph Smith and his comrades in deception and blasphemy?

In this short paper I shall not attempt to record the many thousand of changes that have been made since the first edition was published, but direct the reader's attention to such works as that published by a brilliant scholar, once a member of the Mormon church, by the mame of Lamoni Call, of Bountiful, Utah. His work is entitled "Two Thousand Changes in the Book of Mormon." The reader will notice his name "Lamoni," and the name of the city he resides in "Bountiful," are both names taken from the Book of Mormon, so this scholar ought to know what he is writing about. That Mr. Call has not misrepresented the facts I call your attention to the report of a committee selected by the Reorganized church to examine and compare the many different editions of the Book of Mormon with the Manuscript of the book, then in the possession of one of the three witnesses, David Whitmer. This committee was presided over by Joseph Smith, president of the Reorganized church and son of the founder of the church. Their report is recorded in the Herald for Aug. 23rd, 1884. The report practically admits all that Mr. Call and others have said as to incorrect spelling and horrible grammar and thousands of changes, they publish a great number of instances and add, "The alterations are too numerous to publish in detail.." Yet they do publish a great many hundreds of them and occupy ten columns over nine feet of solid matter in their published report. Did God make these mistakes or are they the blunders of **Joseph Smith and his confederates in deception?**

Many Parts Taken From The Bible and Other Books

A careful examination of the Book of Mormon will reveal to the Bible student that there are thirty-eight pages in the Book of Mormon that is found in the Bible, whole sentences of Paul's writings, six hundred years before Paul wrote a word, whole chapters of the Old Testament are quoted and complete sentences from the New Testament giving the exact language hundreds of years before the one who uttered it lived. One writer states that "by actual count the plagiarisms from the New Testament of paragraphs, phrases and sentences are over 500, the quotations of phrases amount to hundreds. There are over ten in each page of Rigdon's sermon against Infant Baptism, pages 330-341. Whole chapters are quoted, Isaiah 11, 14, 21, 48, 50, 52, 54; Malachi 3; Matthew 5, 6, 7; 2 Corinthians 13. Braden Kelley debate, page 153.

Not only have they stolen the religious portion of the Book of Mormon from the Bible, but they have quoted the great English poet, Shakespeare, as also from Pope's Essays on Man, The Westminster Confession of Faith, and other leading authors of the last few hundred years, thus showing beyond a doubt that the fraud was written by someone living in these latter times and not by the hands of prophets and seers residing in America hundreds and thousands of years ago, some of them before the time of Abraham.

Before leaving this part of the examination I wish to say that Joseph Smith claimed that God had inspired him to translate the Bible, both the old and new testament. He did so, and has made thousands of corrections, taking out hundreds of verses and placing in hundreds. In this way he has given us a new Bible by inspiration, they claim to believe in the Bible as held by all Christians. This is a false position for the bible given them by Joseph Smith is published and used by the Mormons in this city. I have one in my possession and have traveled with some of their apostles that have no other Bible but the Smith one.

Speaking on the corruption of the Christian churches, the revelation of Smith, found in the Book of Mormon says: "For behold they have taken away from the gospel of the Lamb **many parts which are plain and most precious and also many covenants of the Lord have been taken away,** and all this have they done that they might pervert the way of the Lord, that they might blind the eyes and harden the hearts of the children of men." This hypocrisy in his revelations in the Book of Doctrine and Covenants, in which he is commanded to translate the scriptures. See Book of Mormon, 1 Nelphi, 3, 40; D. C. 42, 15, 6, 12, 90, 12.

Now the folly of it all is that while Smith condemns the King James translation of the Bible, and corrects thousands of its mistakes in his new Bible, when we take up the Book of Mormon (printed before his new bible), the same mistranslations of King James' translation are found by the dozens, in the Book of Mormon. Question, if as stated by the Mormon church, "the whore of the whole earth, the Roman Catholic and Protestant churches combined" have changed the Bible in order to deceive the people, why did God, when giving the Book of Mormon word by word to Joseph Smith, stand in with the "whore of all the earth" in presenting their mistakes to Joseph Smith as found in King James' translation of the Bible? Can we ask for greater proof to show that God had nothing to do with the Book of Mormon, but that Joseph Smith and his confederates in the deception, knew no other Bible to quote from than the King James and they quoted that as the words of God, and then Joseph and Rigdon, a few years later, forgot the trap they had set for themselves and professed to correct and translate by inspiration the Bible, and in their attempt to expose the Christian Bible they destroyed the faith of many of their followers in the divine authenticity of the Book of Mormon.

Notwithstanding all these blunders, we are told by the Reorganized church authorities "No book ever came before the race of mankind with such an august message as the Book of Mormon." Saints Herald, Nov. 6th, 1918. To this agrees the great Apostle Pratt. "The Book of Mormon claims to be a divinely inspired record—it professes to be revealed to the present generation for the **salvation** of all who will receive it, **and for the overthrow and damnation of all nations who reject it**—the nature of the message in the Book of Mormon is such that if true, no one can **possibly be saved and reject it."** Divinity of Book of Mormon, p. 1.

Early History of America.

There is one other claim made for the Book of Mormon, one that has deceived thousands of people, which I wish to expose before I show the real true history of the Book of Mormon. It is this: That the Book of Mormon gave to the world the first account or history of the early settlers of America, that the fact that America was once a civilized part of the world, and that the inhabitants built large cities and all that was unknown till revealed by God in the great revelation known as the Book of Mormon. This delusion has been circulated by their books and preachers all over the country, and it is false. That I once believed that and taught it and sent my sermons out by the thousands is quite true, but thank God, the darkness and superstition is fled away and I am disillusionized, but to the proofs.

"The fact is that there were a considerable number of works on science and travel and adventure published in the English language before 1830 which contained descriptions of the ruined cities of Mexico, Central America and Peru—the following are the names of a number of works in the English language before 1830, describing the antiquities of Central America and Mexico. They are either quoted from or referred to in the writings of Bancroft, Prescott and other later writers:—

"Conquest of Mexico, De Solis, London, 1735; History of America, Herrera, London, 1740; History of America, Robertson, London, 1777; Origin of the Tribes and Nations of America, Barton, Philadelphia, 1797- Account of the Settlement of Hundurus, Henderson, London, 1812; Re; searches, Humboldt, London, 1814; Researches in America, McColoch, Baltimore, 1817; Spanish America, Bonneycastle, London, 1818; Travels in North America, Bingley, London, 1821; Description of an Ancient City, Del Rio, London, 1822; Six Months' Residence in Mexico, Pollock, London, 1823; History of Cautemala, Juarros, London, 1824; History on Mexico, Mill, London, 1824; Notes of Mexico, Poinsett, London, 1825; Mexico Illustrated, Beaufoy, London, 1828; Mexico in 1827, Ward, 1828.

"We might continue the list but will be content to say the American Antiquarian Society was organized in Worcester, Mass., 1812, and the American continent was well known then. 'North American Indians' was published in London by the celebrated Adair in 1775 and such men as Hunter, Barton, Colden, Loskiel, Stoddard and Charlevoix, wrote more or less extensively on the subject of antiquities and Indian life before 1830." Cumorah Revisited Shook, pp. 133-134.

The celebrated Josiah Priest wrote a work entitled "The wonders of Nature and Providence." It was copyrighted by him June 2, 1824, in the office of R. R. Lansing, clerk of the district of northern New York and printed in Rochester, N. Y. in 1824. Will the reader remember that the Book of Mormon was copyrighted by Joseph Smith in the **same office by the same R. R. Lansing,** June 10th, 1829, and printed in Palmyra, N. Y. just twenty miles from Rochester in 1830.

This book of Josiah Priest quotes from many of the authors I have named above, and it is beyond all question that the writers of the Book of Mormon had opportunity to study many of these books and hence the positions taken in the Book of Mormon agree with many of those books. For instance, it has been known from the conquest of Mexico by Cortez, that there were three civilizations in Mexico; it has been known since the conquest of Peru by Pizarro that there had been three or more civilizations there; Baron Humboldt visited America and described the Ruins of Central America in his book published in both England and America in 1806. But why take time and space to prove further that the claims made by Mormons that the Book of Mormon gave the first real history of these things, is a monstrous falsehood. We leave this part believing that none but those who are prejudiced by their priestcraft and superstitions will attempt to refuse to believe the position that I have taken.

The Spaulding Story, or Manuscript Found

I shall be as brief as possible in giving the real origin of the Book of Mormon. The reader can read the complete story from the Encyclopedias and history of the times, but I shall content myself in giving a brief outline of the matter which will show beyond doubt that the claim made for the Book of Mormon is fraudulent.

Solomon Spaulding was born in 1761, preached for a time and leaving the ministry he became an infidel, kept tavern for a time and when his health failed, he started to write a novel on the early inhabitants of America. He was a great reader and had studied many of the works that I have had occasion to make reference to in this paper.

He wrote one entitled the "Manuscript Story." Later he wrote others, one of which was called **"Manuscript Found."** This first work called the **"Manuscript Story"**, was set aside and in time was discovered and was loaned to Hulbert, who gave it to Howe to prepare for publication to prove it was the foundation for the Book of Mormon. They soon discovered that it was not the right one. This manuscript became lost with a host of other papers of the office, in time the office and contents changed hands and many years after was discovered, the Mormons heard that it had been located and rushed for it, and obtained a copy and printed it to show that it was not the original of the Book of Mormon. This they think they have done, but the cat is out of the bag when we discover that there were two or more manuscripts written by Spaulding, the one they run down as the Manuscript Story, and the one that was the **real foundation** of the Book of Mormon was **"The Manuscript Found."** They have confused these two stories till the superficial reader has them as one and the same manuscript. I know that, for I both believed it and preached it myself. My writings prove that, but when I was made to

MORMONISM—ITS EARLY HISTORY 19

understand that the Manuscript Found was the real foundation of the Book of Mormon, I could see how easily people could be mistaken in taking the "Manuscript Story" for the "Manuscript Found." Knowing this, the Mormons have made the most of it to their eternal discredit.

The clear statements made by Spaulding, his wife, his daughter, his partner in business and many others who knew him well and read the Manuscript Found are in evidence, that he wrote the Manuscript, placed it in the printing office for publication, he died in 1816 and that Sydney Rigdon, who was in turn a farmer, preacher for the Baptists, Deciples and Mormons, was well acquainted with a printer who either loaned him the "Manuscript Found" or gave him opportunity to steal it. That Rigdon had the Manuscript and spent much of his time in reading it and intended "to make a great thing out of it some day," is proved by his wife and several preachers with whom he conversed. That he made secret visits to Joseph Smith during the time Smith was arranging to spring his Book of Mormon on the world is a well attested fact. That he let P. P. Pratt into the secret, and had Pratt go to the Mormons and profess conversion, and then come to Rigdon and profess to present to him the Book of Mormon for the first time, and that Rigdon in a few days was baptized and knew from God the Book of Mormon was true, is all too well known to need reiteration here. I will content myself by presenting for the reader the testimony of those who knew, and if there is any credence to be given to human testimony, then it is well sustained that the book of Mormon is a fraud stolen from the Spaulding Manuscript Found, and that Rigdon and Smith placed the religious part of it, stealing that from the King James translation of the Bible, which book they afterwards assailed with all the infidelity within them by setting it aside for their own translation of the Bible.

I will now present to you the sworn statement of Solomon Spaulding's wife, his brother, his sister-in-law, his partner in business and a number of other neighbors who heard him read the Manuscript Found, and the reader will note that this combination of evidence is as good a description of the Book of Mormon as any Mormon could give to-day: Braden and Kelly debate, pages 35-42.

Mr. Spaulding's brother John:—"It was a historical romance of the first settlers of America, and endeavored to show that the American Indians are the descendants of the Jews, or the Ten Lost Tribes. It gave a detailed account of their journey from Jerusalem, by land and sea until they arrived in America under the command of Lehi and Nephi. They afterwards had quarrels and contentions and separated into two distinct nations, one of which he denominated Nephites, the other Lamanites. Cruel and bloody wars ensued, in which great multitudes were slain. They buried their dead in large heaps which caused the mounds, so common in this country. Their arts, sciences and civilization were all brought into view, in order to account for all the curious antiquities found in various parts of Northern and Southern America. I well remember that he wrote in the old style, and commenced almost every sentence with, "And it came to pass," or "Now it came to pass."

Solomon Spaulding's Sister-in-law:—"I was at the house of Solomon Spaulding shortly before he left Coneaut. He was then writing a historical novel founded on the first settlers of America. He presented them as an enlightened and war-like people. He had for many years contended that the aborigines of America were the descendants of some of the Lost Tribes of Israel; and this idea he carried out in the book in question. The lapse of time which has intervened prevents my recollecting but a few of the leading incidents of his writings, but the names Lehi and Nephi are yet fresh in my memory, as being the principal heroes of his tale. They were officers of the company which first came off from Jerusalem. He gave a particular account of their journey by land and by sea, till they arrived in America, after which disputes arose between the chiefs which caused them to separate into bands, one of which was called Lamanites, the other Nephites. Between these there were recounted tremendous battles which frequently covered the ground with slain and these being buried in large heaps was the cause of the many mounds in the country. Some of these people he represents as being very large."

Henry Lake, Solomon Spaulding's business partner, testifies: —"Solomon Spaulding frequently read to me from a manuscript which he was writing, which he entitled the "Manuscript Found," and which he represented as being found in this town. I spent many hours in hearing him read said writings and became well acquainted with their contents. The Book represented the American Indians, as being the descendants of the Lost Tribes of Israel, and gave an account of their having left Jerusalem and of their contentions and wars which were many and great. I remember telling Mr. Spaulding that so frequent use of the words "And it came to pass," "Now it came to pass" rendered the book ridiculous."

Aaron Wright testifies:—"One day when I was at the home of Solomon Spaulding he showed and read to me a history he was writing of the Lost Tribes of Israel, purporting that they were the first settlers of America and that the Indians were their descendants. He traced their journey from Jerusalem to America. He told me his object was to account for the fortifications, etc., that were to be found in this country and said that in time it would be fully believed by all except learned men and historians."

Oliver Smith testifies:—"Solomon Spaulding boarded at my house six months. All his leisure hours were occupied in writing a historical novel, founded upon the first settlers of this country. He said he intended to trace their journey from Jerusalem by land and sea till their arrival in America, and give an account of their arts, sciences, civilization, laws and contentions. In this way he would give a satisfactory account of all of the old mounds so common in this country. Nephi and Lehi were, by him, represented as the leading characters, when they first started for America. Their main object was to escape the judgments which they supposed were coming on the old world."

Nahum Howard testifies:—"In conversation with Solomon Spaulding I expressed my surprise that we had no account of the people once in this country, who erected the old forts, mounds, etc. He told me he was writing a history of that people."

Artemus Cunningham testifies:—"Solomon Spaulding described to me his book. He said it was a fabulous or romantic history of the first inhabitants of this country and it purported to be a record found buried in the earth or in a cave. He had adopted the ancient scriptural style of writing. He then read from his manuscript. I remember the name of Nephi, who appeared to be the principal hero of the story. The frequent repetition of the phrase "I, Nephi" I remember as though it were yesterday. He attempted to account for the numerous antiquities which are found upon the continent."

John N. Miller testifies:—"I perused Spaulding's manuscript as I had leisure, more particularly the one he called his "Manuscript Found." It purported to be a history of the first settlers of America. He brought them off from Jerusalem, under their leaders, detailing their travels by land and sea."

Mrs. Spaulding testifies:—"Mr. Spaulding conceived the idea of writing a history of the long lost race that produced these antiquities. Their extreme antiquity led him to write in the most ancient style, and as the Old Testament was the oldest book in the world, he imitated its style, as much as possible. As he progressed in his narrative, the neighbors would come in from time to time to hear portions read, and a great interest in the book was excited among them. It claimed to have been written by one of the lost nations and to have been recovered from the earth. The neighbors would often ask how Mr. Spaulding progressed in deciphering the manuscript, and when he had a sufficient portion prepared he would inform them, and they would assemble to hear it read. He was enabled from his acquaintance with the classics and ancient history to introduce many singular names, which were particularly noticed by the people and could easily be recognized by them."

Mr. Spaulding's daughter:—"My father read the manuscript I had seen him writing to the neighbors and to a clergyman, a friend of his who came to visit him. Some of the names he mentioned while reading to the people, I have never forgotten. They are as fresh in my memory as though I had heard them but yesterday. They are Mormon, Moroni, Lamanite and Nephi, etc."

Joseph Miller testifies:—"Mr. Spaulding seemed to take great delight in reading from his manuscript written on foolscap. I heard him read most if not all of it, and had frequent conversations with him about it. Some time ago I heard most of the Book of Mormon read. On hearing read the account of the battle between the Amlicites (Book of Alma, Chapter 11) in which the soldiers of one army placed a red mark on their foreheads to distinguish them from their enemies. It seemed to reproduce in my mind not only the narrative but the very words as they had been imprinted on my mind by reading Spaulding's manuscript."

Ruddick McKee testifies:—"I was a boarder at Spaulding's tavern in Amity, Pa., in the fall of 1814. I recollect quite well Mr. Spaulding spending much time in writing on sheets of paper torn from an old book, what purported to be a veritable history of the nations or tribes that inhabited Canaan. He called it "Lost Manuscript" or some such name. I was struck with the minuteness of its details and apparent sincerity and truthfulness of the author. I have an indistinct recollection of the passage referred to by Mr. Miller, about the Amlicites making a cross with red paint in their foreheads to distinguish them from their enemies in the confusion of battle."

Mr. Abner Jackson testifies:—"Spaulding frequently read his MS. to the neighbors and commented on it as he progressed. He wrote it in Bible style, "And it came to pass" occurred so often that some called him "Old come to pass." The names Mormon, Moroni, Nephi, Nephite, Laman, Lamanite, etc., were in it. The closing scene was at Cumorah where all the righteous were slain."

Rev. John Winter, M. D., testifies:—"In 1822-3 Rigdon took out of his desk in his study a large manuscript stating that it was a Bible romance purporting to be a history of the American Indians. That it was written by one Spaulding, a Presbyterian preacher whose health had failed and who had taken it to the printers to see if it would pay to publish it. And that he (Rigdon) had borrowed it from the printer as a curiosity."

James Jeffries testifies:—"Forty years ago I was in business in St. Louis. The Mormons then had their temple in Nauvoo, Ill. I had business transactions with them. I knew Sydney Rigdon, he acted as general manager of the business of the Mormons (with me). Rigdon told me several times, in his conversation with me, that there was in the printing office with which he was connected in Ohio, a manuscript of the Rev. Spaulding, tracing the origin of the Indians from the lost tribes of Israel. This manuscript was in the office several years. He was familiar with it. Spaulding wanted it published but had not the means to pay for printing. He (Rigdon) and Joseph Smith used to look over the manuscript and read it on Sundays. Rigdon said Smith took the manuscript and said, "I'll print it," and went off to Palmyra, N. Y."

From the above testimonies we think we have proven that Solomon Spaulding's Manuscript Found was the real foundation of the Book of Mormon. They have beyond doubt shown that the features found in the Book of Mormon and the Manuscript Found, both as to plot, names of the leading actors, and names of places are absolutely the same. We now present briefly, the following features found in the Book of Mormon and the Manuscript Found, being in complete harmony, as stated in those two books and nowhere else as follows:—

"(1) The plot of the Manuscript Found as witnesses describe it was just what Mormons give when describing the Book of Mormon. (2) It purported to be a veritable history of the aborigines of America. So does the Book of Mormon. (3) It attempted to account for the antiquities of America by giving an account of their construction. So does

MORMONISM—ITS EARLY HISTORY

the Book of Mormon. (4) It assumed that Israelites were the aborigines of America and ancestors of the Indians. So does the Book of Mormon, (5) It said the Israelites left Jerusalem, so does the Book of Mormon. (6) They left to escape divine judgments about to fall on their people. So does the Book of Mormon. (7) That they journeyed through and from Southern Asia, by land and sea, so does the Book of Mormon. (8) Their leaders were Nephi and Lehi, so does the Book of Mormon. (9) One Laban was murdered to obtain records. So declares the Book of Mormon. (10) They quarrelled and divided into two nations, called Nephites and Lamanites. So says the Book of Mormon. (11) There were terrible wars between the two nations and the parties into which they divided with awful slaughter. So declares the Book of Mormon. (12) They buried their dead after these slaughters in great heaps, that caused the mounds. So declares the Book of Mormon. (13) In two instances the end of these wars was the total annihilation of all but one who escaped to make record of the final catastrophe. So declares the Book of Mormon. (14) These sole survivors finished the record of the people and buried it. So declares the Book of Mormon. (15) The Manuscript Found gave an historical account of the civilization, laws, customs, arts and sciences of those people. So does the Book of Mormon. (16) One party of these people were the ancestors of our American Indians. So declares the Book of Mormon. (17) The names Nephi, Lehi, Laban, Lamon, Nephite, Lamanite, Mormon, Moroni, Amlicite, Zarahemla, etc were in the Manuscript Found, so they are in the Book of Mormon. (18) The use and characteristics of these names in the Manuscript Found were precisely the same as in the Book of Mormon. (19) The Manuscript Found was written in scriptural style—that is, the style of King James Version. So is the Book of Mormon. (20) "Now it came to pass" occurred too frequently as to render the language ridiculous. Such is true of the Book of Mormon. (21) This ridiculous peculiarity got for the author of the Manuscript Found, the nickname of "Old Came to Pass." The Book of Mormon is just such a book. (22) The original from which the story was translated was taken from the earth. The same is claimed by the Book of Mormon. (23) One party of emigrants landed near the Isthmus of Panama and migrated across the continent in a northeastern direction. So declares the Book of Mormon. (24) The land near the Isthmus was called the land of Zarahemla. So declares the Book of Mormon. (25) In a battle between the Amlicites and Lamanites, one party marked their foreheads with a red cross to distinguish them from their enemies. So declares the Book of Mormon. (26) The destruction of the nation exterminated took place near a hill called Cumorah. So declares the Book of Mormon. (27) The Manuscript Found could have been used as a fraud, an imitation of the Bible, a pretended revelation. The Book of Mormon is just such a fraud. Now then, the reader must do one of the two things, believe that Solomon Spaulding, during a period of from fourteen to twenty-two years before the Book of Mormon appeared, by a miracle wrote a romance that contained these twenty-seven great features of the Book of Mormon—features that no other book except the Manuscript Found and the Book of Mormon ever contained in common, or that Rigdon or someone else stole the manuscript of the Manuscript Found and remodeled it into the Book of Mormon." Deb. B. K.

As a closing thought to this brief history of Mormonism, I wish to bring the four first great and prominent men of Mormonism before you in the light of their own statements regarding each other.

Joseph Smith professed that he has seen God the Father and His Son Jesus Christ, face to face, also talked to such Angels as John the Baptist, Peter, James, John, Nephi, Moroni, and others. That, as a result of his conversation with those sacred beings, he denounced all Christianity as the "whore of the whole earth, the Mother of abominations, the church of the Devil," and was inspired to organize the only true church upon the face of the whole earth, bring forth the Book of Mormon which contains the fullness of the gospel for the salvation of the world and translate the Old and New testament, so as to expose the corruption of the Bible as adopted by the churches.

Oliver Cowdery, David Whitmer and Martin Harris, testify to the truth of all the above claims made by Joseph Smith, and tell us that the voice of God bade them bear witness to the world regarding all this, and that angels appeared to them from time to time in support of it all.

It would require a book to publish all the statements made by these men affirming the above positions, so I will give the reader the opportunity to consult the different books in which these statements are made, I affirm I have the books, all accepted by the church. Book of Mormon, Church History, Vol. 1, Inspired Translation of the Bible by Joseph Smith and Doctrine and Covenants, Revelations of Smith.

Witnesses Leave the Church.

Now it so happens that the three witnesses above named all parted with Smith denounced him as about everything that was bad and left the church in a few years after they had organized it.

Oliver Cowdery says Smith held over him a mysterious power and deceived him—that he tried to destroy his reputation and his life—that he was a false prophet—that he made a tool of him—that the voice of the angel who claimed to be John the Baptist, was strikingly similar with the voice of Sidney Rigdon (this is a mild way of letting the cat out of the bag, that the angel John the Baptist who conferred the Priesthood upon him and Smith, was none other than Rigdon)—that this Rigdon influenced Smith into the formation of a secret band to commit murder.

Cowdery testifies that the Lord revealed himself in person to him and commanded him to leave the church and to denounce the wickedness of Smith, he declared that he can prove that Smith had a band organized to inflict death upon apostates and that he fled to save his life.

This statement was published by Oliver Cowdery in Norton, Ohio, in 1839. See the True Origin of Polygamy by Shook, pp. 49-54.

David Whitmer testifies, left the church in a few years, denied that—"The church was organized April 6th, 1830—agrees with Cowdery that the secret band of murderers was organized in 1838. He says he left the church in 1838, and all of the eight witnesses of the Book of Mormon, who were living, left the church with their families (save the Smiths). The church went deeper and deeper into wickedness. Joseph had a revelation telling Cowdery and others to go to Toronto, Canada, and they would sell the copyright of the Book of Mormon. They went, but could not get a buyer. That proved to them and others that Smith was false—says "I have as much evidence to believe that Brother Joseph received the revelation on polygamy and gave it to the church as I have to believe that such a man as George Washington ever lived." He clearly shows that the leaders of the Reorganization admitted it and that they are now lying out of it and in this they are playing the hypocrite. See origin of Polygamy, p. 41 by Shook, Whitmer's address, p. 26-38.

Martin Harris, the last of the three witnesses, left the church and denounced it in both America and England. This is sometimes denied but the history of the church proves it beyond doubt. Ibid. p. 44.

Now what has Joseph Smith and the church authorities to say of these three witnesses, that they wish us to believe talked with God and conversed with angels. They tell us that Whitmer was so highly favored of God that three angels were sent to spread plaster of Paris on his land, so that he could go with his team of horses and give Joseph Smith a ride. This story is published by the Reorganized church, see Mother Smith's history, pp. 144-145.

Just as soon as these three men discovered they had been fooled by Smith, they denounced him and then all that the pen and tongue of hatred and slander could write or articulate was not vile enough to circulate about these men, in proof of which I submit the following:—

Joseph Smith:—"About this time there were several persons living in Far West, who were cut off the church, these characters were studiously engaged in circulating false and slanderous reports against the saints to stir up our enemies to drive us from our homes, and enjoy the spoils together. They are as follows: Oliver Cowdery, David Whitmer and others." Joseph Smith in Times and Seasons, Vol. 1, p. 80.

Hyrum Smith, Joseph's brother states that:—"While I was away from home persons came to my home, ramsacked it, carried off money and other valuables, among those who treated me thus I cannot help making particular mention of Lyman Cowdery, who in connection with his brother Oliver Cowdery, took from me a great many things and to cap the climax of his iniquity he compelled my father (by threatening to bring a mob upon him), to deed over to him or his brother Oliver, 160 acres of land, to pay a note which he said I had given to Oliver for $165—the note was a forgery. Ibid., Vol. 1, p. 22-23.

Rigdon and 84 others swear that Oliver Cowdery and David Whitmer were guilty of theft and counterfeiting, and says they were blacklegs of the deepest dye." Ibid. Vol. 1, pages 82-84.

There is a report published by the authority of the United States government, and presented in the district court before Judge King, in which 84 leading Mormons state that Oliver Cowdery is charged with stealing, lying, perjury, counterfeiting, and being leader of a gang of blacklegs, congressional document 189, A. D. 1841.

Joseph, writing to the press regarding Whitmer, says:—"Poor Phelps, who professes to be much of a prophet, has no other dumb beast to ride but David Whitmer, or to forbid his madness when he goes up to curse Israel, but this ass (not being of the same kind as Balaam's), therefore notwithstanding the Angel appeared unto him, yet he cannot sufficiently penetrate his understanding but that he (Whitmer) brays out cursings instead of blessings, poor ass, who ever lives will see him and his rider perish like those who perish in the gainsaying of Noah." B. K. D. p. 173.

Joseph wrote of the third witness:—"Martin Harris is so far beneath contempt that a notice of him would be too great a sacrifice for a gentleman to make. The church exerted some restraint upon him, but now he has given loose to all kinds of abominations—lying, cheating, swindling with all kinds of debauchery." Elders Journal, Aug. 1838, p. 49, B. K. D., p. 173.

We could write a book of many pages were we inclined to make report of all the evidence these four leaders have published against each other. We think the above is sufficient to prove beyond a doubt, that their testimony is from such a source that God will never condemn any person for refusing to accept it. If Smith tells a hundredth part of the truth about the three witnesses they were three scoundrels, and as such we should not be expected that such characters would be the comrades of angels and blessed with personal conversations with God and Christ, therefore we are justified in refusing to believe their testimony.

On the other hand, if they tell one hundredth part of the truth about Smith, he was a false prophet, a murderer in his heart, a liar of the deepest dye, and the author of the infamous revelation on polygamy and concubinage, and that he not only taught and practiced these abominations, but that as a result of his life of shame he has prostituted hundreds of thousands of his followers, who have lived in these unhallowed conditions a whole life time and went down to death despised by all who love God and clean respectable conduct.

In this short treatise, I have endeavored to give you the result of my studies and trust that the reader may be benefitted by the efforts I have made to bring the facts to the public.

CHAPTER II.

Was Joseph Smith a Polygamist?

Brief History of Smith and Mormonism

Joseph Smith was born December 23rd, 1805, in Sharron, Vermont, and was killed June 27th, 1844, in Carthage, Illinois. Many thousands regard this remarkable man as a false prophet, one who was guilty of many crimes, including lying, stealing, treason, blasphemy, adultery, concubinage, spiritual wifery, and polygamy, while thousands regard him as a Prophet, Seer, Revelator, Translator, God's sole mouthpiece to give commandments to his church, Christ's Apostle to organize "the only true church upon the face of the whole earth, with which I and the Lord am well pleased," and that Smith's words and commandments were but the voice of the Almighty Doctrine and Covenants, 1, 4-5; 19.

Churches All Wrong

They believe that God came all the way from heaven to introduce Christ to Joseph the very first time that Joseph ever condescended to offer a prayer vocally, and that Christ stood over him while Smith reclined under a tree, and told him that all the sects or churches were wrong, that he must join none of them, that the creeds were all an abomination in his sight, and those professors were all corrupt; they were just giving God lip-service, while their hearts were far from him. In other words, the membership of the Christian church, both member and parson, were a parcel of hypocrites. Church History, Vol. 1, Page 9.

Joseph Smith was informed that the church combined was the church of the Devil, the Mother of abominations; that they had taken many parts away from the Bible, and added much to it, in order to deceive the nations, and that God had now come to appoint Joseph Smith to translate the Scriptures of the Old and New Testaments, and restore hundreds of verses that the great and abominable church had left out, and take out hundreds of verses that "The Mother of Harlots and her daughters" had put in. Hence, Joseph Smith gave us a new Bible. For proof of the above read Preface of Smith's Bible, also Doc. and Cov., 42-15; 42-5; 90-12; 6-12; 34-5. Pratt on Bible, page 19.

They believe that "There are save two churches only, the one is the church of the Lamb of God, and the other is the church of the devil, wherefore whoso belongeth not to the church of the Lamb of God belongeth to that great church, which is the mother of abominations, and she is the whore of all the earth." Book of Mormon, 1 Nephi, e, 220-223.

They believe that Joseph Smith was directed to a certain place on a hill in the State of New York, where an Angel delivered to him a record taken from a stone box. This record, we are told by them, was translated by J. Smith, and was furnished to the world under the title of "The Book of Mormon." This is said to be a sacred scripture belonging to the people who lived upon the continent of America many hundreds of years before the great Columbus discovered it; that it contains the fullness of the Everlasting Gospel, the Everlasting Covenant, and those who refuse to believe in this book will be damned. Evidence of Bible and Book of Mormon, compared, Page 58. D. C. 1-5.

They teach that God so directed that J. Smith obtained several mummies imported from Egypt. Inside the wrappings of one mummy was found a history of the world as written by the hand of Abraham. This is a very valuable book, older than any part of the Bible, and is called the "Book of Abraham." This, they say, God inspired Joseph Smith to translate by use of the Urim and Thummim, see Millenial Star, Vol. 3, July 1, 1842. Pearl of Great Price, pages 48-76. Church History, Vol. 1, pages 568-569. Saint's Herald, Vol. 1, pub. 1860.

Book of Abraham

Joseph Smith published the "Book of Abraham," and with it several illustrations of the Egyptian documents, years past, and at last several world-renowned scholars examined these characters and illustrations, and have showed conclusively that J. Smith again played the base imposter, in that his purported translations are a complete fraud from beginning to end. The Editor of the Saints' Herald, a nephew of J. Smith, wrote at length regarding these exposes. Our space forbids us to follow at great length, but we wish to puncture one glaring false statement, in that he makes claim that if J. Smith's translation of the "Book of Abraham" is proved false, it does not injure his claim to translate the Book of Mormon, as the Book of Mormon was translated by a divine gift through the **Urim and Thummim,** while there is no claim of divine help in the translation of the "Book of Abraham," and he triumphantly affirms: "Certainly the **Urim and Thummim** was not used." It is both painful and disgusting to follow some members of the Smith family in their deceptive efforts to hide the awful trickery of their relative, Joseph Smith. Listen, now, for another Mormon lie exposed by their own paper, published during the lifetime of the Prophet Joseph Smith: "We have much pleasure this month in being able to give an illustration and extract from the Book of Abraham, a book of higher antiquity than any portion of the Bible. Singular is the providence by which this ancient record fell into the hands of the servant of the Lord, Joseph Smith.

The record is now in course of TRANSLATION BY THE MEANS OF THE URIM AND THUMMIM, and proves to be a record written partly by the father of the faithful, Abraham, and finished by Joseph when in Egypt." The Latter Day Saint Millennial Star, Vol. 3, p. 45-47, July 1st, 1842. When Pres. E. A. Smith wrote the false statement in Herald for October 20th, 1915, he had doubtless felt sure the statement printed above in 1842, could not be found to expose him. Shame.

Hence the world is requested to believe, under the penalty of damnation, that God has inspired Joseph Smith as his prophet and mouthpiece to this generation, to organize the true church of Christ, Translate a new Bible, The Book of Mormon , the Book of Abraham, the Doctrine and Covenants, as also to expose the Christian churches as being a mass of hypocrisy, and to save us from such. He has inspired Joseph to organize "The only true and living church upon the face of the whole earth with which I, the Lord, am well pleased." D. C. 1-5, 1 Nephi 3-220-223.

Smith Vile, Yet True Prophet

Here we present the two sides of this momentous question, if the first position be true, can we accept the second position as true. Some of the leading men of the Mormon Church, including Joseph Smith, the son of the man in question (and because he was his son he was made President of one branch of the Mormon Church), says, when speaking on this part of the matter which we are considering "While I do not accept the proofs offered by you that my father was a pluralist or polygamist, as conclusive, I repeat that whether he was or was not, the gospel of Christ, as it was taught by Christ, and as recommitted through Joseph Smith, is complete and sufficient for the salvation of man, nor is it essential to the validity of that gospel that my father be proved to be a polygamist, or that I be compelled to believe that he was."—Joseph Smith's fourth letter to L. O. Littlefield, p. 4.

"I am frank to say, however, that if all you allege in your letter to me, namely, that Joseph Smith sanctioned polygamy, that the Order of Enoch is a wicked organization, are true, I do not see how that justified your action in withdrawing from the church."—Letter of H. C. Smith, church historian, in reply to R. C. Evans, August 1, 1918.

Brigham Young is reported to have said: "I don't care if the prophet Joseph acted like the devil. He brought forth a doctrine that will save us. He may have got drunk every day of his life, slept with his neighbor's wife every night—I never embrace any man in my faith."—Braden and Kelley Debate, p. 98. "I have many times, in this stand, dared the world to produce as mean devils as we can. We have the greatest and smoothest liars in the world, the cunningest and most adroit thieves, and any other shade of character that you can mention. We can pick out Elders in Israel right here who can beat the world at any game. We can beat them because we have men here that live in the light of the Lord, **that have the holy priesthood and hold the keys of the kingdom of God,** but you may go through all the sectarian world, and you cannot find a man capable of opening the door of the kingdom of God to admit others in. We can do that. We are not to be beat."—Journal of Discourses, Vol. 4, p. 77.

Now, I have taken some space to give you the facts as I find them in the books of the church, both the Utah and Reorganized Church, and both from the Prophet and his son, and Brigham and other leading lights of both factions, so it cannot be said that I am unfair. We may be wrong, but we have concluded that if Joseph Smith was guilty as charged, then it has much to do with our accepting his testimony. Jesus said: "Beware of false prophets." "Ye shall know them by their fruits. Do men gather grapes of thorns or figs of thistles? Matt. 7, 15-21.

Now, we betake ourselves to examine the evidence as to his character. His friends say his death was like that of the Saviour, As Christ said, "My God, my God, why hast thou forsaken me," so Joseph said, "O, Lord, my God." Some say that his words, as above given, were not like the Master, but were part of a signal of distress, uttered by a secret society, of which he had once been a member, but which he had disgraced. However, they claim he said he was "Going as a lamb to the slaughter," and they write of him as having shed his blood to seal the Book of Mormon, which was the covenant given for the salvation of the world, and hence they sing of him as follows:

"Hail to the prophet, ascended to heaven,
    Traitors and tyrants now fight him in vain,
Pleading with God, in behalf of his brethren,
    Death cannot conquer that hero again,"

Saints' harp 760; D. C., 113, 4-7; Mill. Star, Vol. 13, p. 15.

Joseph Smith escaped from Ohio charged with many sins. He escaped from Missouri charged with treason and other crimes. He was at the time of his death charged with treason against the State of Illinois, and other crimes, and his last act was to kill two men and shoot the arm off a third, and he tried to kill others, but his pistol missed fire, and he jumped out of the window, and they caught him and shot him.—Journal of History, October, 1918; p. 410-416.

Paul informs us in 1 Timothy, 2, 5: "For there is one God and ONE MEDIATOR between God and man, the Man, Jesus Christ." The teaching of the Mormon church is, that Joseph Smith has gone to heaven to assist Christ in this work. See the above hymn, "Pleading with God in behalf of his brethren." The Bible plainly teaches that Christ shed His blood to seal the Covenant by which man may be saved, but J. Smith again comes to the rescue, and we are told that J. Smith shed his blood to bring forth the Book of Mormon, for the salvation of a ruined world.—D. C. 113. Shall we place J. Smith and his Book of Mormon on a par with Christ and the Bible? Is the blood of Christ sufficient? Will His pleadings prevail or do we require J. Smith to go to heaven to help Him as a mediator?

The current history of the times says that the Smith family bore an unsavory reputation. "He was a lazy, drinking, fellow; loose in his habits in every way," the family were a pack of liars, too low to associate with. Joseph and his father wandered over the country with a peep stone and a witch hazel rod, pretending to find waterways and lost treasures, buried gold, and finally Joseph claimed to find the gold plates of the Book of Mormon, and while he says God protected the Urim and Thummim for the purpose of translating the Book of Mormon, at times he says he used those spectacles, and at other times it is said he discarded them and used the peep stone. No man living can make the leading

Mormon statements agree on the Urim and Thummim and peep stone story. Here is a blank contradiction. Let the reader look up the notes Braden Kelley Debate, p. 47, 119; Chambers Ency. Art Mormonism; Ency. Britt. Art Mormonism; Two Thousand Changes in the Book of Mormon, by Lamoni Call, p. 18-25; Myths of the Manuscripts Found, p. 71-83.

The revelations say he must translate with the Urim and Thummim. Some say he did. And such persons as Joseph's wife and David Whitmer are strong on the point that Joseph used the Seer stone, while he put the peep stone in his hat, shut out all light, while the plates layed ? covered up on the table or somewhere else. Question is, why not have left the plates in the Hill if he could translate them without looking at them? Why did the Lord carry the Urim and Thummim back and forth over the ocean, as the Book of Mormon claims, when Joseph could get along with the translation without them?

The history shows they were given to Jared's brother about 2230 B. C., carried back over the ocean and given to Moses and Aaron about 1406 B. C., then carried back to America and given to Lehi about 600 B. C., and "hid up" till 1827, when the Lord gave them to Joseph to do the translating with, yet he set them aside and did the trick with the peep stone (see David Whitmore's address, pages 12-30-31-32, 37, 42, 56; Joseph the Prophet, page 793-794; Myth of Manuscript Found, page 20; H. A. Stebbins, Herald, Dec. 30, 1908; Mosiah, page 1-2-3; Mormon, page 200, D. C., 3-1, 15-1.) The peep stone is said to have been found when digging a well and Joseph took it.—Braden Kelley debate, page 47.

With all this history of silly contradictions which are impossible of belief, and with all the statements as to his character, are we compelled under pain of damnation to accept Joseph Smith as a prophet of the Lord and all his self-contradicting books as the word of God?

Was Joseph Smith Immoral?

My next position is that if it be true that Joseph Smith was guilty of gross immorality all through his life, and that he was the originator of that abomination, Mormon polygamy, and the author of that blasphemy entitled "A Revelation in Regard to Celestial Marriage," that has been the ruination of thousands of men and has broken the hearts of thousands of women, blasting the peace, joy, happiness and virtue of tens of thousands, then I say, if there is any credence to be given to the test made by Jesus Christ, "By their fruits ye shall know them," Matt. 7, the Smith claim to be a prophet, seer, revelator, God's mouthpiece and the translator of the Book of Mormon, and Book of Abraham and all his other revelations, must fall to the ground, and that it is not true that all those living in this generation will be damned if they reject him and his claims, and now to the history.

Passing over the general history of his lewdness, as presented in many of the leading histories of the world, we will try and be as careful as possible to give reference for all we state; it is recorded that:

"**Dr. McIntyre,** family physician of the Smiths in Manchester, N. Y., declared that the house of Joseph Smith, Sen., was a perfect brothel."

"**Eza Pierce, Samantha Payne** and other school-mates of the Smiths testify that Smith was lewd, and so were the family."

"**Levi Lewis** testifies that while Smith was pretending to translate the plates, he tried to seduce Eliza Winters, declaring that adultery was no sin."

"**Eli Johnson** led a mob against Smith for being intimate with his sister, Marinda, who afterwards married Orson Hyde. Brigham Young twitted Hyde with this fact, and Hyde put away his wife."

"**Fanny Brewer** testifies that Smith had serious trouble in Kirtland arising from his seducing an orphan girl."

"**Mr. Moreton** told his daughter and her husband that Emma Smith detected Joseph in adultery with a girl by the name of Knight, and that Joseph confessed the crime to the officers of the church."

"**Dr. John Stafford** testified he was a school-mate of Smith's and that he (Smith) was a great admirer of Mohammed and the Koran, and that polygamy was right and that nature and the Bible taught it."

"**W. W. Phelps** stated that while Smith was translating the Book of Abraham he declared that polygamy would yet be a practice of the Saints." Braden-Kelley Debate, page 202.

Polygamy

Turning from these scattered testimonies, running through the early years of Smith's life, we now come to the more public time of his life. Joseph F. Smith, a relative of the original Joseph, and standing high in the councils of the Mormon church, speaking of the revelation as written on polygamy, July 12th, 1843, says: "This, however, was not the time this principle was first known to the Prophet Joseph Smith, for as early as 1831 the Lord revealed the principle of celestial and plural marriage to him, and he taught it to others." Origin of Plural Marriage, by Joseph F. Smith, page 92.

This same Apostle of the church, speaking of the marriage of "Aunt Lucy Walker, Smith Kimbel, to Joseph Smith, May 1st, 1843, says: "The strong point which he attempts to make is the fact that Lucy was married to the Prophet Joseph Smith on May 1st, 1843, while the revelation on plural marriage was dated July 12th, 1843. No one knew better than she did that the REVELATION WAS GIVEN AS FAR BACK AS 1834, and was first reduced to writing in 1843." Discussion between Joseph F. Smith and R. C. Evans, page 69. The statements of Joseph F. Smith agree with that made by Martin Harris and others that polygamy or spiritual wifery was taught and practiced by Joseph in Kirtland in the early thirties.

Some affirm that the revelation given through Joseph Smith, April 6th, 1830, known as Section 19, Doc. and Cov., is the first foundation for polygamy. It says: "Wherefore, meaning the church, thou shalt give

WAS JOSEPH SMITH A POLYGAMIST? 33

heed unto all his words and commandments, which he shall give unto you, as he receiveth them—for his words ye shall receive, as if from mine own mouth in all patience and faith."

Here you have it; think not that all the membership of the church were wicked people; many loved God and tried to serve him, and regarded Smith as the mouthpiece of God, and when the revelation on polygamv came, their faith was so strong that they, with broken hearts, bowed in submission to the foul mandate.

Now, we come to a little matter that has caused me trouble with the son of Joseph Smith, at the time thousands of my sermons on polygamy were burned by his order, because I inadvertently convicted his father. Here it is: Brigham Young was in England. He had a manifestation on polygamy. Speaking on polygamy he said: "While we were in England (in 1839 or 1840, I think), the Lord manifested to me by visions, and his spirit, things that I did not understand. When I returned home, and Joseph revealed those things unto me, then I understood the reflections, which were upon my mind while in England. This was in 1841. The revelation was given in 1843, but the doctrine was revealed before this." Desert News, July 1, 1874.

Now, will the reader note this point: Brigham confessed that he had some spiritual manifestation in England on polygamy. He comes home and tells it to Joseph. Then Joseph tells him he had revelations on the same matter, and in time it was written and given to the church. But just a moment, dear reader, what think you? After Brigham Young had his revelation on polygamy, and Joseph Smith had his, and they talked the matter over as Brigham says, then we are asked to believe that the Lord spoke through Joseph to Brigham Young and made him the president of the Twelve Apostles, and gave him "the keys to open the authority of my kingdom upon the four corners of the earth, and after that to send my word to every creature," Doc. and Cov., 107-40.

Joseph F. Smith states that Orson Pratt testified that Lyman Johnson told him that Joseph Smith had a revelation on polygamy as early as 1831. Pratt makes the above statement in his sermon "Does the Bible Sanction Polygamy," p. 140. This is in keeping with the Elders' Journal, edited by Joseph Smith, No. 2, page 38, published in Kirtland, November, 1837, where Joseph in an editorial says we were asked daily and hourly by all classes of persons while we were travelling, "Do Mormons believe in having more wives than one?" Martin Harris told J.M. Atwater, Mr. Chapp and others that polygamy was taught and practised by Smith and others in Kirtland. B. K. D. p. 202

Some writers on the question say they could print scores of affidavits of old Mormons that prove Joseph Smith practiced spiritual wifery and polygamy from 1830 to his death, and it is admitted in the Doctrine and Covenants that their conduct was of such a character that in 1834 they were compelled to make the following statement: "Inasmuch as this church of Christ has been reproached with the crime of fornication and **polygamy**, we declare that we believe that one man should have one wife and one woman but one husband." D. C., 111-4. Three points we wish to notice here. This statement does not call polygamy a crime, but fornication. If they meant polygamy they would have said crimes of fornication and polygamy, but, reader, notice the wording, "With the CRIME of fornication, and polygamy," again, "One man should have ONE WIFE." It does not say he should have **only** one, or **but** one, but when it comes to the woman, "one woman **but** one husband." Who cannot see the deception in this statement?

Mormon Excuse For Lying About Polygamy in Early Years of The Church.

When the following questions were propounded, the following answers were given, much was said, we give but a brief, yet true report:

Q.—"Have not the Latter Day Saints denied that a plurality of wives existed in their midst, when such was actually the case?"

A.—"Doubtless some have because they did not know that such was the case."

Q.—"Have not some Elders of the Latter Day Saints denied that polygamy was practised, when at the same time they positively knew that it was?"

A.—"That is a personal question, and must be answered accordingly. I have not, neither have I heard any other Elder."

Q.—The question may arise in your mind—If a plurality of wives has been prevalent in the church so long, why have not the Elders publicly preached the doctrine?"

A.—"The answer is very plain, BECAUSE NEITHER THE BODY OF THE SAINTS NOR CHRISTENDOM WERE PREPARED FOR IT—Neither is it wisdom in the Elders to publish all knowledge the moment it is revealed to them. Your little child asks you various questions respecting its origin, or its course when it shall arrive at maturity, and makes most amusing remarks on the subject, you sit and smile at it, YOU DO NOT TELL IT THE TRUTH ABOUT THESE THINGS—but you consider it proper and wise to EVADE its interrogations, or to refuse to answer them. It is just so in God's dealings with His church, and if God acts so, His servants, to be like him, must do so too. By reading the Doctrine and Covenants, 20, 16x36, 6-7, you will learn that many things were to be withheld from the saints and the world, and only to be revealed at a fitting time and season. If the doctrine of POLYGAMY had been publicly preached by the Elders when the church was in its infancy, and when the saints were comparatively ignorant and weak in the faith, it is probable that very few indeed would have been able to endure." Elder John Jaques, "Polygamy," Mill Star, Vol. 15, p. 165.

Doctor John C. Bennett had a career that was at once most spectacular and gorgeous; baptized in 1840, he helped draft the bill for the incorporation of the city of Nauvoo. He was elected first mayor of the city, chancellor of the Nauvoo University, major-general of the Nauvoo legion. In his patriarchal blessing from Hyrum Smith, brother of Joseph, he was given the holy priesthood, was to have visions and dreams and the mysteries of God were to be given to him in dreams and visions, have power to heal the sick, cause the lame to walk, the deaf to hear, dumb to speak, be like Paul, and to become a patriarch. He also received a splendid revelation from the Lord through Joseph the prophet, D. and C., 107-6, and then the Lord made him one of the first presidency of the whole church until Rigdon's health should be restored.—Times and Seasons, Vol. 2, page 387.

Well, after all this Bennett started to expose Smith, claiming he was guilty of adultery, that he seduced a number of single and married females; he tried to seduce Nancy Rigdon. The story of Miss Rigdon is one of the most foul in history. The girl refused to submit and told Bennett and her parents and brother. I have before me the sworn statement of **John W. Rigdon,** brother of the girl and son of Sidney Rigdon. Time and space is too precious to relate it all, but we leave the horrid matter by saying that Rigdon and Smith quarreled over it and Smith soon had Rigdon out of harm's way, sending him to Pittsburg, where Rigdon lived till after the death of Smith.

Rigdon was Joseph Smith's strongest man—his first counselor—but he left the church and published a work in 1844, denouncing Smith in the broadest terms of unspeakable wickedness. He declares that, "The leaders of the church were monsters in human form; that Joseph was cut off for his transgression, that Joseph Smith departed from the living God, and like David and Solomon he contracted a whoring spirit and that the Lord smote him off from the earth." He says he loved Joseph, but when he found that he was teaching the unholy spiritual wife doctrine secretly and denying it openly, he was compelled to lose faith in him and denounce him.—Messenger and Advocate, Vols. 1 and 2. Many pages are covered with his denunciations of Smith and his polygamist villians. Here as a concluding statement we give the following from the second volume of the Messenger and Advocate: "This system of polygamy was introduced by the Smiths some time before their death, and was the thing which put them in the power of their enemies and was the immediate cause of their death."—Vol. 2, page 475.

William Law was baptized near Toronto and soon went to Nauvoo. He was brilliant and wealthy, and soon Joseph had him place his money in property which Joseph had to sell. Joseph had a revelation from the Lord making Law his counselor in the first presidency of the church. He was to cast out devils and raise the dead and do many wonderful works.—D. and C., 107, 30.

William Law became convinced that Smith was an imposter and tells us in a sworn statement that Hyrum Smith, brother of the prophet Joseph read the revelation on polygamy before the high council, and then gave it to him to take home and read to his wife. Law read it to his wife, then took it to Joseph, and Joseph bore testimony that he had received it from the Lord. Law collected several of the leading men of the church, who with him had become disgusted with Smith's vile life, such men as Wilson Law, Charles Irvins, F. M. Higbee, C. L. Higbee, Robert Foster and Charles Foster; and they bought press and type and printed a weekly paper. In this first issue several of them exposed the revelation regarding adultery, polygamy and concubinage given to Smith July 12th, 1843, and many other vile actions on the part of Smith and others. Then Smith as prophet of the church and mayor of the city called the people out, held a meeting and ordered the press and type destroyed and thrown into the streets, and some was carried to the river. The proprietors of the press escaped with their lives, went to the county seat, swore out a writ for Smith. He escaped, but was sent for by his friends, returned, was bailed to appear at the next sitting of the court, but the same day was arrested on the charge of treason against the State of Illinois and placed in jail, where he shot two men dead and shot the arm off another and would have killed more but his six-shooter missed fire three times, when he jumped out of the window, and in trying to escape was shot dead.

For a complete account of the above matters the reader is requested to read Nauvoo Expositor, June 7th, 1844; the Weekly Tribune, Salt Lake City, August 4th, 1887; Joseph the Prophet, p. 746, Journal of History, October, 1918.

After the paper published by these men, called the **Nauvoo Expositor,** under date of June 7th, 1844, had been destroyed, the people all over the country became aroused and to stem the tide, Joseph Smith called the city council together to discuss **The Revelation of Polygamy,** as referred to by those making sworn statements as published therein, the minutes of that council was published in a paper called the **Nauvoo Neighbor.** The same may be found also in the **Millennial Star,** Vol. 23, p. 754, 770, 816. We quote the following statements made by Joseph Smith and his brother Hyrum, which contradict each other:—"Councillor H. Smith referred to the revelation read to the High Council of the church, which has caused so much talk about a MULTIPLICITY OF WIVES, that said revelation was in answer to a question concerning things which transpired in **former days, and had no reference to the present time."**

"Then Mayor Joseph Smith said: They make a criminality for a man to have a wife on the earth while he has one in heaven, according to the keys of the Holy Priesthood—that he had never preached the revelation in private as he had in public—had not taught it to the annointed in the church in private, which statement many present confirmed, that on inquiring **concerning the passage in the resurrection concerning "They neither marry nor are given in marriage,"** etc., he received for answer: Men in this life must marry in view of eternity, otherwise they must remain as angels, or be single in heaven, which was the amount of the revelation referred to, and the Mayor spoke at considerable length in explanation of this principle." Nauvoo Neighbor, June 19, 1844.

Here these brothers admit that there was a revelation on the marriage question. One says it referred to the past, and the other that it referred to the future, after the resurrection. But the admission is fully made and is in complete agreement with sworn statements made by those

WAS JOSEPH SMITH A POLYGAMIST? 37

who heard the revelation read and others who read it and with the Revelation as published in Doctrine and Covenants, Sect. 132, Utah edition, part of which I submit in this paper.

Three Witnesses.

Permit me to expose one of the most deceptive works of the reorganized church. They fill their church papers with the pictures of the three witnesses of the Book of Mormon, tell over and over again their testimony to the Book of Mormon, doubtless written for them by Joseph Smith. They never weary of saying they never denied their testimony but, dear reader, just think of it, those three witnesses all denounced Joseph Smith as a bad man, and accused him of most everything, and left the church in less than ten years after the Mormon Church was organized.

I have already placed the statement of **Martin Harris** before you, that Smith taught and practiced polygamy before they left Ohio. **David Whitmer** says Joseph changed the revelations and was guilty of many evils, and prints a book in which he says, "I now have as much evidence to believe that Brother Joseph received the revelation on polygamy and gave it to the church as I have to believe that such a man as George Washington ever lived," and he scores the reorganized church for trying to lie out of it, and declares that God directed him to leave the corrupt church.—David Whitmer's address, pages 38-45.

Oliver Cowdery, the man who wrote nearly all of the Book of Mormon for Smith, and was a president and most prolific writer, says that Christ commanded him to leave the church because of its corruption, and shows how Smith led them into sin. He declares that a society was formed with the knowledge and sanction of Joseph Smith to inflict death upon their enemies. Whitmer's book gives quite a history of this band organized for murder. It was in full swing in 1838, when these three with many other men left the church and fled for their lives. See Cowdery's defence, published in 1839; Shooks' True Origin of the Book of Mormon, page 50-61.

Pres. Lorenzo Snow swears that on his return from England in 1843 Joseph Smith explained the doctrine of plurality of wives to him, how the Lord commanded him to have women sealed to him as wives, how Joseph saw the trouble that would follow and sought to turn away from the commandment, that an angel from heaven then appeared before him with a drawn sword and threatened him with destruction unless he went forward and obeyed the commandment. He then told him how he had Eliza R. Snow (this man's sister) sealed to him as his wife for time and eternity. Snow when an old man closed this affidavit in these solemn words: "I solemnly declare before God and holy angels, and as I hope to come forth in the morning of the resurrection, that the above statement is true." (Sworn August 28th, 1869, Origin of Plural Marriage, pages 81-82.)

One hundred or more affidavits in relation to the introduction of celestial and plural marriage are on file in the historian's office, Salt Lake

City, and are the expressions of eye and ear witnesses, who know that the prophet Joseph Smith introduced and taught celestial and plural marriage. (Origin of Plural Marriage, by Joseph F. Smith, page 81.)

At the risk of being tedious, I submit the names of a few of the women who make affidavits that they were married to Joseph Smith, and lived with him as his wives:

Lucy Walker Smith Kimbel says: "I was a plural wife of the prophet Joseph Smith and was married for time and eternity in Nauvoo, State of Illinois, on the first day of May, 1843, by **Elder William Clayton.** The prophet was then living with his first wife, Emma Smith, and I know that she gave her consent to the marriage of at least four women to her husband as plural wives, and she was well aware that he associated and cohabited with them as wives. The names of these women are **Eliza** and **Emily Partridge** and **Mary** and **Sarah Lawrence.**" (Origin of Plural Marriage, pages 82-83.) See affidavit of Lucy Walker Smith.

Melissa Lot Willes, upon her oath saith "that on the twentieth day of September, 1843, at the city of Nauvoo, she was married or sealed to Joseph Smith, president of the Church of Jesus Christ of Latter Day Saints, by Hyrum Smith, according to the laws of the said church regulating marriage, in the presence of her parents, Cornelius Lott and Parmelia Lott." Origin of Plural Marriage, page 87.

When in Salt Lake City I called at the residence of Patriarch John Smith, brother of Joseph F. Smith, and son of Hyrum Smith, nephew of the original prophet John Smith, and while there his wife, Helen, told me, among many other interesting things, that "Melissa Lott told me that when a girl she sewed for Emma Smith and took care of the children. Joseph had to pass through her room to go to Emma's room. She said Joseph never had sexual intercourse with her but once and that was in the daytime, saying he desired her to have a child by him. She was barefooted and ironing when Joseph came in, and the ceremony was performed in the presence of her parents." (R. C. Evans).

Lucy Walker Smith states that when young Joseph was in Utah he called on her and asked the question, "Did my father have more (other) wives than my mother?" I answered truthfully without hesitation. Afterwards he went to Lehi, called on Melissa Lott, with whom he had been associated from early childhood, and asked, "Will you answer me one question? I come to you, knowing you will tell me the truth; were YOU MY FATHER'S WIFE?" "Yes, Joseph, I was." "Where is your proof?" She stepped to the stand and took the family Bible, opened to the family record, placed it upon his knee and asked: "Do you recognize the handwriting?" "Certainly, that is your father's (Cornelius Lott's) handwriting; know it as well as my own." Then read the marriage certificate of prophet Joseph Smith and Melissa Lott.—Origin of Plural Marriage, pages 73-74.

I could produce these affidavits in full and submit many more that are in my possession, but will present part of a letter written by **Elder William Clayton,** who wrote the revelation known as section 132, in the book of Doctrine and Covenants, Utah edition, at the dictation of the prophet Joseph Smith, July 12th, 1843: "I am ready to testify to all the world, I did write the revelation on celestial marriage, given through the prophet Joseph Smith, July 12th, 1843. When the revelation was given there was no one present except the prophet Joseph, his brother Hyrum and myself. It was written in the small office upstairs in the rear of the brick store which stood on the bank of the Mississippi river; the same night a copy was taken by Bishop Whitney, which copy is now here (in the historian's office), and which I know and testify is correct. The original was destroyed by Emma Smith. I again testify that the revelation on polygamy was given through the prophet Joseph Smith on the 12th of July, 1843, and that the prophet both taught and practiced polygamy I do positively know. In April, 1843, he sealed to me my second wife, my first wife being then living. I had the honor to seal one woman to Joseph under his direction."—William Clayton, Origin of Plural Marriage, pages 92-93.

Having followed Joseph Smith to his untimely death, as he says, all through that cursed spiritual wife doctrine, I leave the general church and point to the reader that nearly all the factions practiced polygamy in some form. I care not what they called it, it meant the sexual act with women other than their legal wives. **William Smith,** brother of the prophet, left Brigham Young, started a church of his own and practiced polygamy. The Utah people say he was in polygamy before his brother's death, and his three wives lived in Utah till their death, **Priscilla M. Smith, Sarah** and **Hannah Libby.**—Origin of Plural Marriages page 58; Temple Lot Evidence, page 395; Church History, vol. 3, page 200; The Messenger, vol. 2, Joseph Smith letter to Davis.

James J. Strange taught and practiced it in his church till his murder, and he professed till death that Joseph ordained him his successor.

Lyman Wight taught and practiced it, **Sidney Rigdon** practiced it in his little church, **Gladden Bishop** practiced it. (See young Joseph's letter to Mr. Davis, October 13th, 1899, Origin of Plural Marriages, page 58.)

The Reorganized Church has ever denounced polygamy. But, as David Whitmer says, they have displeased God in trying to deny that Joseph Smith taught, practiced and sanctioned polygamy and had revelations commanding its practice. This to my mind is the great sin of the Reorganized Church.

For many years the leading men of the Reorganized Church preached and wrote freely, admitting that Joseph Smith had the revelation on polygamy and that it was practiced in Nauvoo during his presidency till his death, and that it was the curse of the church and caused his death. For proof of this I now present to you their statements in as brief a manner as possible to give you the facts. I abbreviate to save time and space, which mean expense in publication.

Joseph Smith, The Son of The Prophet.

"I believe that during the later years of my father's life there was in discussion among the elders, and **possibly in practice,** a theory like the following: That persons who might believe that there was a sufficient degree of spiritual affinity between them, as married companions, to warrant the desire to perpetuate that union in the world to come and after the resurrection, could go before some high priest, whom they might choose, and there making known their desire, might be **married for eternity,** pledging themselves while in the flesh unto each other for the observance of the rights of companionship in the spirit; that this was called **spiritual marriage,** and upon the supposition that what was sealed by this priesthood, before which this pledge was made on earth, was sealed in heaven, the marriage relation then entered into would continue in eternity. That this was not authorized by command of God or rule of the church, but grew out of the constant discussion had among the elders; and that after a time it resulted in the wish (father to the thought) that married companionship rendered unpleasant here by incompatibilities of different sorts, might be cured for the world to come by securing through this means a congenial companion in the spirit; that there was but brief hesitancy between the wish and an attempt to put it into **form and practice.** That once started, the idea grew, spiritual affinities were sought after, and in seeking them the hitherto **sacred precincts of home were invaded;** less and less restraint was exercised, the lines between **virtue and license** hitherto sharply drawn, grew more and more indistinct; spiritual companionship if sanctioned by a holy priesthood, to confer favors and pleasures in the world to come, might be antedated and put to **actual test here**—and so the enjoyment of a spiritual companionship in eternity became a companionship here; a **wife** a spiritual wife, if congenial; if not, one that was congenial was sought, and a wife in fact was supplemented by one in spirit, which in easy transition became one in essential earthly relationship. From this, if one, why not **two or more, and plural marriage, on the plurality of wives was the growth."**—"Life of Joseph the Prophet," page 798-800. This book was printed by the Reorganized Church and advertised by them in their papers until they destroyed the type because it told too much.

Comment. Here the son is trying to make the position as easy as possible, yet he admits that during the latter years of his father's life there was in discussion among the elders, **and possibly in practice,** three stages or steps that brought the church to polygamy and destruction and to his father's untimely death.

First step, a spiritual affinity between married companions, who went before some Mormon priest and were married for eternity.

Second step, that married companionship rendered unpleasant might be cured for the world to come by securing a congenial companion, that this was put into **practice,** that in thus practicing this spiritual wifery, the sacred precincts of home were invaded, less and less restraint was exercised, the lines between license and virtue grew indistinct, and that his spiritual companionship sanctioned by the holy priesthood to confer favors in the world to come might be antedated and put to actual test here, and that plural marriage or plurality of wives was the growth, this being the third step.

In the same paper he tries to protect his father, makes a feeble attempt to state that when his father became convinced that the world would make the discovery and the church would be destroyed by this abominable prostitution, he tried to stop it, but was powerless. But it was too late, and he met his untimely death, and so Brigham continued to lead the people in the way of sin, and finally grew bold, and openly preached and practiced the crime which in secret they had practiced but denied for years.

That Joseph Smith is said to have repented of his connection with polygamy, and burned the **revelations that commanded the faithful to practice it,** and so confessed a few days before his death, is admitted by others of the Reorganized Church, but the great sin of it all is that now that nearly all these old books are destroyed and the victims of his polygamy are dead, the Reorganized Church leads their people to believe that Joseph Smith was innocent of it all, and that Brigham Young was the scoundrel that had the revelations and introduced its practice.

Emma Smith.

Before we leave this book I present what is often styled the death-bed statement of Emma Smith, legal wife of Joseph, as made in answer to questions propounded by her son, Joseph.

"What about the revelation on polygamy? Did Joseph Smith have anything like it? What of spiritual wifery?"

"There was no revelation on either polygamy or spiritual wives; there were some rumors of something of the sort, of which I asked my husband. He assured me that all there was of it was that **in a chat about plural wives he had said:** "Well, such a system might be, if everybody was agreed to it, and would behave as they should. But they would not, and besides it was contrary to the will of Heaven." No such thing as polygamy or spiritual wifery was taught publicly or privately before my husband's death that I have now, or ever had any knowledge of." Life of Joseph the Prophet by Tullidge, page 792.

Comment. Is it not strange that for many years Joseph was challenged to ask his mother, but he waited till she was about ready to enter the grave before he approached her on this momentous question? Then it is recalled that this purported statement is not signed or written by Emma nor did she give it under oath. Then it must be remembered that the sworn statements to the contrary of the Laws and Cowles published twenty days before the prophet's death and corroborated afterwards by the affidavits of Fullner, Grover, Soby Robinsons, and the sworn statements of many others, and lastly the statements made by Marks, Sheen and hundreds of others, including several women, who made oath that they were the wives of Joseph Smith, and many affirming that Emma knew that her husband had the revelation, practiced polygamy and that she burned the revelation. Brigham Young says: "Emma burned the revelation." Isaac Sheen says: "Joseph had the revelations on that subject burned." William Law swears: "Mrs. Smith complained to me about Joseph keeping his young wives in her house and elsewhere, and his neglect of her. She spoke freely about the revelation and its threat against her life (eight years after the revelations were published by Brigham Young, and contains the threat upon Emma's life, as stated by her to President Law, R. C.). She seemed to have no faith in it whatever, from what she said to me, and from what I learned from other sources, I have good reason to believe that Joseph and Hyrum Smith and others in the church had been practicing polygamy for a long time before the revelation came forth." Mormon polygamy, page 191.

Emma admits they were discussing polygamy, she admits she heard rumors, she says her husband said **"such a system might be if everybody was agreed to it and would behave as they should."** Can anyone fail to see guilt there. This is in keeping with his position all along. The people were hard to manage, they talked too much. Some were not content to practice polygamy and keep quiet about it. The world would soon know the secret. That was his trouble. The command was **"thou shalt not be found out."** Keep the strong meat from the world; feed them on milk. D. C., 18, 2.

To say the least, the above makes the **last testimony of Emma Smith look slightly suspicious.** Thousands contradict her story.

Much more could be presented from this old book, the type of which was destroyed lest the admissions of Joseph and his mother would be urged against the husband and father. But I leave that book and go to another book which I found within the last two months. I had seen some garbled quotations from it in my hurried reading in the past, but the book itself is presented to me. It is a bound volume composed of the True Latter Day Saints' Herald, volume 1, and I quote from the best authority ever produced by the Reorganization, surely they will not deny it, for I confess, hurt as it did, my honor compelled me to admit the truth contained therein, though it well nigh broke my heart.

Isaac Sheen Testifies.

Vol. 1, No. 1, page 8-9: The editor of the paper is making claim that polygamy is sinful in the sight of the Lord, and showing not only the guilt of Joseph Smith, but trying the best he can to excuse him. Here are his words:

"In Ezekiel, 14, 1-5, the prophet says: "Then came certain of the elders of Israel unto me, and sat before me. And the word of the Lord came unto me, saying, 'Son of Man, these men have set up their idols in their heart, and put the stumbling block of their iniquity before their face; should I be inquired of at all by them? Therefore, speak unto them and say unto them, thus saith the Lord God; every man of the house of Israel that setteth up his **idols in his heart,** and putteth the stumbling block of his iniquity before his face, and cometh to the prophet; I, the

Lord, will answer him that cometh according to the multitude of his idols; that I may take the house of Israel in their own heart because they are all estranged from me through their idols."

"We have shown you that God gave a revelation unto us in which he commanded that every man should "cleave unto his wife and none else," and that he commanded us, saying, "repent and remember the Book of Mormon and the former commandments which I have given them, not only to say, but to do, according to that which I have written," and that in that book there is much testimony against polygamy. All these instructions were sufficient for our guidance, but "men have set up their idols in their hearts, and put the stumbling block on their iniquity before their face." **This adulterous spirit had captivated their hearts and they desired a license from God to lead away captive the fair daughters of his people and in this state of mind they came to the Prophet Joseph.**

Could the Lord do anything more or less than what Ezekiel hath prophesied? The Lord hath declared by Ezekiel what kind of an answer he would give them, therefore he answered them according to the multitude of their idols. Paul had also prophesied that "for this cause God shall send them strong delusion, that they should believe a lie, that they all might be damned who believed not the truth, but had pleasure in unrighteousness." Both these prophecies agree. In Ezekiel's prophecy, the Lord also says: "I will set my face against that man and will make him a **sign and a proverb and I will cut him off from the midst of my people;** and ye shall know that I am the Lord. And if the **prophet** be deceived when he hath spoken a thing, I, the Lord, have deceived **that prophet,** and I will stretch out my hand upon him, and will **destroy him** from the midst of my people, Israel. And they shall bear the punishment of their iniquity; the punishment of the prophet shall be even as the punishment of him that seeketh unto him; that the house of Israel may go no more astray from me, neither be polluted any more with all their transgressions; but that they may be my people and I may be their God, saith the Lord God."—8, 11 v.

"We have here the facts as they have transpired, and as they will continue to transpire in relation to this subject. The death **of the prophet is one fact that has been realized,** although he **abhorred and repented of this iniquity before his death."**

This branch of the subject we shall leave to some of our brethren who are qualified to explain it satisfactorily. Those who have practiced these abominations have become "a sign and a proverb" among men in accordance with this prophecy. These are the "false teachers" prophesied of by Peter, of whom he said: "Many shall follow their pernicious ways, by reason of whom, the way of truth shall be evil spoken of, and through covetousness shall they with feigned words make merchandise of you; whose judgment now of a long time lingereth not, and their damnation slumbereth not." **The reason why the Lord destroyed the prophet and made those who "set up their idols in their hearts,"** "a sing and a proverb," made them bear the punishment of their iniquity is worthy of our earnest attention."

Comment. Here is plain admissions to the following: The church had fallen under an adulterous spirit. They desired a license from God to lead away the fair daughters of his people. They went to Joseph Smith, the prophet (not Brigham Young, as we so often taught) with this idol in their hearts; he received the revelation commanding polygamy, but just before his death he repented of this iniquity, and abhorred it; but we will permit Isaac Sheen, the editor, to make his own statement:

"The Salt Lake apostles also excuse themselves by saying that Joseph Smith taught the spiritual wife doctrine, but this excuse is as weak as their excuse concerning the ancient kings and patriarchs. Joseph Smith repented of his **connection with this doctrine,** and said that it was of the devil. **He caused the revelations on that subject to be burned,** and when he voluntarily came to Nauvoo and resigned himself into the arms of his enemies, he said that he was going to Carthage to die. At that time he also said that if it had not been for that accursed **spiritual wife doctrine** he would not have come to that. By his conduct at that time he proved the sincerity of his repentance, and of his profession **as a prophet.** If **Abraham and Jacob,** by repentance, can obtain salvation and exaltation, so can **Joseph Smith.''**

Comment. Joseph repented of his connection with this doctrine (the spiritual wife doctrine is under consideration). He said it was of the devil. **He caused the revelations on that subject to be burned. When he went to Carthage to die** he said: "If it had not been for that accursed spiritual wife doctrine, he would not have come to that. By his conduct at that time he proved the sincerity of his repentance and of his profession as a prophet." All this cannot be denied, and as it is supported by hundreds of others, whom we were unwilling to believe in the past. But now that it is admitted by the leading men of the church, why should the present leaders try to excuse Joseph and place the blame on Brigham. Here Isaac Sheen concurs with President William Law, and Pres. Brigham Young that Emma not only knew of the revelation, but that it was burned. The two presidents say Emma burned it, the editor says Joseph had it burned."

William Marks Testifies

Now we call attention to William Marks on the question of polygamy. He was president of the High Council at Nauvoo at the time of Joseph Smith's death. He supported the claims of Sidney Rigdon for a time, then went with the polygamous apostles under Brigham Young, then it is said he left them and joined the Stranite faction, then he joined the little church called the Baneemytes, and after all this running around he united with the Reorganized Church and ordained Joseph Smith to be the prophet, seer and revelator of the new faction. This man wrote in the Saints' Herald, under date of Oct. 23, 1859, published in that paper on pages 25-26 of first volume, the following:

"I feel desirous to communicate through your periodical a few suggestions made manifest to me by the spirit of God in relation to the church of Jesus Christ of Latter Day Saints. **About the first of June, 1844** (situated as I was at that time, being the presiding elder of the Stake of Nauvoo, and by appointment the presiding officer of the High Council), I had a very good opportunity to know the affairs of the church, and my convictions at that time were that the church, in a great measure, had departed from the pure principles and doctrines of Jesus Christ. I felt much troubled in mind about the condition of the church; I prayed earnestly to my Heavenly Father to show me something in regard to it, when I was **wrapt in vision,** and it was shown me by the spirit that the **top, or branches,** had overcome the root in sin and wickedness, and the only way to cleanse and purify it was to **disorganize it,** and in due time the Lord would reorganize it again. There were many other things suggested to my mind, but the lapse of time has erased them from my memory.

"A few days after this occurrence I met with Bro. Joseph. He said that he wanted to converse with me on the affairs of the church, and we retired by ourselves. I will give his words verbatim, for they are indelibly stamped upon my mind. He said he had desired for **a long time** to have a talk with me on the subject of **polygamy.** He said it eventually would prove the overthrow of the church, and we should soon be obliged to leave the United States unless it could be speedily put down. He was satisfied that it was a cursed doctrine, and that there must be every exertion made to put it down. He said that he would go before the congregation and proclaim it, and I must go into the High Council, and he would prefer charges against those in transgression, and I must sever them from the church unless they made ample satisfaction. There was much more said, but this was the substance. The mob commenced to gather about Carthage in a few days after, therefore there was nothing done concerning it.

"After the Prophet's death, I made mention of this conversation to several, hoping and believing that it would have a good effect, but to my great disappointment, it was soon rumored about that Brothers Marks was about to apostatize, and that all he said about the conversation with the Prophet was a tissue of lies."

Comment. The Lord shows him a vision of the corruption of the church and that the only way to purify it was to disorganize it. That the "top had overcome the root in wickedness." (Joseph was the top, and wicked) that Joseph told him he desired **for a long time to have a talk with him on polygamy.** It had made such headway that it would eventually overthrow the church; they would soon have to leave the United States unless it could be put down, and advised that all who would not repent should be cut off the church, but in a few days the mob came and Smith was shot to death.

The reader should remember that according to the above, polygamy was extensively practiced **for a long time in the church.** Joseph had now been converted that it was wrong. He repented of his connection with it, abhorred his past conduct and would now try and put it down.

He was the mayor of the city, he was the prophet, seer and revelator. He had been a crowned king, he was lieutenant-general of the Nauvoo Legion, he was the only one that had the right to give a revelation that the church is to receive. As if from the mouth of Christ, for the support of this blasphemy and autocracy, read Doc. and Cov., 19, 243, 1. So that Smith was absolute in power, and if revelations were given and polygamy was practiced, then he had those revelations, and he practiced the abomination. His own revelations and the testimony of hundreds of his victims prove this beyond question.

Joseph Smith's Last Revelation on Polygamy.

Now I will quote from the book containing the revelations of Joseph Smith, as published in the Book called the "Doctrine and Covenants"— a book that is held to be superior to the Bible, for the reason the revelations in the Bible, they say, are unreliable, while Joseph Smith, the "Mouthpiece of God" to the church, delivered the revelations as published in the Book of Doctrine and Covenants. Now here is part of the last famous revelation as published in their own book under date of July 12th, 1843. It contains sixty-six paragraphs and covers ten pages, telling all about how to practice polygamy and concubinage, and states that a man is not guilty of adultery even if he have ten women at one time as his wives, and let the reader remember that in the revelation several times over **damnation is promised to those who refuse to enter into polygamy, and the highest glory is only secured by the practice of polygamy.** But to the revelation, "Revelation on the eternity of the marriage covenant, including plurality of wives, given through Joseph, the Seer, in Nauvoo, Hancock County, Illinois, July 12th, 1843":—

1. "Verily thus saith the Lord unto you, my servant Joseph, that inasmuch as you have inquired of my hand to know and understand wherein I, the Lord, justified my servants Abraham, Isaac and Jacob; as also Moses, David and Solomon, my servants, as touching the principle and doctrine of their having many wives and concubines."

2. "Behold, and lo, I am the Lord thy God, and will answer thee as touching this matter."

4. "For behold I reveal unto you a new and everlasting covenant; and if ye abide not that covenant then are ye damned, for no one can reject this covenant and be permitted to enter into my glory."

6. "And as pertaining to the **new and everlasting Covenant,** it was instituted for the fulness of my glory and he that receiveth a fullness thereof, must and shall abide the law, **or he shall be damned,** saith the Lord."

15. "Therefore, if a man marry him a wife in the world, and he marry her not by me, nor by my word, and he covenant with her so long as he is in the world, and she with him, their covenant and marriage are not of force when they are dead, and when they are out of the world, therefore they are not bound by any law when they are out of the world."

16. "Therefore, when they are out of the world they neither marry nor are given in marriage, but are appointed Angels in heaven, which angels are ministering servants, to minister for those who are worthy of a far more and exceeding and an eternal weight of glory." (To those who abide in the covenant is this great promise made).

20. "Then shall they be GODS, because they have no end, therefore they shall be from everlasting to everlasting, because they continue. Then shall they be above all, because all things are subject unto them. Then shall they be GODS because they have all power, and the angels are subject unto them."

21. "Verily, verily, I say unto you, except ye abide my law, ye cannot attain to this story."

26. "Verily, verily, I say unto you, if a man marry a wife, according to my word, and they are sealed by the Holy Spirit of promise, according to mine appointment and he or she **shall commit any sin** or transgression of the new and everlasting covenant whatsoever, and all manner of blasphemies, and if they commit no murder, wherein they shed innocent blood, yet they shall come forth in the first resurrection and enter into their exaltation."

27. "And he that abideth not this law can in no wise enter into my glory, but shall be damned, saith the Lord."

32. "Go ye therefore and do the works of Abraham, enter ye into my law and ye shall be saved."

33. "But if ye enter not into my law, ye cannot receive the promise of my father, which he made unto Abraham."

34. "God commanded Abraham, and Sarah gave Hagar to Abraham to wife, and why did she do it? Because this was the law and from Hagar sprang many people. This, therefore, was fulfilling among things, the promises."

35. "Was Abraham, therefore, under condemnation? Verily, I say unto you, Nay, for I, the Lord, commanded it."

37. "Abraham received concubines, and they bear him children, and it was accounted unto him for righteousness—as Isaac also and Jacob did none other things than that which they were commanded. They have entered into their exaltation and sit upon thrones and are **not Angels, but are Gods.**"

38. "David also received many wives and concubines, as also Solomon and Moses my servants, from the beginning of creation until this time, and in nothing did they sin, save in those things which they received not of me."

52. "And let mine handmaid Emma Smith (Joseph's first wife, R. C. E.) **receive all those that have been given unto my servant Joseph,** who are virtuous and pure before me."

61. "And again, as pertaining to the law or the priesthood; If any man espouse a virgin, and desire to espouse another and the first give her consent; and if he espouse the second and they are virgins, and have vowed to no other man, then he is justified, **he cannot commit adul-**

tery, for they are given unto him, for he cannot commit adultery with that that belongeth unto him and no one else."

62. "And if he have **ten virgins** given unto him by this law **he cannot commit adultery,** for they belong to him, and they are given unto him, therefore, is he justified."

64. "And again, Verily, verily I say unto you, if any man have a wife, who holds the keys of this power, and he Teaches unto her the law of my priesthood, as pertaining to these things, then shall she believe and administer unto him, or **she shall be destroyed,** saith the Lord our God, for I will destroy her, for I will magnify my name upon all those who receive and abide in my law."

Here is the law from their own book, given by Jesus Christ to Joseph Smith, which states clearly that polygamy and concubinage is a new and everlasting covenant. Those who obey it and enter into the practice of polygamy will pass by the Angels and **become Gods,** while good men who have not had the privilege of practising polygamy will only be Angels to serve these polygamist gods, and those who have had opportunity to enter into polygamy and refuse to do so, **will be damned.** Joseph Smith's first wife had rebelled and was herein told to receive **all those that have been given unto my servant Joseph,"** showing that he was guilty of polygamy before this revelation was given. Just think we are asked to believe under pain of damnation that Paul who had no wife will be an Angel-servant to Joseph Smith or Brigham Young who had many wives. Doc. and Cov. 132. Comment is needless.

It is but justice to say that the branch of Mormon church to which I belonged for forty-two years, known as the Reorganized church of Jesus Christ of Latter Day Saints, have never practiced polygamy, their great sin is not in practicing polygamy, but in making lies their refuge, in that for many years no part of the Mormon church including the Reorganized church ever thought of denying that Joseph had the revelation on polygamy and that he had several wives, and that it lead to his untimely death. This is clearly admitted in their public journals and private letters, but the sin of it is that after the son of the prophet decided to take his father's place at the head of the Mormon church, a council was called and the question was discussed, some leaders said, let us tell the truth, while others argued we can never make headway in the new organization if with one voice we affirm that Joseph Smith was a true prophet, seer, revelator, and God's sole mouth-piece to the church, and with another voice declare that he was playing the base hypocrite and deceiver, in that he denied publicly the ·charges urged against him by those leaving the church, and those outside of the church, regarding his having the revelation of polygamy and concubinage and his practising those secret abominations, and so it was decided of the two evils to accept what appeared to them to be the least, and so they entered into covenant, so we are informed, to just deny his guilt and throw the burden of proof upon those making the charges, for they argued, in a short time, there will be none living who were guilty with him and the papers, few in number as they were in those far distant years, will be all lost, and so the coast will be clear and thus the deception grew till now many who hold membership in the Reorganized church believe, as I did for many years, that Brigham Young and not Joseph Smith, was the author of the revelation on polygamy. When I became convinced that Joseph Smith taught, practiced and sanctioned polygamy and concubinage, and was the author of the infamous revelation on polygamy, it was the first shock to my faith, but when my eyes were opened to that, it was not long before I began to see the cruel deceptive system as it really is, and I thank God for the light He has sent into my soul, that I have been enabled to abandon the foul system and receive Christ and the Gospel as it is found in the sacred scriptures; and while I mourn the wasted years, yet I am glad of the opportunity that is left to tell the world the facts as they have come to me and I trust that God will preserve my life till I have done my part in unmasking Mormonism.

Joseph Smith's Idol—Polygamy.

"Verily thus saith the Lord unto you, my servant Joseph, that inasmuch as you have inquired of my hand to know and understand wherein I, the Lord, justified my servants **Abraham, Isaac and Jacob;** as also **Moses, David and Solomon,** my servants, as touching the principle and doctrine of their having many wives and concubines."

Comment. Smith had the word of God, and the nations of the civilized world before him all condemning polygamy. If he loved his own wife he should know that polygamy was a heart-crusher, that which must channel the face of pure womanhood with tears of unutterable woe, and yet he came before the Lord, as Ezekiel said, with the idol of polygamy and concubinage before him. All can see who wish to see truth that the very revelation shows he was guilty before he received this revelation, and that it bears proof as stated by others that he was in the cess pit of polygamy before this revelation was given, and that this was but an enlargement of other revelations which many say he had before on the subject.

W. W. Blair Testifies.

Now let us hear the testimony of another great leader in the Reorganized Church, W. W. Blair, one of the early men of the church, and the counsellor to Joseph Smith the Prophet. He says:

"The plurality-wife revelation was never **given unto the church by Joseph,** and when it was made public the first organization of the church had ceased. The church had been rejected of God, and counterfeit churches under the direction of greedy wolves had supplanted the true church. The church was not commanded to give heed unto revelations which were not given unto them, but only those which Joseph gave unto them, **and as that revelation was withheld from the church, and was repudiated and denounced by him, and as it was only intended for those who (according to the prophecy of Ezekiel) had "set up their idols in their hearts," therefore the church was not commanded to receive it."** True Latter Day Saints' Herald, March, 1860, page 64.

Comment. Here it is admitted by Brother Blair that the revelation on polygamy was in existence before Smith's death, and that it **"was repudiated and denounced by him,"** that it was not given to the church as a body. This is proof that the position taken by the Reorganization that it was not given in his time, but later, and by Brigham Young is absolutely false. The entire testimony shows that Smith taught that it was not time to give it to the world, and that many in the church could not stand the strong meat, but for the time should only have the milk. But that he had it, and taught it to the priesthood, and they to their female victims, and that he with them practiced it is beyond question.

J. W. Briggs Testifies.

Jason W. Briggs, one of the founders of the Reorganization and the President of the Twelve Apostles for many years, until he, like many hundreds of others, had his eyes opened to the false positions taken and left the church, was called to testify in the temple lot suit, said: "I heard something about the revelation on polygamy when I was in Nauvoo in 1842; I heard there was one; there was talk going on about it at that time, and continued to be." Record p. 349-505.

Writing to J. T. Clark under date of February 13th, 1888, he said: "I was at Nauvoo in 1843, the year it was found necessary to legalize polygamy by a revelation. No, I have no doubt as to the authorship of that (socalled) revelation of July 12th, 1843. It has all the ear-marks to identify it as the production of the mouthpiece of those days." Joseph is called the mouthpiece in the revelation found in Doc. and Cov., Sec. 19, in these words, "wherefore, meaning the church, thou shalt give heed unto all his words and commandments—for his words ye shall receive as if from my own mouth—in all patience and faith. Yes, and it required faith and patience on the part of those broken-hearted women who submitted to the revelations because they were persuaded that God had commanded. They were not bad women, but were the victims of misplaced confidence, and many of them found rest in hopeless insanity or the cold grave.

Ebenezer Robinson Testifies.

Ebenezer Robinson united with the church in 1835. He became clerk of the High Council in 1838; was joint editor of the Times and Seasons until 1842. He folllowed Rigdon after Smith's death, and was his counsellor. He joined the Reorganization in 1863, made affidavit in 1873, as did also his wife.

"To whom it may concern:

We, Ebenezer Robinson and Angeline Robinson, husband and wife, hereby certify that in the fall of 1843, Hyrum Smith, brother of Joseph Smith, came to our house in Nauvoo, Illinois, and taught us the doctrine of polygamy. And I, the said Ebenezer Robinson, hereby further state that he gave me special instructions how I could manage the matter so as not to have it known to the public. He also told us that while he had heretofore opposed the doctrine, he was wrong and his brother Joseph was right; referring to his teaching it.

(Sgd.) Ebenezer Robinson.
Angeline E. Robinson.

Sworn to and subscribed before me this 29th day of December, 1873.
J. M. Smallee, Notary Public.

"To whom it may concern:

This is to certify that in the latter part of November, or in December, 1843, Hyrum Smith (brother of Joseph Smith, President of the Church of Jesus Christ of Latter Day Saints) came to my house in Nauvoo, Illinois, and taught me the doctrine of spiritual wives, or polygamy.

He said he heard the voice of the Lord give the revelation on spiritual wifery (polygamy) to his brother Joseph, and that while he had heretofore opposed the doctrine he was wrong, and his brother Joseph was right all the time.

He told me to make a selection of some young woman and he would send her to me, and take her to my home, and if she should have an heir, to give out the word that she had a husband who had gone on a mission to a foreign country. He seemed disappointed when I declined to do so.

(Sgd.) E. Robinson.

Davis City, Iowa, Oct. 23, 1885.

Subscribed and sworn to before me, a notary public, in and for Decatur Country, Iowa, this 24th day of October, A D., 1885. Z. H. Gurley, Notary Public."

The reader should remember that this man Robinson was a member in high standing in the church during the life work of Joseph Smith, and while it is true that Joseph Smith is not accused by him of polygamy directly, yet Hyrum Smith was Joseph Smith's brother and his chief advisor, counsellor and the presiding Patriarch of the church. If he told the truth, Joseph was guilty; if he lied, then Hyrum Smith was a liar. His testimony is corroborated by hundreds, hence it will be taken as good evidence that Joseph was guilty as stated.

This man Robinson came into the Reorganized Church and was prominent in it for years, and testified to these things through the years. Those having the Inspired Translation of the Bible, as published by the Reorganized Church in 1867, will see that Robinson, with Joseph Smith and Bishop Rogers, was a committee to publish said Bible, and as he made his affidavit in 1873 and did not leave the Reorganized Church until 1888, that he was about fifteen years holding membership in the Reorganized Church, all the while affirming under oath that Joseph and Hyrum Smith were guilty as per his statement. Why did not the Reorganized Church take action to stop this man, if he was slandering the Prophet and Patriarch? They knew better, and they know to-day that many of their leading men now believe that Joseph had the revelations on polygamy and practiced that accursed doctrine.

Many of them make arguments that Joseph Smith did not have the revelation, **but they excuse themselves under the cover "well he**

did not have it just as it is published by the Brighamite Church."
The facts are, many believe he had it, but that Young enlarged upon it. One leading man said to me in Dow City, Iowa: Joseph had the revelation all right, but any man with brains can see that no one person was the author of the revelation **as it now appears.** "What do you mean," I said. He replied, "Well, I mean this—Joseph had the revelation on polygamy and Brigham Young or some of his apostles made certain changes and additions to it, made it to read more grammatically, so that **gives us a chance to make argument that Joseph Smith did not have that revelation."**

This little piece of trickery to evade the real facts is in keeping with the one in which twelve leading men and nineteen leading women signed the following:

"We, the undersigned members of the Church of Jesus Christ of Latter Day Saints, and residents of the City of Nauvoo, persons of families, do hereby certify and declare that we know of no other rule or system of marriage than the one published from the Book of Doctrine and Covenants, and we give this certificate to show that Dr. John C. Bennett's secret wife system is a creature of his own make, as we know of no such society in this place, nor never did.

S. Bennett
George Miller
Alpheus Cutler
Reynolds Cahoon
Wilson Law
Wilford Woodruff

N. K. Whitney
Albert Perry
Elias Higbee
John Taylor
E. Robinson
Aaron Johnson

"We, the undersigned members of the Ladies' Relief Society, and married females, do certify and declare that we know of no system of marriage being practiced in the Church of Jesus Christ of Latter Day Saints save the one contained in the Book of Doctrine and Covenants, and we give this certificate to the public to show that J. C. Bennett's secret wife system is a disclosure of his own make.

Emma Smith, President.
Elizabeth Anne Whitney, Counsellor.
Sarah M. Cleveland, Counsellor.
Eliza R. Snow, Secretary.

Mary C. Miller
Lois Cutler
Thyrsa Cahoon
Ann Hunter
Jane Law
Sophia R. Marks
Polly Z. Johnson
Abigall Works.

Catherine Petty
Sarah Higbee
Phebe Woodruff
Lenora Taylor
Sarah Hillman
Rosannah Marks
Angeline Robinson

The Josephites claim that the above statement positively denies the existence of the plural wife system in the church at all. While the Brighamites declare that they were aimed solely at the "secret wife system" of John C. Bennett, which they tell us was "as far removed from the plural marriage system set forth in the revelation had by Joseph Smith July 12th, 1843, as lechery is from virtue and foulness is from purity."

"So with that spiritual wife doctrine which lustful men attempted to promulgate at that period. Joseph the Prophet was just as much opposed to that false doctrine as anyone could be. It was a counterfeit. The true and divine order is another thing. The errors which those ladies who signed the affidavits declared were not known to them as doctrines of the church were not, are not, and never will be part of the creed of the Church of Jesus Christ of Latter Day Saints. They were conscientious in their statements." Deseret News of May 20th, 1886.

The different Mormon churches have each a different method of their own, each denounces the other, but a careful reading will show that the seed of all their systems of female defilement is found in the Revelations of their first Prophet, Joseph Smith. They differ in wording, but it reaches the same end, the satisfying of the lust of the men and the assassination of the virtue of their female victims. To prove this the reader may read up the systems employed by Joseph Smith, Brigham Young, Sidney Rigdon, James J. Strang, William Smith, John C. Bennett, Lyman Wight and others, whose names defile the pages of American history.

It is apparent that Joseph Smith desired a monopoly in this marriage business and had trouble with others desiring a share in the honor, and it was hard work for him to keep them into line as the following will show. When answering his wife regarding polygamy, he said: "Well, such a system might be, if everybody was agreed to it and would behave as they should, but they would not."—Life of the Prophet, by Tullidge, page 792. Poor Joseph, he could not get his folk to **behave** when practicing polygamy. This must have been a sore trial for him, and, as he said, it would lead him to his death, and it surely did.

"As we have lately been credibly informed that an elder of the Church of Jesus Christ of Latter Day Saints, by the name of Hiram Brown, has been **preaching** polygamy and other false and corrupt doctrines in the County of Lapeer, State of Michigan;

"This is to notify him and the church in general that he has been cut off from the church for his iniquity; and he is further notified to appear at the special conference on the 6th of April next to make answer to these charges. (Sgd.) "Joseph Smith,
"Hyrum Smith,
"Presidents of said church."

Comment. Hiram Brown's iniquity' consisted not in believing or practicing, but in **preaching polygamy**. Brown was the wrong man to preach it, and Michigan the wrong place, as may appear from the following:

Taken from President Joseph Smith's diary for October 5th, 1843:
"Gave instructions to try those persons who were preaching, teaching or practicing the doctrine of plurality of wives; for, according to the law, **I hold the keys of this power in the last days;** for there is never

but one on earth at a time on whom the power and its keys are conferred; and I have constantly said no man shall have **but one wife at a time unless the Lord directs otherwise.**"

We are requested to believe that the Lord advised the church by revelation through Joseph Smith to be careful and not teach the secrets of the church until the proper time came for the world to know them.

"Until the open enunciation of the doctrine of celestial marriage by the publication of the revelation on the subject in 1852, no elder was authorized to announce it to the world. The Almighty has revealed things on many occasions which were for His servants and not for the world. Jesus enjoined His disciples on several occasions to keep to themselves principles that he made known to them. And this injunction, "Cast not your pearls before swine lest they trample them under their feet and turn again and rend you," has become as familiar as a common proverb. In the rise of the church the Lord has occasion to admonish His servants in regard to revelations that were afterwards permitted to be published.

"I say unto you, hold your peace until I shall see fit to make all things known unto the world concerning this matter."

"And now I say unto you, keep these things from going abroad into the world until it is expedient in me."

"But a commandment I give unto them that they shall not boast themselves of these things, neither speak of them before the world, for these things are given unto you for your profit and your salvation." Doct. and Cov.

Under these instructions elders had no right to promulgate anything but that which they were authorized to teach. And when assailed by enemies and accused of practicing things which were really not countenanced in the church, they were justified in denying those imputations and at the same time avoiding the avowal of such doctrines as were not yet intended for the world. This course which they have taken when necessary, by commandment, is all the ground which their accusers have for charging them with falsehood.

From the hundreds of leading men and women of the church, under Joseph Smith, the prophet, I herewith submit the evidence of a few to show beyond question, many of them under oath, that Joseph Smith had revelations authorizing the practice of polygamy and that he had many wives, sealed to him, who lived with him in all the earthly relationship touching married life, many of the women under oath testifying to this fact.

It is a great sorrow to me to have given forty-two years to the defence of this man, schooling myself to believe that those who had testified against him had misrepresented him, and then to discover that I was mistaken, and that he was guilty. But what distresses me more than anything else is that the leaders of the Reorganized Church admitted his guilt, as shown in this paper, and when they concluded that the witnesses were nearly all dead, or soon would be, and the few papers printed which proved his guilt were nearly all destroyed, that they would deny all guilt on the part of Smith and place the guilt on Brigham Young. When I became fully convinced of this monstrous deception, in which I with thousands of others had been victimized, I could do but one thing, and that was to denounce it and sever my connection with the rulers who have agreed to make lies their refuge, and under falsehood hide the guilty.

To take this step has cost me much that is dear in life. Thousands throughout the world who love me will now despise me and think that I have forsaken the way of the Lord and become the enemy of truth. Ah, could they feel what I feel, they would know that it is stern duty and love of the right that compels me to take the step that hurls me out of their lives forever. I shall do what I can to show them the sunny way of Christ untarnished with this hideous bugbear and to this end have I devoted my life.

The Last Straw

Let me say that the leaders of the Reorganized Church, since I tendered my resignation and left them, have written several tracts and have published more than 200 feet long, and a column wide of matter in their three church papers against me, claiming that I have admitted that I was convinced of all this polygamy and other infamous conduct of Joseph Smith and his people, for more than ten years before I left their church, and thus they argue that I was a hypocrite and a liar all these years when representing the church. In reply to that I wish to say they cruelly misrepresent me. I nowhere have asserted that I was convinced of all that dirt ten years before I left them. The truth is simply this: it is true that for years I have read and heard stories concerning Smith, but I had such confidence in him that I refused to believe them, first because many of those stories were told by those who were guilty of polygamy themselves, or by those who never were Mormons, and could only give hearsay statements. I admit they at times staggered me, but when I read the positive and at times sworn statements of the leading men and women of the Reorganized Church, such as Joseph Smith, his mother, W. W. Blair, Isaac Sheen, the Robinsons, President Briggs, President Marks, the Gurlies and a host of others, I was made powerless to oppose longer. I then began to measure the statements made by the people who had testified against him from his childhood till his untimely death with those of the Reorganized Church, and my last effort of resistance was taken from me.

One straw would not break the camel's back, but continue to pile straw on, then it is said "the last straw breaks the camel's back." One drop of water would not drown a person, but let the drops come faster and faster and in larger and larger quantities and sufficient water will come to drown the man. I carried the burden till it broke me down. I battled mid the surging waters till the waves overcame me. For some years I had little to say concerning Joseph Smith's private life, nor did I try hard to defend him on the question of polygamy. When men at times took extravagant positions concerning him, I tried to show the weakness of their position. On one or two occasions I examined their evidence, and I did this among my fears and doubts, still hoping that light would come, but the more I read and the more I studied, the more I was silenced. One by one the former arguments were demolished, position after position was broken down, until I was finally convinced that Joseph Smith early in life was dishonest and lewd, and that long before polygamy was established in his church by the publication of a written or printed revelation, he practiced evil and he had several revelations on the matter and finally gave the famous revelation under date of July 12th, 1843, which hurried him on to his untimely death. That this is the true position regarding the matter I am now fully convinced.

Some argue that I have committed an unpardonable sin because I have changed my mind and become converted from darkness to light. Abraham (Josh. 24, 2), Moses (Exodus, 2), changed their minds. The apostles (Matt. 18: 1, 3), after years of intimacy with Jesus had to become converted to the great light. Paul, honest and sincere, was wrong and had to change, Acts. 9: 1-2. Millions of honest people have had to change. Why should I be slandered because I have grown in grace and in the knowledge of the truth?

Mormons Teach That Both God and Christ Had Many Wives and That Polygamists Will Become Gods and Preside Over Worlds Like God.

That the doctrine of polygamy and many gods was taught by Joseph Smith is already proven in this work, but we purpose to give quotations from the leading works of Smith and other prominent Mormons that tell the story in their own words.

"You have got to learn to be Gods yourselves—the same as all other Gods have done,—by going from one small degree to another until you are able to sit in glory as does those who are enthroned in everlasting power." Joseph Smith, King Follett Sermon.

We have given a brief history of the Book of Abraham, as translated by Joseph Smith, elsewhere in this book. That this book was considered the Word of the Lord, we quote from both the Utah and Reorganized Mormon leaders:

"The Book of Abraham translated from Egyptian Papyrus through the **Gift and Power of the Holy Ghost,** by Joseph the Seer." O. Pratt, The Seer, page 68.

"The Book of Abraham was translated by the **Gift and Power of the Holy Ghost by Joseph Smith.**" Reorganized Church Herald, 1860, page 270.

"We propose to prove that all the revelations which Joseph Smith gave unto the church, we are bound to give heed unto, if the first edition of that book is divine (Doctrine and Covenants) all the subsequent revelations which are contained in the Book of Covenants, **In the Book of Abraham, etc., Are Equally Divine.**" Saints' Herald, 1860, p. 63. Shook on Polygamy, page 162, shows Pres. Blair wrote the article from which I quote from the Saints' Herald.

WAS JOSEPH SMITH A POLYGAMIST? 57

"This record (Book of Abraham) is now in course of translation **by means of the Urim and Thummim."** Editor of Mill Star, July, 1842, pages 45-46.

Here we have it stated by themselves that the Book of Abraham was translated by the gift and power of the Holy Ghost, by means of the Urim and Thummim, and is equal to any revelation given by God to Smith. Now we will show that in this Book of Abraham, the doctrine of many gods is presented to the world by Smith, and that both the Utah and Reorganized Churches taught and believed it.

"The Scriptural evidences show that the revelations in the New Translation of the Bible (Smith's new bible), and in the Book of Abraham **concerning the Gods** all harmonize together." Saints' Herald, 1860, page 283.

Statement Quoted From Book of Abraham.

"And the Gods said, 'Let there be light'; the Gods called the light day; and the Gods organized the earth; and the Gods said, 'let us prepare the waters'; and the Gods prepared the earth; and the Gods took counsel among themselves; the Gods went down and organized man; and the Gods planted a garden; and the Gods said, 'let us make a helpmate for Adam'; and the Gods formed every beast of the field." Book of Abraham. See Mill Star, July 1842, also the Pearl of Great Price, 1888, Saints' Herald, 1860, page 284.

We have shown from Joseph Smith and the Utah and Reorganized church publications their defense of the many Gods, none can deny this.

"Now hear it, O inhabitants of the earth, when our Father Adam came into the garden of Eden, he came into it with a celestial body and brought Eve **one of his wives** with him. He is **our Father and our God and the only God with whom we have to do."** Brigham Young Sermon, Mill Star, Vol. 15, page 769, 1853.

God and Christ Both Had Many Wives and Christ Was Not Begotten by The Holy Ghost But By Adam, Who is the God of This World.

When the virgin Mary conceived the child Jesus, the Father had begotten him in His own likeness, **He was not begotten by the Holy Ghost,** and who is the Father? He is the first of the human family, and when he took a tabernacle, it was begotten by his father in heaven, after the same manner as the tabernacles of Cain and Abel and the rest of the sons and daughters of Adam and Eve. Now, remember from this time forth and forever, that Jesus Christ was not begotten by the Holy Ghost." Sermon by Brigham Young, Mill Star, Vol. 15, pages 769, 1853.

"The Gods who dwell in the heavens from which our spirits came, are beings who have been redeemed from the grave in a world which existed before the foundation of this earth was laid. These Gods being redeemed from the grave with their wives, are immortal and eternal, and will die no more, but they and their wives will be supremely happy. All the endearing ties of congugal love, which existed in their bosoms when terrestial and fallen beings, are now greatly increased and perfected." Apostle Pratt, in Seer, Vol. 1 and 2, pages 23-24.

"Celestial beings beget children composed of fluid which circulates in their veins, which is spiritual, therefore their children must be spirits and not flesh and bones. This is the origin of our spiritual organization in heaven. The spirits of all mankind, destined for this earth, were begotten by a father and born of a mother in heaven, long anterior to the formation of this world. In the heavens where our spirits were born there are many Gods, each one of them has his own wife or wives. Each God, through his wife or wives, raises up a numerous family of sons and daughters, indeed there will be no end to the increase of his own children, for each father and mother will be in a condition to multiply forever and ever. As soon as each God has begotten many millions of male and female spirits, he, in connection with his sons, organizes a new world after a similar order to the one which we now inhabit, where he sends both the male and female spirits to inhabit tabernacle of flesh and bones. Thus each God forms a world for the accommodation of his own sons and daughters." Ibid No. 3, page 37.

God and Jesus Polygamists.

I had thought to pass by this most awful position taken by the Mormons, but some opine it is my duty to show the world the real teachings of this degraded system, called Mormonism, so we will give the reader a few brief quotations from their own writings as I find them in print in their leading journals.

"The fleshy body of Jesus required a mother as well as a father, therefore the father and mother of Jesus, according to the flesh must have been associated together in the capacity of husband and wife, hence the virgin must have been, for the time being, **the lawful wife of God the Father.** It would have been unlawful for any man to have interfered with Mary, who was already espoused to Joseph, but God having created all men and women had the most perfect right to do with His own creation, according to His holy will and pleasure. He had a lawful right to overshadow the virgin in the **capacity of a husband.** Inasmuch as **God** was the first husband to her, it may be that he only gave her to be the wife of Joseph in this mortal state, and that he intended, after the resurrection, to again take her as one of his own wives to raise up immortal spirits in eternity."

"Now, let us inquire whether there are any intimations in Scripture concerning the **wives of Jesus**. One thing is certain, that there were several holy women, that greatly loved Jesus, such as Mary and Martha, her sister, and Mary Magdalene, and Jesus greatly loved them and associated with them much. He appeared first to these women, or at least to one of them, Mary Magdalene. Now it would be very natural for a husband in the resurrection to appear first to his **own dear wives.** The psalmist David prophecies in particular concerning the **wives of the Son of God.** We quote from the English version of the Bible, translated about three hundred and fifty years ago: 'All thy garments smell of myrrh and aloes, and cassia when thou comest out of the ivory palaces where they have made thee glad, **king's daughters were among thine honorable wives, upon thy right hand did stand the queen in a vesture of gold.'** Pages 45, 8-9.

"Let it be remembered that the Son of God is expressly represented as having honorable **wives**. King James' translators were not willing that this passage should have a literal translation, lest it should give countenance to **Polygamy,** therefore they altered the translation to **honorable women,** instead of **wives.**" Apostle Pratt, in "The Seer," Vol. 1, No. 10, pages 158-9, 160.

"We have now clearly shown that God the Father had a plurality of wives, one or more being in eternity, by whom He begat our spirits as the Spirit of Jesus, His first born, and another being upon the earth by whom He begat the tabernacle of Jesus as His only begotten in this world. We have also proved most clearly that the Son followed the example of His Father, and became the great bridegroom to whom king's daughters and many honorable wives were to be married." Ibid, No. 11, pages 172-173.

"If at the marriage at Cana of Galilee, Jesus was the bridegroom, and took unto him Mary and Martha, and the other Mary, whom Jesus loved, it shocks not our nerves if there was not an attachment and familiarity between our Saviour and these women highly improper, only in the relation of husband and wife. Then we have no sense of propriety, or of the characteristics of good and refined society. Wisely then was it concealed; but when the Saviour poured His soul unto death, when nailed to the cross, **He saw His seed of children,** but who shall declare **His generation."** Apostle O. Hyde, Sermon, Beadle, page 304.

This man Hyde was baptized in 1831, ordained an Apostle in 1835. Seeing the wickedness of the leaders, he left the church and made oath against Joseph Smith, swearing to terrible things. He returned to the church, was sent to bless the land of Palestine, was faithful to Joseph Smith and Brigham Young till death, which occurred in Utah, 1878.

I could fill a volume of this kind of teaching from the leaders of the church, but will drop the curtain on the awful blasphemy.

In conclusion, I draw your attention to this point, that we have shown by the sermons and books of Joseph Smith, Brigham Young, the two first prophets and seers of the Mormon church, as also from Apostle Pratt, the most powerful man Mormonism has produced, and prominent leaders of the Reorganized Mormon church as recorded in the Saints' Herald, that they believed in many Gods, No one can deny this point from their own leading men of both branches of the Mormon Church.

In justice to the Reorganized church, let me say that during the forty-two years of my connection with it, I never heard their leaders teach the doctrine of many Gods, that they did endorse the "Gods" theory, is shown in their writings of early years.

Now, it is clear that from the doctrine of the Gods many Mormons have argued that polygamy makes the Gods, for the more wives the larger the families and so they become Gods. Now we will show from the last revelation Smith had on polygamy, that the Gods have an important part to play in that revelation.

The revelation given to Joseph Smith, July 12th, 1843, has sixty-six paragraphs in it, and as I have quoted largely from it in another part of this work, I will only quote briefly from it here.

First paragraph states that Joseph prayed the Lord to show him wherein God had justified Abraham, Isaac, Jacob, David, Solomon and others in the principle of having many wives and concubines. The other sixty-five paragraphs reveal the secret and give him to understand, stating in the following terms, he that would receive a fullness of his glory "Must and shall abide the law (touching polygamy and concubinage) **or he shall be damned,** saith the Lord."

Paragraphs 15, 16, 17 state those who marry the one wife for time and refuse to keep the law of polygamy, will not have a chance to get more wives in eternity, and so will not be Gods, but only Angels. "These angels did not abide my law, therefore they cannot be enlarged, but remain separately and single, without exaltation in their saved condition to all eternity, and from henceforth **are not Gods but are Angels of God forever and ever."**

The 19th paragraph states those who abide the law (of polygamy) "They shall pass by the Angels." Their glory shall be a fullness and a continuation of the **seeds forever and ever."**

Pratt has told us that this seed matter means that they with their many wives will bear children forever, and the twentieth paragraph, speaking of those polygamists says, "Then shall they be Gods, because they have all power and the Angels are subject unto them."

Here is the corner stone of Mormonism from their prophets and Apostles, sermons and books. Just think, such men as Paul and Peter shall be merely Angels to wait on and be subjected to Joseph Smith and Brigham Young. Poor Paul without even one wife, and Peter with but one, is to be but the humble servants of Mormon polygamists through eternity. We leave it with you. No words could describe its filthiness like their own.

CHAPTER III.

Mormonism Against The World

There Are But Two Churches

In Mormon theology there are but two churches, one is the church of Christ, the other the church of the Devil. In proof of this, I will quote from the standard books of Mormonism and the leaders of that body.

Hypocritical priests of Mormonism sometimes deny this and attempt to curry favor from the press and pulpit of Christianity, but it is only when they wish a favor of some kind, or desire to make inroads upon the gullibility of the people. But to the proof:

"Behold, there is, save it be **Two Churches:** the one is the church of the Lamb of God, and the other is the church of the Devil. Wherefore, whoso belongeth not to the church of the Lamb of God belongeth to that great church, which is the mother of abominations; and she is the **whore** of all the earth." Book of Mormon, page 40, First Nephi, 3 ch., v. 220-223.

In the first revelation published in the book known as the Doctrine and Covenants, Jesus Christ when speaking to Joseph Smith, is reported to have said, speaking of the Mormon church, as "The **only true and living church** upon the face of the whole earth, with which I, the Lord, am well pleased." D. C. 1-5.

Orson Pratt, the most eloquent Apostle, and the greatest writer of Mormonism, says: "Since the church with its authority and power has been caught away from the earth, the great Mother of Harlots, with all her descendents, has blasphemously assumed authority of administering some of the sacred ordinances of the gospel." Revelation Necessary, by O. Pratt.

To this may be added the statement made by Apostle W. H. Kelley, President of the Apostolic Quorum of the Reorganized Church: "The priesthood having been caught up to heaven, no man on earth has authority to minister in gospel ordinances, and hence the necessity for new revelation." Presidency and Priesthood, page 224.

We could fill a large volume in support of the above positions, but let it be sufficient for me to say, that the position taken by the Mormon church of every stripe, is, that the church as established by Christ fell into apostasy, lost the priesthood, or authority to preach the gospel and administer in the ordinances of the church, and that the Roman Catholic Church is the Mother of Harlots, and the Protestant churches are her daughters, all imposters devoid of priesthood authority, and hence form the **Church of the Devil,** while Joseph Smith and others have been called of God by direct revelation from heaven and some of them have been ordained by Angels to administer the gospel and work the works of God, as directed by direct revelation.

God and Christ Visit Joseph Smith.

In support of this I quote the first vision that Joseph Smith professed to have: "He got religion" and went to pray under the shadows of a great tree in the rear of his father's farm, when he had offered what he called his "first audible prayer," he declares that God came down from heaven and brought Jesus with him, and when God introduced Jesus to Joseph, he seems to have lapsed into silence and Joseph at once asked Jesus which of all the sects was right, and Christ is reported to have answered: "The churches are all wrong, their creeds are an abomination before me, and their professors are all corrupt." See Church History Vol. 1, page 10. And from that day to this Mormonism has denounced every church on the earth as corrupt, drawing near God with their lips but having their hearts far from him, In a word, those men and women who have sacrificed their lives to tell the heathen world of Jesus and His love, are a combination of hypocrites. And every mother who, in the dimming shadows of eventide hath gathered her children around her knee and taught them "Gentle Jesus" or "Our Father" has been guilty of deception toward their little ones, only "drawing near God with their lips while their hearts were far from him," and so the world has been filled with this Mormon delusion and many thousands have believed it, and the time has come that liberty has come to us and we hope to say something that will help the world to know Mormonism as it really is, and that for the good of the deluded Mormons, as well as those who stand in jeopardy from their deceptions.

Reorganized Mormons Deny That God and Christ Appeared to Joseph Smith.

Before we leave this angel matter and the different stories concerning it, let us draw the readers' attention to the conflicting accounts of the first heavenly message Smith is supposed to receive.

The Reorganized Mormons in the last few years are ashamed of this lying story by which Christ is made to denounce every honest man in all the Christian churches as vile hypocrites, and the churches as abomination in his sight, and they misrepresented this vision and, when writing the last history, they tell it so differently that no one would think it was the same place or occasion. The visit of God and Christ is entirely expunged from the story and four times in the first page, we are told that it was an Angel who came to Smith. It starts out as follows: "The history of the church begins with the **visit of an Angel** to a young man named Joseph Smith. The angel came to him while he was out in the woods praying aloud," and what was said is misrepresented in an inexcusable manner. Surely Mormonism has made lies their refuge. See Young Peoples' History of Church, Vol. 1, page 1.

John the Baptist Ordained Smith and Cowdery.

The general claim made by Mormonism is that Joseph Smith and Oliver Cowdery were called of God to the Aaronic priesthood by an Angel, who said he was John the Baptist; that this Angel ordained them by the laying on of hands, and thus the Aaronic priesthood was restored to earth May 15th, 1829. Tullidge Hist., page 43, Church Hist., Vol. 1, page 34.

With regard to this ordination by John the Baptist, Oliver Cowdery a few years after, when he left the church and denounced Joseph Smith as guilty of most every kind of sin, including murder, says "Smith held a mysterious power over him, tried to destroy his life, and that the voice of the Angel who claimed to be John the Baptist was strikingly similar with the voice of Sidney Rigdon (this is a mild way of telling the world that the Angel who ordained Smith and himself was none other than Sidney Rigdon). This statement was made by Cowdery and published by him in Norton, Ohio, in 1839. Shook's Origin of Book of Mormon, pages 49-54.

Baptized Each Other—Holy Ghost Before Ordination or Confirmation.

Having learned from the Mormon authorities that there is no true church on earth save the Mormon church, and that that is the true church because their ministers are called to the priesthood by direct revelation from God to preach, baptize for the remission of sins, and confirm those baptized by the laying on of hands for the gift of the Holy Ghost; this brings sinners to Christ and adopts them into the church and Kingdom of God, and outside of this organization there is no true church. Now, let us look at the inconsistency and deception of Mormonism.

First let me show that according to Joseph Smith's own story, while he and Oliver Cowdery were translating the Book of Mormon they came to a place which showed them that water baptism was for the remission of sins. They went to the woods to pray, when John the Baptist as an Angel, came down from heaven, laid his hands upon them and ordained them to the Aaronic priesthood. He commanded them to go and baptize each other. Smith baptized Cowdery and Cowdery baptized Smith, then Smith ordained Cowdery to the Aaronic priesthood, and afterwards Cowdery ordained Smith to the Aaronic priesthood. These ordinations were performed by the laying on of hands. The story continues, saying after they had baptized and ordained each other, the Holy Ghost fell upon them both immediately, so much so that both enjoyed the spirit of prophecy. Tullidge, Life of Joseph Smith, pages 43-44, Church Hist. Vol. 1, page 36.

The reader will notice here that Smith and Cowdery placed little value on the ordination of the Angel, for they each ordained the other, but remember the ordination of each other did not take place till after they had baptized each other; in a word, if the Angelic ordination was of any value, why ordain each other. If of no value, then we have the two leading Mormons administering baptism before their ordination, and worse and more of it, Smith baptized Cowdery before he was baptized himself. But we are told that the Angel John told them "The Aaronic priesthood had not the power of laying on of hands for the gift of the Holy Ghost, but that this would be conferred upon them later, when three angels known as Peter, James and John would confer the Melchisedec priesthood upon them." Ibid, page 43.

But wonders shall never cease. This Holy Ghost that could not come but by a Melchisedec priest laying on hands to impart it, has slipped out before this priesthood came and Joseph tells us here how the Holy Ghost came upon them as soon as they were baptized and they both delivered prophecies in great power.

Here then we have Mormonism starting by an unbaptized man baptizing another man, then being ordained by the same man, and receiving the Holy Ghost without the laying on of hands or confirmation. This story destroys Mormonism, and exposes its leading opposition a against the Catholic and Protestant churches.

But we proceed: Within a month of their baptism they had baptized Samuel Smith and Hyrum Smith (brothers of Joseph), and David and Peter Whitmer. They all received the Holy Ghost and obtained revelations from God direct. Yet remember, the great baptism of the Spirit, the gift of the Holy Ghost, could not then and cannot now, according to Mormon theology, be enjoyed until a Melchisedec priest lays hands upon you for the giving of that Holy Ghost. There was not yet a Melchisedec priest on the earth.

Ordained Elders Confirmed For Holy Ghost Long After They Had It.

The history shows that Joseph soon discovered that something had to be done, if they could receive direct communication with God, see and talk to Angels, have the Holy Ghost and prophecy, all without the Melchisedec priesthood, all without even an Elder, let alone Apostles and High Priests, why bother with them, but he must have this greater priesthood or the first Angel message of John the Baptist would be proved false, so he informs us that they betook themselves to prayer and the Lord told him to ordain Oliver Cowdery to be an Elder in the church of Jesus Christ, and that he should ordain me to the same office. They met, took bread and wine, ordained each other, and then laid their hands on the others whom they had previously baptized, for the gift of the Holy Ghost. Tullidge, page 73.

The reader will see the farce, They ordained each other and confirmed all the others by laying on of the hands for the gift of the Holy Ghost, when if they tell the truth they had the Holy Ghost long before the conferring of it.

We understand by the History of the Church, that the ordination of Cowdery and Smith to the Melchisedec priesthood took place April 6th, 1830, in Peter Whitmer's house, the same day the church was organized with six members. Ibid, page 75, D. C. 17, 1.

The reader will see that several were baptized, ordained Aaronic priests, received visits from Angels, enjoyed the gift of the Holy Ghost, saw visions, and spoke in prophecy, all before they were in possession of the Melchisedec priesthood, and had not organized the church. The day the church was organized the two leaders were ordained Elders, and confirmed the others for the gift of the Holy Ghost, long after they had received it.

Smith and Cowdery Ordained by Peter, James and John.

Now, we are told that Joseph was commanded that day to ordain Cowdery an Elder, and Cowdery was to ordain Joseph an Elder, which they did on April 6th, 1830. But may we enquire, what about the promise of the Angel John the Baptist made, saying "Peter, James and John held the keys of the Melchisedec priesthood." Has Joseph been in too great a hurry, has he robbed these three Melchisedec Angels out of their job, by ordaining Oliver and having himself ordained by Oliver? No, Joseph has a way out of it, and so we turn to a revelation found in Doctrine and Covenants, Sect. 26, which looks like a frame-up: "Listen to the voice of Jesus Christ—during a long revelation Christ says, "And also with Peter, James and John by whom I have ordained you and confirmed you to be Apostles and special witnesses of my name."

Cowdery speaking of this Angelic ordination says: "I was present with Joseph Smith when the Higher or Melchisedec priesthood was conferred by the Holy Angel from on high. This priesthood was then conferred on each other by the will and commandment of God." Church Hist., Vol. 1, page 64. Myth. of Manuscript Found, page 80.

Joseph Smith tells us where this Angelic ordination took place, he says: "The voice of Peter, James and John in the wilderness between Harmony, Susquehanna County and Colesville, Broome County, on the Susquehanna River, declaring themselves as possessing the keys of the kingdom, and of the dispensation of the fullness of times." D. C. 110, 20.

So the ordinations of Smith and Cowdery are about as big a mess as anything that has ever found its way into history.

The Aaronic priesthood conferred by ordination under the hands of the Angel John the Baptist, but counted as a thing of naught, for Smith ordained Cowdery and Cowdery ordained Smith to this same priesthood. Then Peter, James and John ordain these same two men to the Melchisedec priesthood, and again they set this at naught and proceed to ordain each other. What would we think of the twelve apostles of Bible times after Jesus had ordained them and said: "Ye have not chosen me but I have chosen you and **ordained you,"** John 15, 16, if they were to set that ordination aside and proceed to ordain each other again. So much for the Smith ordinations he and Cowdery knew well that the Angelic ordinations were invented by Smith. Cowdery as already referred to, admit in effect that the John the Baptist was Sidney Rigdon, the dark horse of Mormonism.

Pratt on Angelic Ordination.

Orson Pratt, perhaps the greatest Apostle of Mormonism, when writing of this Angelic ordination says: "Mr. Smith testifies that Peter, James and John came to him in the capacity of ministering angels and by the laying on of hands ordained him an apostle and commanded him to preach, baptize, lay on hands for the gift of the Holy Ghost and administer all other ordinances of the gospel as they themselves did in ancient days." Divine Authority, page 4. Mill Star, Vol. 1, 15, page 491.

Young Joseph Says No Angels Came.

We could fill a volume of Mormon statements regarding this angelic ordination, but shades of Smithanity, what will we do when we turn to the son of Joseph Smith, who, when writing the history of the church, denies that Peter, James and John ever really came to ordain Joseph Smith and Oliver Cowdery. After making a long article on the matter, he concludes by saying: "Nor is their any evidence that Peter, James and John were present either when the instruction was given to ordain, or when the ordination took place." Ch. Hist., Vol. 1, pages 64-65.

Here we have Joseph Smith and Oliver Cowdery showing that the Angel John the Baptist ordained them to the Aaronic priesthood, and told them that Peter, James and John would come to ordain them to the Melchisedec, then we have Cowdery telling that they did come, and we have Joseph Smith telling the spot on the Susquehanna River, then Pratt tells the same story, and then to expose the lie and try to bury it so that Mormonism will not be required to meet it any longer, we have young Joseph Smith, the prophet and successor, telling us "'Taint so." We have Smith, Cowdery, Pratt and all Mormonism testifying to this Angelic ordination for eighty years, and we have the latest production of Mormonism in the form of Smith's son denying it.

Ministry Must Be Called By Revelation.

Now let us leave these Angelic muddles and return to the call of the priesthood. The Mormon cry is and has ever been, "A man has no authority to preach, baptize or act as a Christian minister unless he has been called by God through a revelation given by the Holy Ghost or some Angel." This cannot be denied by any man in Mormonism; it is the most prominent and distinctive plea of every branch of Mormonism.

Now, we have seen that Smith's story about John the Baptist and Peter, James and John, is contradicted by himself and others, and denied by his own son in regard to most of them. We have seen that under the direction of that same son a new history has been published that denies the visit of God and Christ to his father. Now let us see that the Mormons have not lived up to their own creed in regard to the call of the ministry by direct revelation.

Priests Not Called By God.

The Mormon church baptized people as early as 1829, and the church was organized in 1830, yet no Apostles were chosen till 1835.

So the church could and did exist without Apostles for five years. If that be true, why not forever? But when they were called surely after all the business with God, Christ, Angels and the Holy Ghost, and the great denunciation of all churches 'with a man-made ministry,' these apostles will be called by an Angel or God or Christ or by Revelation. But were they? No, no, dear reader, they are man-made if Mormon history be true. "Joseph stated that the first business of the meeting was for the Three Witnesses of the Book of Mormon to pray, and then proceed to **choose twelve men** from the church as apostles, to go to all nations, kindreds, tongues and people. The Three Witnesses, namely, Oliver Cowdery, David Whitmer and Martin Harris united in prayer. They were then blessed by the laying on of the hands of the Presidency, and then proceeded to make **choice of the twelve as follows:**" Church Hist., Vol. 1, page 541; Tullidge, page 150.

Here you have it from their own history, after all the talk of "No man taking the honor of priesthood unless called of God by revelation," here we have it, the Three Witnesses **made choice of the twelve apostles.** We may stop to enquire what became of those twelve men. We must be brief for a darker history of apostasy and criminality could scarcely be written of twelve men than can be written and has been written of many of those men. Five of them got into trouble with Smith and they denounced him as about everything that was bad and left the church. One of them was killed in a fight, and six of them went into polygamy and became the scoundrels of the darkest kind of Mormon infamy, Brigham Young being among them, with the two Pratts and Kimball. It is said that when the Three Witnesses refused to select William Smith as one of the Twelve, Joseph compelled them to place his brother William as one of the Twelve Apostles, yet this William Smith was a low-down drunkard, and had three wives at one time, and gave his brother Joseph a sound thrashing. Ch. Hist., Vol. 1, pages 592-624; Tullidge, page 577.

Apostles Led Church Into Great Sin.

The Mormons affirm we must have Twelve inspired Apostles in the true church, and they quote 1 Cor. 12, to show these inspired Apostles should be in the church for the **"perfecting of the saints,"** for the edifying of the body of Christ, etc. But, let the world look for a more degrading set of men than the majority of the Mormon Apostles of the early days, and they will be disappointed. They led the church into murders, adulteries, Adam-God worship, polygamy and made Mormonism a stench in the nostrils of civilization.

Now we have seen that neither Smith, Cowdery or the Twelve Apostles were called of God in the first organization of the Mormon church, and that system led their followers into most every evil. Now let us turn to the coming forth of what is known as Reorganized Mormonism, and commonly called the Reorganized Church of Jesus Christ of Latter Day Saints.

CHAPTER IV.

History of The Reorganized Church of Jesus Christ of Latter Day Saints

Jason W. Briggs.

Jason W. Briggs was baptized in the year 1841, ordained an Elder in 1842, followed Brigham Young till 1846, then preached for and belonged to James J. Strang's church till 1850; was called an Apostle in the church of William Smith in 1851. He testifies that all these churches taught polygamy, and he left them.

In November, 1851, Jason W. Briggs claims that the Lord gave him a revelation which caused him to leave the William Smith church and look for the coming of the seed of Joseph Smith to become president of the church. He sent this revelation around to several places.

In June, 1852, he, with a few others, called a conference over which he presided. They resolved to denounce all leaders and wait for the seed of the prophet to come and preside over the church. The next October they had another little conference, Briggs presiding. At this conference they presented to the Lord the question "Is polygamy of God?" They had a revelation that the Lord regarded it as an abomination. The conference of 1853 elected J. W. Briggs president and he was at that conference ordained one of the Twelve Apostles. A committee of three was chosen to select seven men to be ordained Apostles, and Briggs was one of the seven, so that the first Apostles of the Reorganized Church were chosen by men and not by revelation.

Nothing of special importance transpired until 1860, when Joseph Smith was chosen and ordained president of the Reorganized Church. Briggs does not appear to have attended that conference. Z. H. Gurley was president of the conference, and presented Joseph Smith, the church. J. W. Briggs was present at the June conference of that year. At this time he was made president of the Apostolic Quorum, and retained that position till he left the church in 1886. Ch. Hist., Vol. 3, pages 737-742.

Now this great man, after being the leading man in the reorganization for many years, and the first church historian and perhaps the strongest man that ever occupied in the Reorganized church, left it, stepping first from the first presidency of the church, to the Apostolic Quorum, and from that out into the world apart from Mormonism where he died in 1889.

Before his death he testified that he "heard about the revelation on polygamy while in Nauvoo in 1842," that was before the last revelation was given by Smith on that subject. He said further, "I was in Nauvoo in 1843, the year it was found necessary to legalize polygamy by a revelation." "No, I have no doubt as to the authorship of that so-called revelation of July 12th, 1843. It has all the earmarks to identify it as the production of the mouth-piece of those days." Joseph Smith is called the 'mouth-piece.' D. C. 19. See Record, page 349-505, and later in a letter to J. T. Clark, Feb. 13, 1888.

Here we have the man who had the first revelation regarding the Reorganization, the First President of it, the First President of the Apostolic Quorum becoming convinced that Joseph Smith had the revelation on polygamy, and other evils existing in the church, so much so that he left it and died out of the church.

William Marks.

William Marks joined the church sometime before 1837, as the history states that he was a member of the High Council that year. In 1839 he was chosen President of the Nauvoo State. He had some trouble with Joseph Smith and Joseph wrote insinuating that Marks was a traitor to him and the church. Mill. Star, Vol. 22, page 631.

Marks was rejected as president of the Nauvoo State in October, 1844. When the church split after the death of Joseph he went with Sidney Rigdon into his church. He soon left Rigdon's church and wrote a letter to the Times and Seasons, Vol. 10, page 115, affirming that he had been deceived by Rigdon, and testifying that Brigham Young and the Twelve were the proper persons to lead the church.

In 1846 he was counsellor to James J. Strang in his church. In 1849 Strang rebuked him by revelation for his bad conduct. See Gosp. Herald, Vol. 5, page 17. He retained his position as one of the first presidency in the Strangite Church till 1850, or after. He next leaves Strang, and we find him with a faction organized by Charles B. Thompson. He soon left the Thompson church, and we find him in 1855, a member of the church organized by Apostle John E. Page. He left that church and then joined the Reorganized Church in 1859.

When Joseph Smith came into the church in 1860, William Marks assisted to ordain him President of the High Priesthood, President of the Church, Prophet, Seer and Revelator. Marks was ordained Counsellor to President Joseph Smith. He retained that position till his death which occurred in 1872. Ch. Hist., Vol. 3, pages 721-726.

William Marks admits that polygamy was taught and practiced in the church to an alarming degree during the lifetime of Joseph Smith, and that the Lord revealed to him, that the church had become corrupt by departing from the true principles and doctrines of Christ, and that it would be disorganized. He also states that just before Joseph Smith was killed, that Smith came to him, had a long talk to him about polygamy, stating that polygamy would prove the overthrow of the church, and suggested methods by which the practice should be abandoned by the church. This statement implicating Smith on the polygamy question is recorded in Herald, Vol. 1, pages 25-26, 1860.

Zenos H. Gurley.

Zenos H. Gurley, was baptized in Canada in 1838, ordained an Elder same year. Some claim he was ordained a Seventy, but the records do not show this. After the death of Joseph Smith, Gurley investigated the claims of the various leaders, and accepted those of James J. Strang, and travelled extensively for that church. Late in 1850 he preached a funeral sermon in Yellowstone, Wisconsin. This was the first Latter Day Saint sermon preached in that County. He baptized a number, and formed a branch of the Strangite church there. Years after they were the first to make a move towards the reorganization of the church. The history shows that the Strangites were then practicing polygamy.

A number of the Yellowstone branch, in the absence of Gurley, passed a resolution refusing to adopt polygamy or follow those who were practicing it. This was published in the Point Tribune in Galena. Gurley returned, called them together and said: "What are you going to do next?" He could not shake them in their resolution to protest against polygamy, so he suggested to take it to the Lord in prayer, the result was the branch rejected Strang's church and stood apart from all churches looking for the coming of the seed of Joseph Smith.

Gurley met J. W. Briggs and they with others organized what is now known as the Reorganized Church. It was first called the "New Organization." Gurley was ordained an Apostle of the New Organization in 1853 by J. W. Briggs, and others. He presided at the conference in 1860, when Joseph Smith was ordained and appointed President and Prophet of the Reorganization, he assisting in that organization. He (Gurley) died in 1871. His family remained with the church for some years, his son Zenos became an apostle and was regarded as one of the strong pillars of the church, but in time the family, with others of the first organizers, left the church. Apostle Gurley and the family left the reorganized church when President Briggs left it in the year 1886. Apostle Gurley printed a pamphlet exposing the church in which he makes some damaging statements. He claims that his father was an over-ardent admirer of the "Choice Seer"; that he would not oppose him in anything; states that baptism for the dead and polygamy was revealed to the church in 1841, and that his father believed these doctrines just as fervently as any part of the gospel. He gives as authority for the introduction of baptism of the dead and polygamy, Tract on Polygamy, page 8, or T. & S., Vol. 5, page 715. After Smith's death he prepared to follow Brigham Young to Utah, but his wife opposed him and he was prevented from going by his horses dying, so that he could not make the trip. He then left Brighamism and joined the Strangite church, moving to Voree and then Yellowstone, Wis., where they rejected polygamy and made ready for the coming of Joseph to take his father's place. The son and apostle, after leaving the reorganized church, exposes the hypocrisy and deception of the reorganized church in publishing visions and revelations regarding the coming of Young Joseph, when they knew that those revelations had failed in part. They publish the parts that refer to the coming of young Joseph, but not the parts that were proven false at the time resulting in the poverty of many because they trusted in them and obeyed the directions there till they lost all they had. I refer to one from the Gurley expose. The Reorganization publishes with great flourish that Julia Gurley, the daughter of Z. H. Gurley and sister of the late Apostle, when fifteen years of age, hearing her father talk of the coming of young Joseph, professed to have a revelation saying, "It is his right by lineage." She further had revealed to her the place where her father and others should "dig for lead," her father and others were then mining. She said: "In the name of God it is there." They say, "She was almost carried to the spot, they sunk the shaft, spent their pile of money, lost all, then the spirit informed her that it was three feet to the north. They tried and failed, then came another revelation from the Lord given in great power, "Dig another fifteen feet to the north, and behold it is there." Gurley states that the family and others sunk their all in the rock shaft. The reader will see that Gurley claims that these revelations on mining were the same revelations that told of young Joseph's coming. The church quotes the part referring to Joseph, but is silent as to the mining part is manifestly dishonest. The old statement is recalled, "The truth half told is the worst lie in the world," and so we have but to wait for a time and every one of the Gurley family became disgusted with the lying and deception and false revelations of Mormonism and left the church. Think of these three men above referred to and ask yourself the question how much truth is the Reorganization built upon?

For full account, read Z. H. Gurley, Jr. read History of Reorganization.

William W. Blair.

William Blair was baptized by William Smith. He remained in that faction till the summer of 1852, when he left Smith's church because of its corruption. This William Smith was a brother of the original prophet, Joseph Smith, was an apostle in the first church, quarreled with Joseph, denounced him, threatened to expose Mormonism, was a drunkard, gave the prophet a severe thrashing, but he knew too much about the foundation of Mormonism, and so Joseph patched it up with him. After the death of his brother, he was ordained patriarch in the church of Brigham Young, but soon was cut off for his bad conduct and then he formed a church of his own and had several wives, three of them died in Utah, having left him. Blair could not stand for his conduct so left him, and associated himself with Baneemyism under Thompson. After a while he left them and started in with the church organized by John E. Page, a former apostle of the first church. Soon left them and finally drifted into the Reorganization church, being baptized by Z. H. Gurley, and ordained an apostle. In 1873 he was ordained one of the First Presidency, he held that position till his death which occurred April 18th, 1896. Ch. Hist., Vol. 3, pages 726-731. Pres. Blair confessed that Joseph Smith had the revelation on Polygamy, but did not make it public. Herald 1860, page 64.

Samuel Powers.

Samuel Powers was baptized by Z. H. Gurley in 1852, was ordained a seventy in 1854, ordained an apostle in 1855. He assisted to ordain Joseph Smith in 1860, died 1873.

I have carefully followed the history of the leaders and organizers of the Reorganized church, and those who ordained Joseph Smith to be prophet, seer, revelator and sole mouth piece to the church and president of the church in April, 1860. Let us make a hurried recapitulation:

First—J. W. Briggs was an Elder in the first church, held office in the four polygamist churches, under Joseph Smith, then Brigham Young, J. J. Strang and William Smith; became president of the Reorganized church, then president of the quorum of Apostle, then left the church and wrote extensively against it. Pray tell me what authority did he hold from God to organize a church? He admits he had no authority by leaving the church and denouncing it.

Second—William Marks, admits the church during the life time of Smith was corrupt and that polygamy was going to destroy it. He was very prominent in the following churches: Rigdon, Brigham Young, J. J. Strang, Thompson, John E. Page, then joined the Reorganized church and became one of the first presidency and ordained Joseph Smith. In the name of consistency, who will say that a man holding priesthood in several polygamist Mormon churches, seven different churches, held the true priesthood all through that murky stream of polution and lust. If Joseph Smith's ordination as a prophet of God cannot find any cleaner and more solid foundation that the man Marks, who was a traitor to. his father and a backslider from all these churches, then he is to be pitied. No sane man will admit he held priesthood authority through all that dirt, and moreover the revelation accepted by the Reorganization, as given in answer to prayer by Angels during their conference, shows clearly that the ordinations which took place in these corrupt churches were not accepted of God. Tullidge Hist., page 595. If these Angels told the truth, then Marks held no more priesthood than Judas Iscariot, or Brigham Young, or William Smith after they fell.

Third—Zenos H. Gurley was ordained in the first church. His son says he accepted baptism of the dead and polygamy in 1841, under Joseph Smith, followed Young for a time, then J. J. Strang and endorsed polygamy under Strang, then denounced it and helped to organize the new church and ordain Joseph Smith successor to his father. May I ask, what priesthood could he hold or confer, after believing the doctrine of polygamy under Smith, Young and Strang. His son shows that he was deceived by the false revelations regarding both young Joseph and the digging for lead, and that the family finally left the church, denounced both the first and the Reorganization.

Fourth—W. W. Blair never was a member of the first church, if the Reorganized angel story be correct that those ordained in the factions hold no priesthood, then Blair held no priesthood. The angel is said to have denounced William Smith, the man who baptized him, he was a polygamist, he left the William Smith church, joined the Thompson church, then the Page church and then was baptized into the Reorganized church, and assisted to ordain Joseph Smith. No authority there.

Fifth—Samuel Powers never belonged to the first church, and was baptized into one of the factions, and God's angel to the Reorganized church refused to acknowledge the authority of those in the factions. Powers had no authority from God to assist in the ordination of Joseph Smith.

We need follow the Reorganization leaders no further and shall now direct our attention to the claim made for Joseph Smith, the son of the founder of the original church, as prophet, seer, revelator and president of the church of Christ upon the earth.

Joseph Smith the Second

Now let us examine the claims of young Joseph to the prophetic office and presidency of the church, perhaps we can discover that he has authority as God's prophet, seer, revelator and the church president.

First—The claims made that he was called to that position when a boy through his father by blessing, revelation and annointing.

Second—That the position is his by lineage or birthright.

Third—That he was called by revelation through himself.

Fourth—That he was ordained by those holding legal authority.

We shall examine these four claims in their order named:

First—That he was called to that position when a boy through his father, by revelation, prophecy, annointing and blessing. If he was we will show that he knew nothing about it, or if he did he had no faith in it, and second that the leaders of the church knew nothing about it, and no one said anything about it for years.

Joseph Smith, speaking of his approaching death to Stephen Markham, said: "I want Hyrum to live to lead the church but he is determined not to leave me." Tullidge Hist. of Joseph, page 491. Question, why did he not tell the people then that his son was consecrated to that position. Joseph and Hyrum were killed, leaving Sidney Rigdon of the Presidency. He should have known it if Joseph was to take his father's place, but Rigdon claimed it as his right, and when Young and the Twelve cut him off the church, he organized one of his own. Not a word of young Joseph being the successor of his father. Brigham Young was President of the Apostolic quorum, he knew nothing of young Joseph's claim, and was made President of the church, and the Apostles of Joseph's day, several of them in turn, became president of the church, every one of them ignoring any statement regarding young Joseph.

James J. Strang and a host of others, laid claim to be Joseph Smith's successor and organized churches galore, not one of them claimed to know of the claim set up by the Reorganized church.

David Whitmer became president of two different factions, but lived many years and never recognized the claim of young Joseph. He declared that Joseph Smith ordained him to be his successor. Strang claimed his appointment direct from Joseph Smith. Whitmer's address, page 55.

The Smith family had no respect for young Joseph's claim. Lucy Smith, the mother of the first Joseph, and grandmother of the second Joseph, published a vision given her by the Lord showing her that William Smith, her son, and the brother of Joseph the first and the uncle of Joseph the second, had the legal right to the presidency, and he accordingly organized a church and was president of it till it was wrecked on the rock of polygamy. Succession to Presidency, page 20. Hyrum Smith's sons had no faith in the claim of young Joseph, both followed Brigham Young, and Joseph F. Smith became president of the Utah Mormon church, having six wives.

Not a single apostle of the old church ever recognized Joseph's claim and came into the Reorganized church, but his uncle William, the man cut off from the Brigham Young church, and who started a church of his own, went into polygamy and finally staggered into the Reorganized church to die. He proved by his life that it was an afterthought. Why was it that from 1844 to 1860 the wife of Joseph the first, and mother of Joseph the second, is not on record as to Joseph designating his son to the prophet office, through the years she is silent.

Joseph when speaking of a blessing received by his father, says "before the death of my father and Uncle Hyrum, I was blessed by the first in the presence of quite a number of then prominent Elders in the church, this blessing being confirmed just prior to the tragedy at Carthage." Joseph the Prophet, page 744. That he may have been blessed is admitted, but that he was called, ordained, or appointed to be a prophet, seer, revelator, or president of the church is not hinted at by him, and his word which I shall give as published by him, will show that for many years he never had an idea that he would have anything to do with Mormonism, to say nothing of being the president of the church and a prophet of God.

There is a story told by Lyman Wight, to the effect that Joseph Smith blessed his son Joseph, but the man contradicts his own statement. At one time he says the child was blessed by his father "in Liberty Jail," Mo. Reorganized Successor, page 3.

When telling the story again, he says he received this blessing "shortly after we came out of jail." Here we have the blessing given while in jail, and then he says it is "shortly after we came out of jail." Northern Islander, July, 1855, Successor to Presidency, page 50.

Query—If Wight knew this in 1839, why was he silent in 1844 when the matter was discussed in Nauvoo, why did he wait till 1855 to make his statement, and why contradict himself as to the place and time. And lastly, why did he collect a band together himself and introduce polygamy and practice it, and die outside of the Josephite church, if he knew that young Joseph was the rightful successor. Why did he not join the Reorganization? We must conclude that he contradicted statements together with his failure to support young Joseph, but to make a gathering of his own together with his having fallen into polygamy, destroys his testimony.

No one confirms the testimony of Wight. Two others were with Wight and the Smiths in Liberty Jail at the time, Baldwin and McRae. They told much that went on in the jail, but neither of them say one word about this perported blessing, but if he was blessed by his father in 1838-9, it is to be remembered that the church believes in the blessing of children and Joseph was about six years old at the time. There is no evidence, even if he were blessed, that he was ordained prophet, seer, and president of the church, so the story of Lyman Wight falls by its own weight.

Now let us hear from young Joseph himself, the claim has been made that he was called by revelation through his father to be prophet, seer and revelator and president of the church to succeed his father. He said, when under oath, "I do not know whether the revelation was given or not, so far as I am concerned I did not, and have not made any such a statement—personally I do not know whether there was or was not such a revelation. No, sir, I did not state that I was ordained by my father. I was not ordained by my father as his successor." Temple lot case, pages 63-79.

Joseph Smith was killed June 27th, 1844, his son Joseph assumed the leadership April 6th, 1860. Let us see what he was doing during these many years. Did his mother say, "Joseph you are to take your father's place, so prepare." Not a word touching the matter for sixteen years. He worked at farming and made a dead failure of it, he tries storekeeping and failed again, then he took a contract of getting out ties for a railroad and lost what little he had in that. Then he started to study law, but poverty made him abandon that and to use his own words, "I was in debt, and I kept soul and body together by labor and my fees as Justice of the Peace." Joseph the Prophet, page 769.

There is not evidence that he made any profession of religion. He says he studied spiritualism for a time. His mother married a spiritualist, who had no faith in Mormonism, and never joined the church even when his step-son became president and prophet of the Reorganized church.

At last some members of the Utah church came to talk to him and he started to think. James J. Strang came to see him and some of the Elders of the Reorganization called. They were not very well treated, at least those of the Reorganized church. Joseph says, "that they fussed till he came very nearly putting them out of his house." Joseph the Prophet, page 767.

Finally he admits such thoughts as these came to him: "What part in my father's work, if any, was I to take?" Again, "Is not **polygamy** against which you object a correct tenet?" Joseph the Prophet, pages 760-761. He says, prior to that, "I had never taken the subject of Mormonism into very serious consideration," and still later the question came to him, "Will I ever have anything to do with Mormonism?" He became convinced of some things after prayer, and concluded that polygamy was not right and that the Salt Lake church was in error and last of all that the little band called the Reorganized church was accepted by the Lord. The reader has doubtless concluded by the above evidence that Joseph Smith had no evidence of having been called or ordained to take his father's place as the prophet, seer, revelator, translator and president of the Mormon church.

Having settled these questions he wrote to William Marks on March 5th, 1860, saying: "I have concluded to take my father's place at the head of the Mormon church," and on April 6th of the same year, he was accepted by that little gathering of about one hundeerd and fifty people, and was ordained as prophet, seer, and revelator, as also president of the church as organized in 1852. Joseph the Prophet, page 773.

While under oath, young Joseph said, "I claim to be my father's successor by lineage right, and by his blessing and lastly by the right of selection and appointment. I do not know whether the doctrine of lineal right was a doctrine of the church prior to the death of my father— that is a traditional right of the firstborn to what ever may attach to the parent, that right is expressed or understood in such a way that whatever rights I hold or am gifted with by reason of the position I hold, would descend to my oldest son." Temple lot case, pages 80-81.

Now let us have a look at the question of lineage. The claim is made that Joseph being the eldest son of the prophet, the prophetic honors and presidency of the church rightly falls to him. Let us see, Joseph Smith said, "In Hebrews 7-3, in which it is said the Melchisedec priesthood is **"without descent."** He said, **"The Melchisedec Priesthood holds the right from the eternal God and not by descent from father and mother** that Priesthood is eternal as God Himself having neither beginning of days nor end of life." Hist. of Jos. Smith, Mill. Star, Vol. 22, page 55.

If it is the law of God that the priesthood is to descend from the father to the eldest son, how is it that Joseph Smith was selected as the prophet, in place of his father Joseph? If Joseph the first was selected Joseph would not have been selected, but Hyrum would have been the successor of his father, thus Joseph the first prophet would have been left out and of course his son would have been left out, and the sons of Hyrum would have been selected. They have ever resented the claim of Joseph Smith's son, and Joseph F. Smith, the son of Hyrum has occupied till his death in 1918, the position as prophet of the Utah church.

But let us take a glance at the bible history and see if the eldest son was always selected to take the position under the law of lineage.

Gen. 4: 2, Abel was the younger son of Adam.
Gen. 11: 26, Abraham was the youngest son of Terah.
Gen. 25: 26, Jacob is the youngest son of Isaac.
Gen. 35: 24, Joseph is the second youngest son of Jacob.
Gen. 48: 9-20, Ephriam is the youngest son of Joseph.
Ex. 6: 20, Moses is the younger son of Amram.
1 Sam. 17: 14, David is the youngest son of Jesse.
2 Sam. 12: 24, Solomon is among the youngest sons of David.

Having examined the claims, one by one, we find no evidence that young Joseph was appointed by revelation through his father. No evidence that he was ordained by his father, no evidence that it was his right by lineage and that none of his own visions or revelations claim that he was called to be a prophet, seer, revelator or president.

Now in the face of all this, we ask where is the evidence from God that Joseph Smith, son of Joseph Smith, was a prophet of God? The several revelations that he has had, have been examined in my work, "Why I left the Latter Day Saint Church." I shall only call attention to these which are said to contain proof that his son Frederick Madison Smith should be the prophet, seer, revelator, translator and president of the church. This son Fred is a fine, big fellow, but who that have known him all through the years have accused him of having religion. He was no worse than many other wild thoughtless boys, and it is said that his conduct was not considered overly religious as a boy on the streets of Lamoni, and that while he attended the different colleges, schools and universities, that he gave evidence of being of the earth, earthly. I personally have known him from his early childhood, have attended church at different places all through the years where he resided, and it is well known that he did not attend church very much. I never heard him bear a testimony, or offer a prayer in a prayer meeting in all the years I have known him, until after his ordination.

In the spring of 1897, there was a presentment made to the church by his father which indicated that the sons of the church leaders would be selected to minister in the priesthood. D. C. 124, 7. This gave an opportunity for some one to suggest the name of President Smith's son, Fred, for ordination to the holy office of an elder, so they went at it with a rush. Apostle Lamber who was the missionary in charge showed at the conference that such action was contrary to the law, and that the young man in question "had not been an active worker in the church." That was drawing it mildly, and that he had no spiritual evidence of such a call, but the Apostle was snowed under and Fred Smith and Fred Blair were ordained above the protest of the Missionary in charge. This made the said ordination contrary to the law. Apostle Lamber tried hard to go half way in the matter and have him ordained a priest, but he felt strongly in opposition to his ordination as an elder. Just think, dear reader, even the Apostle would permit him an ordination to a priest, without a call from God, so even he thought little of the Priesthood which holds the gift of administration of Angels according to Smith's revealtions. But, to say the least, this young man was ordained to the Melchisedec priesthood, the order said to be after the order of the Son of God, without a call, being the prophet's son, he won out as against the protest of the Apostle. For a history of the fuss, read Herald of June 23rd, 1897, in which is recorded the Decature District conference and in which the Lambert protest is recorded, pages 401-402.

Now, this is the history of this young man's entry into the ministry. Years flew by, the young man having little to do in the ministry, no one ever heard him preach at a conference or elsewhere that I ever heard of, for years, but he was the son of the prophet according to their way of thinking; he was to be the successor of his father as prophet, seer, and revelator and president of the church of Christ in all the world, or in the words of the Lord in the revelation to Joseph Smith, "The only true and living church upon the face of the whole earth with which I, the Lord, am well pleased." D. C. 1, 6.

And so, to get him ready, his father said he had a vision in which he seen his son, "sitting with the Presidency." Many of the leading men of the church refused to receive this vision as a revelation from Jesus Christ. This same Apostle Lambert, in the quorum meeting of the Apostles, when the vision was being examined, said in my hearing, "I have watched the revelations coming for more than twenty years. They have been weaker and weaker and weaker, and this one is the weakest of them all."

Apostle Joseph Luff, said in the same meeting, "If that thing (the revelation) came from God, then I have never known anything about the Spirit of God in all my ministry." Apostle G. T. Griffith suggested that we return it to the Prophet and all unite to ask the Lord for more light on the revelation. Apostle Luff sprang to his feet, and with emotion said, "**Light, more light! Did you say?** My God, man, if I were to ask the Lord anything about it, I would not ask for **more light,** but for light, for that thing is the darkest thing that has ever be-clouded the face of the church."

The same Apostle said to me, when at the Lamoni station, "Richard, I cannot believe a word of that revelation. I would be willing to walk to California on burning stones if the Lord would show me that He gave that message. All I ask is one ray of light, but all is midnight darkness."

The revelation was accepted by the conference and the ordinations took place.

Those who will examine the revelation in question will see that in it the statement is clearly made that the two young men named as being seen with the presidency, Fred Smith and R. C. Evans, was selected "for the purpose that before the presidency should be invaded by death, these younger men should be prepared by association to be of assistance **to whom so ever should be chosen as president upon the emergency which should occur.** Doc. and Cov., Dec. 126, 4-8.

If language is a science to convey ideas, stated in plain language, here is simply this, that Frederick M. Smith and R. C. Evans were selected as two of the Presidency so as to be associated with the venerable president, so that they would learn his methods and when he would be called by death, that these **two young men were to assist the man who would be called to be the president.** In other words they would be the counsellors to the next president and, knowing the way Joseph Smith conducted matters, they would be of great assistance to the inexperienced president, but the old man became nearly stone deaf and for years was totally blind and suffered excrusiating pains from other afflictions, and something occurred that God alone knows. That revelation with its provisions, was forgotten, and the young, strong son came into prominence before the almost helpless and decrepit father, deaf and blind and sick. He is said to have revelations that finally placed Frederick M. Smith, his son, as prophet, seer, revelator, translator and president of the church, with much difficulty these revelations passed the body and he was, soon after the death of his father, elected to that position and was accordingly ordained.

His grandfather was a despot and an autocrat and polygamist of the first water. If there is any credence to be given to human testimony, his father was a pleasant man to talk to, loved by most men who knew him, quiet and gentle in his manner, a fair preacher, a splendid parliamentarian, he always denounced polygamy. I loved him through forty years of association. I could not agree with all he did, I did not agree with some of his spiritual manifestations, and we had some words over some of them which moved us both to tears. I saw for the last few years when he became blind and deaf and so sorely afflicted, that his son was the power behind the throne and many things that had Joseph's signature and stamp of approval, I have of late years become doubtful of his having much to do with. I know in some things he submitted for peace sake, and have some reason to believe that in others he knew almost nothing about them. Perhaps his worst mistake was, in a sense pardonable, it is hard for one reading the evidence which convicted his father of being a polygamist, and the author of the infamous revelations on polygamy and concubinage and adultery, to believe that he was not convinced of his father's guilt. His most close companions and advisers for years both believed and printed that his father was guilty, but Joseph maintained, "I prefer to believe that my father was a good man,'" yet he did let slip some things that convinced me in the last few years that he knew that his father was a guilty man. See his statement in Joseph the Prophet by Tullidge, pages 798-9. Yet it was his father and perhaps we should not be too hard on a son who would throw the cloak of charity over the misdeeds of his father.

In closing, let us take a look at the present prophet, seer and revelator, translator and president of the church. Since his advent in that high station, he has been the chief cause of changing much of the church rules. Rule after rule have been changed to give him almost absolute power over everything in the church, Sunday School Religion, Ladies' Auxiliary, and he has the first and last word in the appointment of every officer in the church, the resolutions on co-ordination. Not a man can move without his consent. He claims the right to go into a mission, district or branch, or even a Sunday School and make the changes in every office, he can speak and a man is taken from one end of the earth to the other. The Bishops and Apostles are completely under his domination, in fact, he rules with all the power of the former Czar of Russia. Much could be written upon his autocracy, but let us take a short look at the only attempt he has made to give the church the word of the Lord as Christ's mouth-piece to the church.

There has been much trouble over Bishop E. L. Kelley's work in the church and the great body was determined to release him. Several efforts were made to do so, but Smith blocked the wheels. At last, something had to be done, and so he has a revelation, but it looks as if he did not believe it himself for he put it in his pocket and arranged to meet Bishop Blakeslee and his wife in Chicago. Bishop Blakeslee refused to take the position, and then the new prophet came forth with the revelation that he had had some weeks before, calling Bro. McGuire to that position. Just think, God called McGuire to be presiding Bishop, Smith put that revelation in his pocket, spent his money to go to Chicago, tried his level best to persuade Bishop Blakeslee to take the position, as God had selected him in former revelations, he refused. I ask what would Smith have done with his revelation which he hid in his pocket about McGuire, if Blakeslee had accepted the position Smith must not blame me for not believing in his first attempt to be God's mouth-piece and give a revelation, for the facts show he did not believe it himself. Herald, April 19, 1906, page 373.

His methods from that hour show to me clearly that he is neither a prophet, seer, revelator nor God's mouth-piece to the church, but is an autocrat, cruel and tricky, and selfish in his methods.

CHAPTER V.

The Proper Name of The Church

From the organization of the church to the present, there has been much strife and contention as to what the name of the church is. David Whitmer (the sixth person baptized in the gathering, and before the church was organized, one who claims to have seen the gold plates of the Book of Mormon, and conversed with the Angel), together with Harris and Cowdery, the other witnesses, with many other leading men, claim that the proper name is "The Church of Christ." Whitmer's address, pages 73-75.

Many parts of the Book of Mormon show the name of the church was "The Church of Christ." Nephi 12, 3.

In the Book of Commandments, a work containing the revelations of Smith, published in 1833, from start to finish refers to the church as "The Church of Christ." The title page reads, "A Book of Commandments for the government of the Church of Christ."

We are informed by their historians that the church had made several changes in its name in the first four years of its existence, during that short period it had been called "The Church of Christ," "The Church of Jesus Christ," "The Church of God," "The Church of the First Born," but that on May 3rd, 1834, during general conference at Kirtland, Ohio, Sidney Rigdon made a motion which the conference adopted by unanimous voice, that this church be known hereafter by the name of **"The Church of the Latter Day Saints."** Ch. Hist., Vol. 1, 454.

When the revelations of Joseph Smith were published in a book called the Doctrine and Covenants, in 1835, Joseph Smith, Sidney Rigdon, Frederick G. Williams and Oliver Cowdery signed the preface, headed as follows: "To the members of the Church of the Latter Day Saints."

The reader will see plainly that the church had no confidence in the perported revelations of Jesus Christ to Smith, in which the church was called the Church of Christ, for they eliminated the very name of Christ from the church name entirely. It was no longer, if ever, the church of Christ, but only "The Church of the Latter Day Saints."

From the history it would appear that Christ must have felt slighted at being thrown out bodily, so He sought and succeeded in making a compromise with the prophet, and we hear Him telling Smith in the revelation given April 26th, 1838, "For thus shall My church be called in the last days, even the Church of 'Jesus Christ of Latter Day Saints'." Ch. Hist, Vol. 2, page 151.

We have followed the church during the early years of its existence and find, from their own histories, that both their Christ and the people of the church, have been vasilating and fickle minded and ridiculous as to the name of the church, and for very shame sake, if they have any shame, they should not accuse other churches of not having the proper name.

It would seem that the main body of the church which followed Brigham Young to Utah, have respected the name given in 1838, but the little body which came out of the Strangite faction in 1852 and finally succeeded in securing Joseph Smith, son of the "Prophet," to lead them was for some time known as the "New Organization." See article written by Z. H. Gurley in the Herald for 1860. But finally adopted the name "The Reorganized Church of Jesus Christ of Latter Day Saints."

These off-shoots of original Mormonism have been so exposed in the last year or two, that they have tried to hide their identity in some parts by dropping their ministerial titles, such as Apostle, or High Priest, or Elder, and the name of the church is dropped and just say "Saint's church." The proof is seen in their advertisements for Toronto, 1918-1919.

The history of the organization of the church, April 6th, 1830, states that the "Church of Christ" was organized. Times and Seasons, Vol. 3, pages 944-945.

"The Church of Christ........was organized........by the will and commandment of God." April 6th, 1830, Doc. and Cov., Sec. 17, par. 1.

Are They Mormons?

Two letters appear in the Evening Telegram for December 3rd, 1918, one in the same paper for Dec. 4th, and one in the Star Weekly for Dec. 7th, and one in the Sunday World for Dec. 14th, all Toronto, Ontario, papers. The said letters being written by T. W. Williams, a High Priest of the Reorganized church, and some other members of the same body, all claiming that the Latter Day Saints are not Mormons, and that the church should not be called the Mormon church, and that the faith preached by them should not be called Mormonism.

Now, let us examine very briefly these claims in the light of history. "Mormons." "First, a member of the Church of Jesus Christ of Latter Day Saints, because of a belief in the Book of Mormon. Second, a member of the sect called the Reorganized church of Jesus Christ of Latter Day Saints." Webster's Dict. Art Mormon.

"Mormons." The common name given to the church of Jesus Christ of Latter Day Saints, Encyclopedia Britannica.

We will show by the history of the church, written by themselves that they called themselves Mormons, said the church was the Mormon church and that the faith they praeched was Mormonism. We will begin with the mother of Joseph Smith, the first person on earth, so far as we know that called the membership of the church Mormons.

THE PROPER NAME OF THE CHURCH 83

"I told her that we were Mormons." Hist. of Jos. Smith by his mother, page 188. Martin Harris, one of the three witnesses to the Angel's message and the man who paid for the printing of the first publication of the Book of Mormon, long after he had denounced Smith, when thinking of going to Salt Lake City, said: "I feel that the spirit has come across me—the old spirit of Mormonism." Ch. Hist., Vol. 1, page 51.

Apostle P. P. Pratt refers to the church as the "Mormon Church." Persecution of the Saints, pages 31-52.

Five leading men of the church, when writing a letter to the authorities of Missouri, refer to the church several times as the Mormon church. Ch. Hist., Vol. 1, pages 495-517.

P. P. Pratt was the first of these - - - to embrace **Mormonism**." Life of Joseph Smith, pages 94-95.

And this is **Mormonism**; a grand universal scheme of salvation, Ibid 133.

"Joseph the **Mormon** prophet—the genius of **Mormonism**." Ibid. 165.

"Book of Abraham, translated by Joseph Smith contains **Mormon** theology." Ibid. 166.

"The people known as **Mormons** are Israel." Ibid. page 176.

"Mormonism harmonizine the views and Gospel themes of all the ages." Ibid 205.

"In the exalted vision of **Mormon** theology we have a pre-existing domain." Ibid. 311.

"The genius or **Mormonism** is—American." Ibid. page 327.

"Joseph said, 'I am willing to die for a **Mormon'**."—and **"Mormonism."** Ibid. 423.

Emma Smith, wife of Joseph the first, when asked by her son Joseph the seond, and head of the Reorganized Mormon church, "What of the truth of **Mormonism**? replied, "I know **Mormonism** to be the truth." Ibid. page 792.

Now let me present the statements of this Joseph the second in regard to this question, and the reader will discover that he refers to the church as the **Mormon Church,** and to the faith and doctrine of that church as **Mormonism,** and that he claims the authority to take his father's place at the head of the Mormon church.

Calls the citizens of Nauvoo, who were church members, "Mormons." Ibid. 750.

"I had a long conversation respecting **Mormonism**." Page 756.

"Will I ever have anything to do with **Mormonism**?" Page 757.

"There is a large part of the (Smith) family in Utah, they seem to be the only ones making a profession of belief in **Mormonism**. Does not duty demand that I go there and clear my name and honor of the charge of ingratitude to my father's character? Is not polygamy against which you object a correct tenet?" Ibid. 761.

"Joseph informs us that he concluded that "He who had enabled my father to decide, could, if he would, enable me to decide whether I should or should not have anything to do with **Mormonism.**" Ibid., page 762.

Speaking of Nauvoo and the County of Nancock, he says: "The country after the **Mormons** left, was worse than a new one—the County of Hancock had twenty-five thousand Mormons residing there." Page 771.

To conclude this part of the subject let us say that young Joseph admits that for about fifteen years he had no thought of Mormonism, but when he failed to earn a good living at farming, he left that and went to work grading on a railroad and lost his time and eight hundred dollars cash, all he had left, he informs us, was "One alpaca coat, $4.00; $2.50 in cash; an iron crow bar and a log chain, all valued at about $12.00." Page 755 He came home and tried to study law, and "owing to want of means" he went back home and then began to wonder if he would ever take any part in Mormonism It just seemed that there was no money in any other job, and so he wrote to William Marks under date of March 5th, 1860, saying: "I am soon going to take my **Father's place at the head of the Mormon church.**' Speaking of this man Marks, he says: "He had retained his faith in **Mormonism** as taught by Joseph and, Hyrum." Ibid. 773.

The Joseph he refers to was his father, Hyrum his uncle. Now let us see who Marks was. He was president of the Stake at Nauvoo and also of the HighCouncil at the time of Joseph Smith's death. Joseph Smith denounced him, he followed Rigdon's church for a while, then denounced Rigdon and followed Brigham Young's church; then he joined Strang's church, then he joined the Thompson church, then he follows John E. Page's church, then he joined the Reorganized church, ordained young Joseph and died in the New Organization. For proof of the above see Mill Star, Vol. 22, page 631; Times and Seasons, Vol. 10, page 115; Gospel Herald, Vol. 5, page 17; Ch. Hist., Vol. 3, pages 721-726.

Surely this man, after being prominent in seven different warring factions of the Mormon church, should be considered a member of the **Mormon Church and should understand Mormonism well enough to ordain young Joseph the head of the youngest child of Mormonism—The Reorganized Mormon Church.**

Now, in conclusion, let us summarize the above paper:

We have shown that the present high priest of Mormonism in Toronto, with others, has denied that the church is the Mormon church and that its faith should be called Mormonism, and to expose these deceivers who are making lies their refuge, I have proven by their own church histories that from the organization of the first church in 1830, through all the conflicting warring family, they have called themselves **Mormons,** and the faith of the church Mormonism, calling to bear witness the leaders such as Joseph Smith the founder, Emma Smith, his wife, Lucy Smith, his mother, Joseph Smith his son and prophet of the Reorganized church, and many other leaders, all testifying that the church is the Mormon church and the faith there of is Mormonism. I commend those who love and make a lie to the tender mercies of a descerning public.

J. Smith said, "Hell may pour forth its rage like the burning lava of Mt. Vesuvius, or of Etna, or of the most terrible of the burning mountains, and yet shall **Mormonism** stand; water, fire, truth and God are all the same, **Truth is Mormonism,** God is the author of it." Mill Star, Vol. 17, page 56.

"I am your friend, and shall sustain your present position as the lawful head and leader of the **Mormon Church."** Uncle William Smith, to his nephew, Joseph Smith. Herald, Vol. 1, Page 172.

Baptism For The Dead.

The claim made by Joseph Smith, and accepted by his followers is susceptible to but one interpretation and conclusion, in regard to the professed mouthings of Smith being the very words of Christ, and therefore binding upon the people, blessing following those who obey and cursing following those who disobey, is clearly announced.

We are commanded to accept Joseph Smith as a seer, translator, prophet, Apostle and Elder. He has been inspired by the Almight y to lay the foundation of the church and build it up in the faith by direct command of Jesus Christ, and because of all this, Christ is supposed to command the church through Smith as follows: "Wherefore meaning the church, **Thou shalt give head unto all His words and commandments,** which he shall give unto you—for his words ye shall receive **as if from mine own mouth."** D. C. 19, 1-2.

"And this ye shall know assuredly, that there is none other appointed unto you to receive commandments and revelations until he be taken, if he (Joseph Smith) abide in me." D. C. 43, 1-2.

"And it shall ge given thee in the very moment, what thou shalt speak and write, and they shall hear it, or I will send them a **cursing** instead of a blessing." D. C. 23, 3.

"No one shall be appointed to receive commandments and revelations in this church excepting my servant Joseph Smith—and thou shalt be obedient unto the things which I shall give unto him." D. C. 27-2.

"Therefore, inasmuch as some of my servants have not kept the commandment, but have broken the covenant, I have cursed them with a very sore and grievous curse, for I the Lord have decreed in my heart, that inasmuch as any man belonging to the order shall be found a transgressor or in other words shall break the covenant with which ye are bound, **he shall be cursed** in this life and shall be trodden down by whom I will." D. C. 101, 1.

Speaking of those who become the enemies of Smith and who reject his revelations and refuse to submit to his commandments the Lord is made to say, "Ye shall curse them and whomsoever **ye curse** I will curse, and ye shall avenge me of my enemies." D. C. 100, 5.

Now this little paper will show that Joseph Smith received revelations from Christ (or he lied) in which he commanded the people to be **baptized for the dead,** and that they **preached, believed and practiced this doctrine during his life and that they still teach it and**

print the said revelations in their books, and the largest part of the church now practice it, and the facts show that the little band calling themselves the Reorganized church of Jesus Christ of Latter Day Saints still hold those revelations through Smith as from Christ, and still print them in their books and are therefore inconsistent in not baptizing for the dead. Are they **honest or fair** in their effort to deny their faith in that doctrine? Let the reader decide when he reads the evidence given under oath in the City of Toronto in June, 1919.

In the Utah edition of the Doc. & Cov. section 110, we are informed that Joseph Smith was in vision in the Kirtland Temple, April 3rd, 1836, Jesus Christ appeared to him, after which Moses appeared to him and committed certain keys, then Elias paid him a short visit, then came the prophet Elijah and handed Joseph certain keys by which he was to be able to turn the hearts of the fathers to the children, lest the whole earth be smitten with a curse.

In the Reorganized church book of D. C. 110, Joseph Smith takes up the subject of baptism for the dead and makes argument in its favor quoting the same Elijah as referred to in the Utah edition, showing clearly that several Angels appeared to him and that the subject of baptism for the dead is the most important matter for the church to attend to, in order to save the dead as well as the living. He makes claim there and also in section 109, that this commandment to baptize for the dead was imparted to him by revelation and again through Angels, and the Reorganized church believes and teaches those revelations to be from God, and yet Bishop McGuire, strongly denied under oath that they believed in that doctrine and blamed the Utah Mormons for it. Can it be possible that McGuire was making **lies his refuge,** in this case, while in the court under oath, but to the revelations in their own book of covenants with which he was confronted and by which he stands exposed, in a very undesirable way.

"Behold I command all ye my saints to build a house unto me, and I grant unto you a sufficient time to build a house unto me and during this time your baptisms shall be acceptable unto me, but hehold at the end of this appointment your baptism for your dead shall not be acceptable unto me and if you do not these things at the end of the appointment ye shall be **rejected as a church with your dead,** saith the Lord your God, for verily I say unto you, that after you have had sufficient time to build a house unto me wherein the ordinance of **baptizing for the dead belongeth** and for which the same was instituted from before the foundation of the world, your **baptism for the dead cannot be acceptable unto me,** for therein are the keys of the holy priesthood ordained that you may receive glory and honor."

The revelation is a long one, and filled with this doctrine and commandment to build a house in which a fount is to be built in which the living are to be baptized for the dead, and it closes with the most fearful curses if they are slothful and the house and fount are not built at a certain time. The Lord told Smith he would pour out cursings, wrath and indignations and judgments upon their heads, and the church would not be recognized any longer by him, but the church and their dead would be rejected. Doc. and Cov., 107, 1-16.

The church baptized for their dead in the Mississippi river till the fount was completed. It was built in the Nauvoo Temple and was a most wonderful piece of art, twelve great wooden oxen upheld the font, but the temple was not completed according to the revelation, and the Reorganized church takes the position that in consequence of their polygamy and many other crimes, God rejected the church with their dead, while the Utah church claims the Temple was completed so far as to admit the baptism font to be used for the baptism for the dead and that they received their different washings and baptisms and sealing of wives in the temple, and that they have gone on according to Joseph Smith, in polygamy, sealing wives to dead men and baptism for the dead and that in baptism for the dead and polygamy and all the rest of the doctrines, revelations and commandments given by God to Joseph Smith that they have followed him closely to prove this I quote from a work published by one of their leading ministers, B. H. Roberts. Pages 109-110.

"The phase of the great Latter Day Work which seemed most to occupy the attention of the prophet Joseph Smith in the last year of his life, was that which relates to the salvation of the dead. Elijah had visited him in Kirtland Temple and had restored the keys of the priesthood which turn the hearts of the fathers to the children and the children to the fathers, lest the whole earth be smitten with a curse. No wonder that this matter occupied his mind when the keys for the salvation of the dead were placed in his hands. The earth will be smitten with a curse unless there is a welding upon some subject or other, and behold what is that subject? It is **baptism for the dead.**"

He then proceeds to show a list of the work done by the Utah Mormon church in keeping with the revelations and commandments given by Joseph Smith, performed in the Temples of St. George, Logan, Manti and Salt Lake City. Read these appalling statistics.

Total number of baptisms for the dead, 683,377.
Total ordinations of priesthood for the dead, 120,232.
Of endowments, 300,511.

Let the readers read this awful work:
Of sealing, including wives and husbands, children to parents (three temples only reporting), 69,749.

Those appalling figures published by the saints themselves in their own books, should tell the people what kind of a prophet Joseph Smith was, and what kind of Christianity they believe and practice.

The Reorganized church does not practice these things now, but why? Is it because they do not believe in it? No, they do believe it and will practice it when they decide the proper time and place arrives. In proof of this, hear their historian and most able man in the Reorganized church: "Baptism for the dead is only legal and acceptable when performed either in Zion or her stakes, or in Jerusalem and in a house dedicated to and accepted by God." The Succession in Church Pres., by H. C. Smith, page 95.

This book is published by the Reorganized church of which presiding Bishop B. R. McGuire is president of that very board of publication. What will honest Latter Day Saints think of their presiding Bishop when under oath denied their faith in baptism for the dead? Will you continue to follow him and other leaders of the Mormon church, or will you become convinced of your error and like Bishop Evans leave the unclean thing that is making lies their refuge.

The readers will see that Smith of the Reorganized church acknowledges baptism for the dead to be a doctrine of Jesus Christ, but he objects to these baptisms taking place in Utah. He says they must only be performed "In Zion or her stakes or Jesusalem and in a house dedicated and accepted by God." That is to say Zion is the State of Missouri, she has a stake in the state of Iowa, but the Temple that is to be erected in Independence, Mo., in this generation, wherein Christ is to bless his saints, is not yet erected. When Christ comes to Independence, Mo., or tells Frederick M. Smith to build the temple for His coming, then the Reorganized church will baptize for the dead, as Joseph Smith did and as their revelations command them to do and the **misleading statements made** under oath and under other conditions by those who believe and preach and sell those revelations commanding the practice of baptism for the dead is to be denounced by every right thinking person.

We may and should pity those who are honestly deceived by the lying wonder of the Latter Days—Mormonism, but there is no excuse for their leaders who promulgate those damnable herecies in secret and deny them when under oath or before the public.

Herewith I submit part of the evidence given by Bishop McGuire at the Toronto trial, May and June, 1919, questions propounded by the lawyers and his replies:

Q. "What about the baptism for the dead? A. Baptism for the dead has never been taught by the Reorganization.

"Q. Is that a doctrine of the Utah Mormons? A. It is a doctrine of the Utah Mormons. They make the pleas that we are not orthodox because we do not teach baptism for the dead."

Under cross examination many of the revelations published by the Reorganized church as coming from Christ to Joseph Smith were read to him, he knowing that his church accepted them as from God, and that he was the presiding Bishop of that Church and president of the board of publication that publishes them. When the lawyer concluded reading the revelations, he said: "Was that present in your mind when you did this swearing you did a little while ago that baptism for the dead was not one of the cardinal doctrines of your church?" McGuire answered: **"It is not a cardinal teaching of the church and has not been."** Q. And you still say so in the teeth of the book? A. Yes." Court evidence, pages 729 and 756.

Will any honest man read the revelations given in the doctrine and covenants regarding baptism for the dead, and the position taken by the historian of the church, and the evidence of Bishop McGuire and then say that man swore "To the truth the whole truth and nothing but the truth?"

The Prophetic Revelations of Joseph Smith Proved False By His Own People, While They Followed Him They Were Comrades of Angels, But as Soon As They Denounced Him They Were Guilty of Most Every Crime.

We will present the **three witnesses** to the Book of Mormon. According to Mormon history, they handled the gold plates, heard the voice of God, conversed with Angels, were high priests and apostles and church presidents. They all left the church in a few years, denouncing Smith as being guilty of most every crime thinkable, and in return he and the church have denounced them, and charged them with most every sin.

Testimony of Joseph Smith and the Church Authorities of the Three Witnesses to The Book of Mormon.

"After Oliver Cowdery had been taken by a State warrant for stealing, the stolen property was found in the house of W. W. Phelps."

"The saints elected Cowdery to be a Justice of the Peace. He used the power of that office to take their most sacred rights from them. He supported a parcel of blacklegs. Oliver Cowdery, David Whitmer and Lyman E. Johnson united with a gang of counterfeiters, thieves, liars and blacklegs of the deepest dye, to deceive, cheat and defraud the saints out of their property. During the full career of Oliver Cowdery and David Whitmer's bogus money business it got abroad that they were engaged in it, they fled to Far West, Cowdery stealing property and taking it with him. The property was later obtained by means of a search warrant, and he was saved from the penitentiary by the influence of two influential men. He brought notes with him upon which he had received pay, and made an attempt to sell them to Mr. Arthur of Clay Co."

This is signed by more than eighty Mormons, and is found in "Documents in Relation to the Disturbances with the Mormons, Missouri Legislature, 1841, page 103. Written by Sidney Rigdon. Linn, Story of the Mormons, pages 81-82; La Rue, page 76.

April 1838, Oliver Cowdery was tried on nine charges before the High Council. He was found guilty of six of them, viz., urging vexatious law suits against the brethren; accusing the Prophet Joseph of adultery; disgracing the church by being connected with the bogus (counterfeiting) business; retaining notes after they had been paid, and forsaking the cause of God. On this find he was expelled from the church. Two days later David Whitmer was found guilty of unchristianlike conduct, and defaming the prophet, and was expelled. Lyman E. Johnson, Thomas B. Marsh and Orson Hyde of the Twelve were expelled. Cowdery and Whitmer fled on horseback for their lives. Elders Journal July 1838; Mill Star, Vol. 16, pages 130-134; Missouri Legislature, 1841, C. H. Vol. 2, page 150.

Joseph writing of David Whitmer, during the Missouri trouble, said: "W. W. Phelps, who professes to be much of a prohpet has no other dumb ass to ride but David Whitmer, or to forbid his madness when he goes up to curse Israel, but this not being of the same kind as Balaam's, therefore, notwithstanding the angel appeared unto him, yet he could not sufficiently penetrate his understanding, but that he brays out cursings instead of blessings." Times and Seasons, Vol. 1, page 82: Linn. 215.

Joseph Smith on Martin Harris—"There are negroes who wear white skins as well as black ones, Granny Parish and others who acted as lackeys such as Martin Harris." Elders Journal, July, 1837.

When Martin Harris left the church, or was cut off, he in time joined the Strangites and was sent to England to preach the Strang doctrine, and was severely denounced as a very wicked man, as stated in Revelation regarding him in D. C. Sect. 5 and 18. Mill. Star, Vol. 18, page 125.

Martin Harris is so far beneath contempt that a notice of him would be too great a sacrifice for a gentleman to make. The church exerted some restraint on him, but now he has given loose to all kinds of abominations, lying, cheating and swindling with all kinds of debauchery." Joseph Smith in Elders' Journal, August, 1838.

Joseph Smith says that Christ told him to tell Harris the following: "And again I command thee that thou shalt not covet thy neighbor's wife, nor seek thy neighbor's life—thou shalt not covet thine own property but impart it freely to the printing of the Book of Mormon." D. C. 18, 3.

The wife of Martin Harris accused him of being intimate with a Mrs. Haggard, and testifies that Harris used to beat her."

Shook, True Origin of Book of Mormon, pages 46-47.

Much more could be presented from the Mormons themselves, to say nothing of those not of the faith, to show that these three men were very vile, wicked and unreliable, yet they are, according to Mormon history, the THREE WITNESSES raised up by the Lord to testify to the world, that God spoke to them, angels talked to them and they saw and handled the gold plates of the Book of Mormon.

Such characters as McLellin, John Whitmer, David Whitmer, Oliver Cowdery and Martin Harris are too mean to be mentioned and we would like to have forgotten them.

Marsh and another whose hearts are full of corruption, whose cloak of hypocrisy was not sufficient to shield them." Mill Star, Vol. 16, pages 626-628.

It may be stated that the very worst that Smith could say about them, can't be any worse than they have written against Smith. They accused him of adultery, concubinage, polygamy, murder, lying and most everything that is low, mean and criminal, and it looks like as if all three witnesses were telling the truth about Smith, and he about them.

Sidney Rigdon.

Sidney Rigdon has been considered by many as the real author of Mormonism. He was Smith's first counsellor. They had visions together, talked to the Lord and angels together, sat in the presidential councils together, were in Zion's Camp together, assisted Smith to translate the Bible, dedicated the Kirtland Temple and the Independence Temple Lot, were sentenced to be shot together, was nominated as Vice-President of the United States, when Smith was presented as President of the United States. Smith was unwilling to sustain him as counsellor in 1843 and Rigdon was soon advertised as one weak in the faith.

Rigdon testified that Smith tried to seduce his daughter Nancy Rigdon. Her brother testifies to this dastardly crime, and J. C. Bennett and others support the story. Shooks True Origin of Polygamy, pages 62-67.

After Rigdon left the church he printed a paper in which I find the following: "Joseph Smith departed from the Living God and like David and Solomon he contracted a whoring spirit and the Lord smote him for this thing, and cut him off from the earth." Messenger and Advocate, Jan. 1, 1845, page 75.

William Law.

William Law was counsellor to President Smith and one of the first presidency. The Lord, through Smith, spake to this man saying: "Let my servant William Law, also receive the keys by which he may ask and receive blessings; he shall heal the sick; he shall cast out devils, and shall be delivered from those who would administer to him deadly poison, and he shall be led in paths where the poisonous serpent cannot lay hold upon his heel, and what if I will that he shall raise the dead, let him not withhold his voice." D. C. Sect. 107, page 30.

Law left the church, lost thousands of dollars in property, had to escape for his life. He denounced Smith as a drunkard, liar, rascal, polygamist. Says Hyrum let him read the revelation on polygamy, that he showed it to his wife, then went to Joseph with it and Joseph told him it was of the Lrd, said Joseph offered to furnish Emma, his own wife with a substitute for him by way of compensation for his neglect of her, in a word he denounced Smith as a rascal of the blackest dye. W. Law's Letters to Weekly Tribune of Salt Lake City, Aug. 4, 1887; also Dr. Wyl's Letter from Law.

Brigham Young was made an Apostle and President of his Quorum and was given many rich blessings, Here is a sample: "The holy priesthood is conferred upon him that he may do wonders in the name of Jesus, that he may cast out devils, heal the sick, and **raise the dead,** open the eyes of the blind—heathen nations shall call him God Himself, if he do not rebuke them." Mill. Star, Vol. 15, pages 206, 207. LaRue, page 30.

Yet it is admitted that this man became the scourge of the earth. History claims that he taught and sanctioned polygamy, concubinage, murder and all kinds of sin and crime, and presided over the Utah Mormon Church.

Lyman E. Johnson

Lyman E. Johnson was given many blessings as well as the Apostleship. "No power of the enemy shall prevent him from going forth and doing the work of the Lord, and he shall live until the gathering is accomplished. He shall see the Saviour come and stand upon the earth with power and great glory." Mill. Star, Vol. 15, pages 206-207; LaRue, page 30.

A short time after this wonderful prophecy, Joseph Smith and others accuse him with others of being united with a gang of counterfeiters, theives, liars and blacklegs of the deepest dye." Linn. pages 81-82.

He was cut off the church and was drowned in 1856. LaRue, page 30.

Orson Hyde

Orson Hyde—"He shall stand on earth and bring souls till Christ comes; he shall have power to smite the earth with pestilence, to divide the water and lead through the saints." Mill. Star, Vol. 15, page 207.

Thomas B. Marsh, was made president of the Twelve Apostles, promised that he should be a mighty man among the nations of the earth. D. C. 105.

Now let us see what Joseph Smith wrote of Apostles Hyde and Marsh when in 1838 they left the church and denounced him as about everything that is criminal. Smith says: **"Thomas B. Marsh,** formerly president of the Twelve, having apostatized, repaired to Richmond and made affidavit before Henry Jacobs, Justice of the Peace, to all the vilest calumies, aspersions, lies and slanders toward myself and the church that his wicked heart could invent. Orson Hyde was also at Richmond and testified to most of Marsh's statements. Ch. Hist., Vol. 2, pages 212-214, 359.

David Patten—"May have power to smite his enemies before him with utter destruction, may he continue till the Lord comes." Mill. Star, Vol. 15, pages 206-207. LaRue, page 30.

As one of Smith's Danites in a fight in Missouri, he was killed. Ch. Hist., Vol. 1, page 649.

William Smith.

William Smith—"He shall be preserved and remain on earth until Christ comes to take vengeance on the wicked." Mill. Star, Vol. 15, pages 206-207.

This apostolic brother of the prophet was a drunkard. He fought and whipped the prophet, denied the revelations given through Joseph, was a polygamist with threee wives and is long since dead. Life of Joseph by Tullidge, page 577. Ch. Hist., Vol. 1, pages 592-3, 614, 620-1.

J. C. Bennett.

J. C. Bennett drafted the bill of incorporation of City of Nauvoo, was mayor of city, major-general of Nauvoo Legion. Smith's revelations to him promised that he would be like Paul, see visions, be a patriarch, was president of church for a time with Smith; was to have power over wind and waves." Times and Seasons, Vol. 2, page 387. D. C. 107. Shook on Polygamy, 46-52.

This Bennett declared that he never believed in Mormonism, just joined the church to get into the secrets, accused Smith of polygamy, adultery, hiring him to commit abortion upon his young victims; tells that Smith offered him the best lot of ground on Front St., Nauvoo, and five hundred dollars if he would secure Nancy Rigdon for his wife, Danites, etc. Shook on Polygamy, 46-59.

Warren Parrish.

Warren Parrish—"Verily thus saith the Lord, my sevrant Warren Parrish, behold it shall come to pass in his day that he shall see great things show forth themselves unto my people, he shall see much of my ancient records and shall be endowed with knowledge of hidden languages. Behold the Lord's scribe for the Lord's seer." Mill. Star, Vol. 15, page 424.

This man left the church after writing Smith's daily journal and early history. He saw and heard so much that he became one of the most powerful enemies of the prophet. LaRue, pages 108-9.

Bishop John Corrill.

Bishop John Corrill organized the counsellors of the church in Missouri, was a great preacher and missionary. D. C. 108, 3, 50, 8, 52, 3.

This man left the church and declares that he left the church because he believed the Bible, and shows that for six years he followed Smith and became convinced that he was a false prophet, and that he led the church into crime, that Smith promised in the name of the Lord that he would lead them to victory, that the day was their own, when in less than a week you were all made prisoners of war and would have been exterminated had it not been for the exertions of deserters. LaRue pages 34-36, Corrill History, page 48.

Missouri Army.

Joseph Smith formed an army to go to Missouri and make war and win that country for his people. They filled their wagons with swords, guns and munitions of war. They formed a munition factory where they made swords, dirks, pistols. Smith had a bodyguard, the Lord gave promise of certain victory, but cholera came and many died, and the Missourians came upon them and they were scattered, and some made prisoners. The entire army scheme fell through. This was in 1834, see Ch. Hist., Vol. 1, 456-487; LaRue, page 35, 180-184; D. C. Sect. 100.

The Nauvoo House was built by command of God. Smith and other men were commanded not to put more than fifteen thousand dollars worth of shares into it. It was called the Lord's boarding house. Smith and his posterity were to have place in that house from generation to generation. It shall be called the Nauvoo House. In the same revelation a great temple was to be erected. The kings of the nations were commanded to bring their gold and silver. The set time to favor Zion had come, baptism for the dead and other mysterious ceremonies were to be performed therein. D. C. 107, LaRue, pages 106-7.

The Nauvoo House

The Nauvoo House was erected, but those who paid their money were robbed and the Mormons, because of their sins, were driven away and Smith shot, and the revelation proved a failure. **The Temple** was erected, the Re-organized Mormons say it was never completed; the Utah Mormons say it was, and the Mormon press shows that it was, and that the Reorganizers are lying about it, as the following will show: "Dedication of the Temple of God in the City of Nauvoo." "This splendid edifice is **now completed** and will be dedicated to the Most High God on Friday the last day of May, 1846. Tickets may be had at the Watch House, near the door of the Temple, at One Dollar each." Hancock Eagle, April 10, 1846, LaRue, page 106.

The Nauvoo House stands a wreck and the Temple was destroyed and the Mormons driven out because of their sins.

The Coming of Christ

Smith had a revelation regarding the Saints going to redeem Zion, in which he said: "They should ordain the ministry to go forth and prune the vineyard for the last time for the coming of the Lord was nigh, even **Fifty Six Years** should wind up the scene." Mill. Star, Vol. 15, page 205.

"I was once praying very earnestly to know the time of the coming of the Son of Man when I heard a voice repeating the following: "Joseph, my son, if thou livest until thou art eighty-five years old, thou shalt see the face of the Son of Man. Therefore, let this suffice and trouble me no more on this matter. LaRue, page 52; Mill. Star, Vol. 20, page 728.

Joseph was born Dec. 23rd, 1805, so if Christ told him the above yarn then He should have come in 1900. Comment is unnecessary.

Slavery Advocated By Joseph Smith.

Most of the Mormons will tell you that Joseph Smith opposed slavery. Let his own words judge him as published by himself.

"If slavery is an evil who could we expect should first learn it? Would the people of the Free States or would the Slave States? All must admit that the latter would first learn this fact. It is my privilege then to name certain passages from the Bible and examine the teachings of the ancients upon the matter, as the fact is inconvertible, that the first mention we have of slavery is found in the Holy Bible, pronounced by a man who was perfect in his generation, and walked with God. And so far from that prediction being averse from the mind of God, it remains as a lasting monument to the decree of Jehovah to the shame and confusion of all who have cried against the south, in consequence of their holding the sons of Ham in servitude, and he said: "Cursed be Canaan, a servant of servants shall be he unto his brethren." "Blessed be the Lord of Shem, and Canaan shall be his servant." The curse is not taken off the sons of Canaan. The scripture stands for itself and I believe that these men were better qualified to teach the will of God than the abolitionists in the world. Mill Star, Vol. 15, pages 739-741. LaRue, page 27.

Question 13th—Are the Mormons abolitionists? Answer—No, unless delivering the people from priestcraft and the priests from the power of Satan, should be considered such—but we do not believe in **setting the negro free.**" Elders' Journal, 1838. LaRue, page 28.

Revelation on War Given Dec. 25th, 1832.

Read it as found in D. C. 132, in edition of 1913. Bays, pages 424-434.

If this revelation was given regarding the Rebellion of South Carolina in November, 1832, as it most assuredly was, then not one word of it came to pass, but if it referred to the rebellion of 1861, then but the first two propositions were even remotely guessed at correctly, the other ten events predicted never came to pass.

1. South Carolina rebelled. 2. Southern States called on Great Britain. 3. No slave ever rose against his master. 4. Britain did not become involved, and did not call on other nations. 5. No alliances with great powers were formed. 6. War was not poured out on all nations immediately following the rebellion of South Carolina. 7. The remnants of the land, the southern armies, did not vex the Gentiles with a sore vexation. 8. The saint was to stand in holy places—they were driven from Missouri. 9. The nations have not been destroyed, not even poor old Turkey. 10. The Lord has not taken vengeance upon the ungodly any more since than before the war.

This revelation was said to have been given Devember 25th, 1832, but not a word was said till it was published in England in 1851. The Doc. and Cov. was published in 1835, not a word of this prophecy.

But it was not a revelation for another reason. The fact as to a rebellion in South Carolina was openly discussed both in Mormon and other papers before the prophecy was given and all the nation looked for some such event occurring, as the following historical reports show.

Joseph Smith's Prophecy on The Rebellion and The War of 1860-4.

If Smith had the prophecy it was not published to the world till after he was dead seven years, and nineteen years after Smith is said to have made it. In 1851 when it was first published it required no prophet to predict a war between North and South Carolina, but the fact of waiting nineteen years before publishing such a prophecy shows that Smith was either afraid it might not come to pass, or else it was a forgery of 1851 that Smith had nothing to do with.

Slavery was first introduced into the United States in 1619 when twenty negroes were sold by a Dutch trader to the colonists. Barnes' U. S. Hist., page 50.

Eleven years before Smith's prophecy there was a discussion as to whether Missiouri would be a free or a slave state. Ibid. 172-3.

"The Protective Tariff Bill passed in 1832 was very distasteful to South Carolina and she declared the law unconstitutional within her boundaries, this became known as the Nullification Act. Students' Ency., page 579.

"A convention assembled in South Carolina in 1832 declared the Acts of 1828 and 1832 to be unconstitutional, and that attempts to enforce them otherwise than through civil tribunals would be resisted by the citizens of South Carolina, and would be deemed inconsistent with longer continuance of South Carolina in the Union, and that the people of the state would hold themselves absolved from all obligations to maintain or preserve their political connection with the people of other states, and would forthwith proceed to establish an independent government and do all the rights that sovereign states have the right to do. Life of Jackson, by Jenkins, page 263.

If Smith had the prophecy that year was it wonderful?

To cap the climax of Joseph's impudence, a few days after he professes to have the above revelation, he published in the churh paper called "The Evening and Morning Star," for Jan., 1833, about every item as found in the so-called prophecy, the cholera spreading over the whole earth, the plague breaking out in India, **the desolution of South Carolina from the Union,** the gathering of Saints to Zion, and adds: **"South Carolina has rebelled against the United States."** Held a state convention, and passed ordinances the same as declaring herself an independent nation, and more than all "Resolved that this convention do recommend to the people of South Carolina the observance of 31st day of January next as a day of fasting humiliation and prayer on which they are invited to implore the blessings of Almighty God on the efforts that are made to restore liberty and happiness to our beloved state. He adds "General Jackson has ordered several companies of artillery to Charleston and issued a proclamation urging submission and declaring such moves as that of South Carolina treason.

So we have it that about the same time that all this was going on, Smith is said to have had the prophecy, that was not published for many years afterwards, and worst of all was not presented for the adoption of the church, but it remained in secret like the revelation on polygamy, as claimed by so many.

Joseph Smith Was Not a Temperance Advocate.

"We then partook of some refreshments and our hearts were made glad with the fruit of the vine. This is according to the pattern set by the Saviour Himself, and we felt disposed to patronize all the institutions of heaven — — I took my mother and Aunt Clarissa in a carriage and accompanied them to Painsville, where we procured a bottle of wine, broke bread, ate and drank and parted, after the ancient order with the blessing of God." Mill. Star, Vol. 15, pages 583 and 744. LaRue, page 57.

Speaking of a meeting in Kirtland Temple, he describes how they washed their feet, prophesied curses upon Missouri. They sent messengers for bread and wine and continued having a good time all night. Mill. Star, Vol. 15, page 727.

Speaking of the drinking habit, in the city of Saints the prophet wrote" I told Theodore Turley that I had no objection to his building a brewery." The brewery was erected and its goods advertised as follows: "Whiskey, beer and cider barrels taken in exchange for beer and ale." Mill. Star, Vol. 20, page 647, and Nauvoo Neighbor, April 10. 1844.

Later we hear what became of this brewery and the temples of the Lord upon which so many prophecies had been delivered.

In the Hancock Eagle, May 29th, 1846, notice is given by one Abram Van Tuyl, to the effect that he has taken over the property of the **"boarding House and fitted it up for a hotel."** This was to be the great home of the prophet and his posterity from generation to generation.

In the issue of the same paper for June 26th, 1846, three advertisements appear authorized by the officers of the church, the Temple of Kirtland, Ohio, the Temple of Nauvoo, and the Brewery at Nauvoo for sale. Here is the great advocate of Temperance, selling his brewery and his two great Temples in which the people were to receive such great blessings.

William Law and other leading men affirm that Smith was a drunkard. Law Letters, 1887.

The same hour that Smith was shot to death, their own history shows that Joseph gave the guards money to buy wine, pipes and two papers of tobacco, and that Smith with the others drank. Joseph the Prophet, pages 522-523.

What a sacred scene, the holy Prophet's last hour spent drinking, smoking and killing two men and shooting the arm off a third and trying to kill three others by firing at them, but his gun missed fire. Was he prepared to meet God under such conditions? Journal of Hist., page 410, October, 1918.

CHAPTER VI.

Book of Abraham

Translated by Joseph Smith.

This book was considered a revelation of God revealed through Abraham and Joseph of Egypt, translated by inspiration, Joseph Smith using the Urim and Thummim with which to translate it, the same as the Book of Mormon. This was the claim made by the old church, and is still made by the main church of Mormons, and was not denied by the Reorganized church till the fraud was exposed and made the laughing stock of the world, then they have tried to lie out of it in the most clumsy way.

"Next month we expect to give some extracts from the Book of Abraham—a relic of greater antiquity than the Bible, written on papyrus and taken from the breast of an Egyptian mummy now in the possession of and translated by Joseph Smith. Mill. Star, July, 1842, page 32.

The history of the Book of Abraham is fully laid out in the paper, Smith and his people having purchased several mummies from a man called Chandler. "The record is now in course of translation **by means of the Urim and Thummim** and proves to be a record written partly by the father of the faithful Abraham, and finished by Joseph when in Egypt, preserved in the family of the Pharaohs and afterwards hid up with the embalmed body of the female with whom they were found." Mill Star, July 1842, pages 45-46.

The entire Book of Abraham is printed in the book published by the Mormon Church entitled "The Pearl of Great Price." Pages 46-70.

That this Book of Abraham was received as an inspired work, translated by the gift of God through Smith was admitted by the Reorganized church for many years, as will appear by the following, "But the Hebrew Patriarch (Abraham) has written his own history, it is contained in the Book of Abraham, translated by Joseph Smith." This extraordinary book has entered largely into Mormon Theology, and has given prominence to some of its most beautiful themes." This reveals a Book of God." Joseph the Prophet, pages 166-169.

That Joseph believed in and taught a plurality of Gods, and that his translation of the Bible and the Book of Abraham taught this doctrine and both the Bible and Book of Abraham were not only considered inspired by the church in the days of Smith and the Utah church to-day, but the Reorganized church admitted and taught it. This is made plain by the following: "By the quotations from our Utah Correspondent from the New Translation of the Bible, and from the Book of Abraham, it will be perceived that a **plurality of Gods** is a doctrine of these books.

It is a doctrine of the common version of the Bible too. The New Translation of the Bible was commenced very soon after the church was organized, and therefore this doctrine was a doctrine of the church at that time. The Scriptural evidences concerning the order of the kingdom in the exaltation of the Sons of God, show that the revelations in the New Translation of the Bible and in the Book of Abraham concerning the Gods all harmonize together: "And the **Gods** formed man from the dust of the ground. And the **Gods** planted a garden eastward in Eden. Unto Abraham the **Gods** said, Let us prepare the earth. And the **Gods** took council among themselves. And the **Gods** said, let us make a helpmate for man. The **Gods** caused a deep sleep to fall upon Adam. The **Gods** formed every beast of the field." Pearl of Great Price, pages 62-70. Herald, 1860, pages 280-285.

Now let us see how this Reorganized church misrepresented the facts about this Book of Abraham, and the position Joseph Smith and the church took upon it from 1842 till some time after it was proved to be a fraud.

"The church has never to our knowledge taken any action on this work, Joseph Smith, as a translator is committed of course to the correctness of the translation, but not necessarily to the endorsement of its historical or doctrinal contents." Ch. Hist., Vol. 2, page 569.

"The Reorganized church has never endorsed the Book of Abraham or accepted it as a standard church work. If he (Bishop Spaulding) is successful in proving that Joseph Smith's translation is unreliable, **that does not effect the Book of Mormon.** There is no vital connection between the Book of Mormon and the Book of Abraham. The power to translate the Book of Mormon was a divine gift, the translation went on with the aid of the **Urim and Thummim.** There is nothing to indicate that the divine help was ever claimed in the translation of the Book of Abraham. Certainly the **Urim and Thummim was not used.**" Pres. A. E. Smith, Herald Oct. 20th, 1915, pages 106-107.

We doubt if a more deceptive misrepresentation was ever penned in so short a space as this statement made by President Smith. Those who read the Book of Abraham, as found in the Pearl of Great Price and Mill. Star, and the description of it and statements made concerning it in the Mill. Star, and Saints' Herald as recorded above, and the history of Joseph Smith, and they will be convinced that Smith claimed inspiration for it, and that he was divinely inspired to translate it by the Urim and Thummim, as well as the Book of Mormon. This has been the claim of every strip of Mormonism from the time Smith obtained the Book of Abraham till the great fraud was exposed, then the Saints' Herald and Historians of the Reorganized church published their misrepresentations as cited above. Did E. A. Smith know all this when he denied that Joseph Smith translated the Book of Abraham by the use of the Urim and Thummim? The fact is that the Mill. Star that makes the statement is quoted by him in his article, so he misrepresented the facts with the paper before him. Having proved that Smith claimed to translate both the Book of Mormon and the Book of Abraham by inspiration through the Urim and Thummim, the proof is apparent that both Books were frauds.

That Bishop Spaulding, Dr. Sayce, Dr. Petrie, Dr. Breasted, Dr. Mase are all leading professors in decifering Egyptian Hieroglyphics, is world-wide admission. They have each examined the work of Smith, and declare with one accord, that the translation of the Book of Abraham by Smith is a "Farrago of nonsense from beginning to end." "None but the ignorant could possibly be imposed upon by such ludicrous blunders." "It may be safely said that there is not one single word that is true in these explanations." La Rue, pages 115-123.

All this being ture, it follows that Smith's claim to translate the Book of Mormon and the Book of Abraham by the Urim and Thummim is false in all its parts, and stamps him as an imposter of the blackest dye.

The latest manifestation of downright misrepresentation and hypocrisy on the part of the leaders of the Reorganized Church, may be read in the Saints' Herald for Nov. 19th, 1919. It seems that the Christian Advocate for Aug. 27th, 1919, has taken the position that Joseph Smith's claim to inspiration has been completely exposed in the fraudulent translation of the Book of Abraham.

In continuing to try to decieve the people, the editor of the Saints' Herald, makes the following false statements, regarding the Book of Abraham:

"The Book of Abraham was printed by the Utah Church in the Pearl of Great Price, as our readers may well know, the Pearl of Great Price is accepted as one of the sacred books of the Utah Mormon church. It was not so included by the original church in the days of Joseph Smith, the founder of the church, nor is it so accepted by the Reorganized Church.'

This monstrous statement is drawing a herring across the path, trying to make out that the Book of Abraham being printed by the Utah Church in the Pearl of Great Price, and therefore, it is not regarded as an inspired book by Joseph Smith or the Reorganized Church.

The facts are, the Book of Abraham was printed in the days of Joseph Smith and by his instruction and authority, while he presided over the very papers wherein it was published, and it was, in those papers regarded as a revelation from God and printed from the translation said to have been made by Joseph Smith through the Urim and Thummim, and was regarded as a revelation from the Almighty. Times and Seasons, Vol. 3, page 704. See also Mill. Star, for June, July and August, 1842.

First the editor of the Mill. Star, 1842, says: "The record (**Book of Abraham**) is now in course of translation by the means of the Urim and Thummim, and proves to be a record written partly by the father of the faithful, Abraham, and finished by Joseph when in Egypt." Here is a direct claim that Smith translated it by the spirit of revelation from God, imparted by the Urim and Thummim, the same instrument and the same way as came the Book of Mormon.

Leaving the Original Church and the Prophet Joseph Smith, let us come to the Saints' Herald published by the Reorganized Church, and we will show the unblushing men of that paper's editorial staff and presidential force who have testified so falsely, that the early editors and leaders of the Reorganized Church quoted the Book of Abraham as equal with the Bible and Book of Mormon, and said that it was inspired of the Almighty.

"**The Book of Abraham was translated through the gift and power of the Holy Ghost by Joseph Smith.** We learn from **this revelation** that the first woman was not begotten and born of parents but created out of the rib of Adam. Here we have four witnesses, Joseph Smith, Abraham, Moroni and Alma, all bearing testimony they were created from the dust of the ground." Saints' Herald, 1860, page 270.

"The new translation of the Bible (Smith's Bible), and the Book of Abraham both teach the doctrine of a **Plurality of Gods.** Although it is an unpopular doctrine, it is the doctrine of the common version of the Bible. The new translation of the Bible was commenced very soon after the church was organized and therefore this doctrine was a doctrine of the church at that time. Some say if we believe in a plurality of Gods, why do we not believe in Adam as a God. The scriptural evidences show that the **revelations in the New Translation of the Bible and in the Book of Abraham concerning the Gods all harmonize together.**" Saints' Herald, Vol. 1, 1860. pages 282-283.

President W. W. Blair of the Reorganized Church, one of the leaders of that body for a life time, writing of the revelations of Joseph Smith says: "Now, we propose to prove that **all the revelations which Joseph Smith gave unto the Church** we are bound to give heed unto. If the first edition of that book (Doctrine and Covenants) is divine all the subsequent revelations which are contained in the Book of Covenants, in **The Book of Abraham,** etc., and which he gave to the church **are equally divine.**" Saints' Herald, 1860, page 63. That Pres. Blair wrote the article, is claimed by Elder Shook. "True Origin of Polygamy." page 162.

Here we have the Presidency and editors of the Reorganized Church, endorsing the Book of Abraham as a revelation from God, given to Joseph Smith by direct revelation, and that it is equally divine with the revelations as given him in the New Translation of the Bible, the Book of Mormon and the Doctrine and Covenants. Why the Reorganized Church Editors and church presidents will wilfully misrepresent this and try to cover up the dirty thing, is one of the lying wonders of the Latter Days.

The Band Called Danites—Organized to Commit Murder.

That Joseph Smith controlled and organized a murderous band, bound under oath-bound penalties to obey the Church leaders, is acknowledged by the leading men who have left the church, and by some of the leading men of the nation who have evidence of such a band.

God Authorized Smith to Curse His Enemies.

According to Smith's revelations, Christ made him the supreme rule of the church and he was in command of every part of it, and every member was under his control

BOOK OF ABRAHAM

He was a "Prophet, Seer, Revelator, Apostle, Translator." D. C. 19, 1.

A High Priest, D. C. 104, 11.

President of the Church, Mill Star, Vol. 18, page 535.

Trustee for the whole Church, Nauvoo Neighbor, Dec. 27th, 1843.

Treasurer of the Kirtland Bank, Journal of Hist., Vol. 2, No. 4.

Grand Chaplain of Masonic Lodge at Nauvoo, Mill Star, Vol. 19, page 152.

Lieutenant-General of the Nauvoo Legion, Mill Star, Vol. 19, page 135.

Judge of the Municipal Court of Nauvoo, Mill. Star, Vol. 19, page 135.

Mayor of the City of Nauvoo, Ibid. 19, 135.

Registrar of Deeds, Ibid. Vol. 19, page 135.

And was at the time of his death a Candidate for the Presidency of the United States, Nauvoo Neighbor, June 26th, 1844. La Rue, pages 50, 51.

He was ordained a King, Herald, Vol. 51, No. 4; Wm. Marks' Records this.

The Lord is reported to have bound the church under a heavy curse if they rejected his words, and he was the only one that the Lord would give revelations to for the government of the church. He was in supreme control.

"Thou shalt give heed unto all his words and commandments. For his words ye shall receive as if from mine own mouth." D. C. 19, 2.

"And this shall ye know assuredly that there is none other appointed unto you to receive commandments and revelations, until he be taken." D. C. 43, 1, 2.

"And it shall be given thee in the very moment what thou shalt speak and write, and they shalt hear it, or I will **send them a cursing** instead of a blessing." D. C. 23, 3.

"No one shall be appointed to receive commandments and revelations in this church excepting my servant Joseph Smith—and thou shalt be obedient unto the things which I shalt give unto him." D.C. 27, 2.

"Therefore in as much as some of my servants have not kept the commandment, I have cursed them with a very sore and grievous curse, for I, the Lord, have decreed in my heart that in as much as any man belongeth to the order shall break the covenant with which ye are bound **he shall be cursed in this life and shall be trodden down by whom I will.** D. C. 101, 1.

Speaking of those who reject the commandments of Smith, the Lord is made to say: "Ye shall **curse them** and whomsoever **ye curse I will curse and ye shall avenge me of my ememies."** D. C. 100, 5.

Now we will show that a society was formed to kill on command

Governor Ford.

Governor Ford of Illinois, made a report to the State Legislature Dec. 17th, 1844. We submit a few statements: "It was asserted that Joseph Smith, head of the Mormon Church, had caused himself to be crowned and annointed King of the Mormons. That he had embodied a band of his followers, called **Danites,** who swore to obey him as God, and to do his command, **murder and treason not excepted."** La Rue, page 38.

President Wm. Law.

Pres. Wm. Law: "Smith taught Polygamy, spoiling (robbing) the Gentiles, **murder,** swindling, lying and many other evils. Joseph Smith told me that he sent a man to kill Governor Boggs—the fellow shot the Governor through a window." Shook, Origin of Polygamy, page 127.

J. C. Bennett.

J. C. Bennett says: "Smith told me to sign that certificate or he would make cat-fish bait of me, or deliver me to the **Danites** for execution." Ibid. page 58.

David Whitmer.

David Whitmer: "In June, 1838, at Far West, Mo., a secret organization was formed, Dr. Avard was put in as leader of the band. A certain oath was to be administered to all the brethren to bind them to support the heads of the church in every thing they would teach." Whitmer's address, page 27.

Oliver Cowdery.

Oliver Cowdery said: "Sidney Rigdon influenced the Prophet, Seer and Revelator to the Church of the Latter Day Saints into the formation of a secret band at Far West, committed to depredations upon Gentiles, and the actual assassination of apostates from the church. A society has been organized among them to inflict death upon those who are deemed apostates, with the knowledge and sanction of the first elder." O. Cowdery's Defence, Mormon Polygamy by Shook, pages 53-54.

Thomas B. Marsh.

Thomas B. Marsh, President of the Twelve, apostatized and swore, saying: "They have among them a company consisting of true Mormons, called **'The Danites'** who have taken an oath to support the heads of the church in all things that they say or do, whether right or wrong. I heard the Prophet say: 'that he would yet tread down his enemies and walk over their dead bodies and that he would make it one gore of blood from the Rocky Mountains to the Atlantic Ocean, and that if he was not let alone he would be a second Mahomet to this generation."

Apostle Orson Hyde said he knew to be true most of the above statement. La Rue, pages 162-163.

Samson Avard.

Samson Avard, who was a leader in the band, after his apostacy, said: "A band called the Daughters of Zion was organized by the members of the Mormon Church. I considered Joseph Smith as the prime mover and organizer of this **Danite Band.** The officers of the band were brought before him at a school house, together with Hyrum Smith and Sidney Rigdon, the First Presidency of the Church. Joseph Smith blessed them and prophecied over them, said it was necessary for the band to be bound together by covenant and those who revealed the secrets of the society should be put to death." La Rue, page 165.

Bishop Corrill.

Bishop Corrill, after he left the church, wrote: "I was afterwards invited to one of these meetings where an oath, in substance the same as testified by Dr. Avard, was administered. At the second or last meeting I attended, the Presidency (to wit, Joseph Smith, Hyrum Smith and Sidney Rigdon) were present. The Presidency pronounced blessings upon each member of the society. Smith threatened at this meeting to be a second Mahomet." La Rue, page 165.

W. W. Phelps.

W. W. Phelps testified that D. W. Patton said he heard Rigdon say: "If any man attempted to move out of the county, any man seeing him attempt to pack his goods **should kill him** and haul him aside into the bush and that all the burial he should have should be a Turkey Buzzard's guts." La Rue, page 165.

The above testimonies are from those who held the leading positions in the church under Smith, who when they left him swore to the above in the trial at Richmond, Mo., when Smith and others were tried for high treason, Nov. 12th, 1838, and is republished by Rev. La Rue, who was a Reorganized Elder for many years, but left the church because of what he knew.

Justice Morse.

Justice Morse, who was a Mormon in the old church and a High Priest in the Reorganized Church, at the time he testified, March, 1887, as follows:

"In the year 1838 at Far West, Caldwell County, Mo., **I was made a Danite** in an organized meeting held for that purpose. Joseph Smith, Sidney Rigdon and Hyrum Smith were present frequently at our meetings, Brother Avard had charge of organizing the band. We held our secret meeting in a deep ravine, in the year 1838. We were instructed by Joseph Smith, Sidney Rigdon and Hyrum Smith that the church could not advance without means, we must get money and means, right or wrong, honest or dishonest, that the church should suck the milk of the Gentiles. To take from Gentiles was no sin." La Rue, page 167. Shook True Origin of Mormonism, pages 168-171.

Rigdon made the Fourth of July speech at Far West, 1838. He said: "It shall be between us and them a war of extermination, for we will follow them till the last drop of their blood is spilled, or else they will exterminate us."

After this speech Smith was on the platform and led off with a shout of "Hosanna and Amen." Church Hist., Vol. 2, page 165; La Rue, page 175.

So we learn that the Mormons were the ones to talk of driving the Gentiles out of Missouri, and milking them and that there would be a war of extermination. Here we append a significant statement to confirm the above: "We are daily told, and not by the ignorant alone, but by all classes of them, that we, the (Gentiles) of this county are to be cut off, and our lands appropriated by them for inheritances." Mill. Star, Vol. 14, page 488.

The Utah Mormons are accused by the Reorganized Mormons of having the Danites still in existence. The Mountain Meadow massacre is a sample, be that as it may, if Utah has the Danites yet, they are but following Smith and the Church over which he had control, and if the Reorganized Mormon does not commit murder, they defame the character, and lie about all those who differ from them and are absolutely heartless and unfair to apostates.

Blood Atonement.

The President of the Reorganized Church, Joseph Smith, and son of the original, Joseph Smith, in attempting to excuse the atrocious crimes and statements made by his father and other leaders of the Danites makes the following statement:

"Whoever counselled or did evil in those times (in Missouri) are responsible personally, therefore; but the church, as such, is no more responsible for it that were the early Christians for Peter's attempt to kill the High Priest's servant when he cut off his ear with a sword. The church, as such, should be judged by its authorized doctrines and deeds, and not by the unauthorized sayings or doings of some of its members or ministers." Blood Atonement, page 44.

"You take great pains to cover up the conditions prevailing which call forth such extreme and in some instances unwise remarks. Conditions in some respects akin to those surrounding the Saints in Missouri in 1838 and 1839, when other unwise remarks were made by members of the leading quorums of the church, but in a sense justifiable and which should be condoned under the trying circumstances that called them forth." Joseph F. Smith in reply to R. C. Evans in Blood Atonement, page 43.

Thus we have the President of the Reorganized Church and son of Joseph Smith admitting, as well as apologizing for the rash statements of his father and other leaders in the old church, and then we have Joseph F. Smith of the Utah church using about the same argument to excuse the language and murderous conduct of the Danites in Utah. All we care to say is reply to both of these descendants of the original prophet and organizer of the Danite Band is, that when the leading members and officers of the church for many years teach and practice, by threats and murders, ascribed to the Danite Band, then we believe the public is justified in denouncing such language and conduct, and affirming it to be the doctrine of the church. We will now quote from the Utah Mormon Church some leading statements made in the public printed sermons of Brigham Young, his counsellors and apostles, regarding the Danites and their murderous conduct under the title of Blood Atonement. These sermons were reported by G. D. Watt and published by the authority of the Mormon Church in a work entitled "Journal of Discourses." Coming from their own church leaders, published by their own church papers, there seems to be little opportunity to deny the genuineness of these statements.

Brigham Young.

Brigham Young said, October 9, 1852: "What shall be done with the sheep that stink the flock so? We will take them, I was going to say, and cut off their tails two inches behind their ears; however I will use a milder term, and say cut off their ears." Journal of Discourses, Vol. 1, page 213.

Brigham again said, March 27, 1853: "I say, rather than that apostates should flourish here, I will unsheath my bowie knife, and conquer or die. Now, you nasty apostates, clear out, or judgment will be pur to the line and righteousness to the plummet. If you say it is all right, raise your hands (all hands up). Let us call upon the Lord to assist us in this and every good work." Journal of Diwcourses, Vol. 1, page 83.

President Brigham Young preached, February 8, 1857, as follows: "All mankind love themselves; and let these principles be known by an individual and he would be glad to have his blood shed. That would be loving themselves even to an eternal exaltation. Will you love your brothers and sisters likewise when they have committed a sin that cannot be atoned for without the shedding of blood? Will you love that man or woman well enough to shed their blood? That is what Jesus Christ meant. He never told a man or woman to love their enemies in their wickedness. He never intended any such thing.

I could refer you to plenty of instances where men have been righteously slain in order to atone for their sins. I have seen scores and hundreds of people for whom there would have been a chance in the last resurrection if their lives had been taken and their blood spilled upon the ground, as a smoking incense to the Almighty, but who are now angels of the devil, until our elder brother, Jesus Christ, raises them up, conquers death, hell and the grave. I have known a great many men who have left this church, for whom there is no chance whatever for exaltation; but if their blood had been spilt it would have been better for them. The wickedness and ignorance of the nations forbid this principle being in full force, but the time will come when the law of God will be in full force.

This is loving our neighbor as ourselves; if he needs help, help him; and if he wants salvation and it is necessary to spill his blood upon the ground in order that he may be saved, spill it." Journal of Discourses, Vol. 4, page 220, or Desert News, Vol. 6, page 397.

Orson Hyde.

Elder Orson Hyde said, April 9, 1853: "Suppose the shepherd should discover a wolf approaching the flock, what would he be likely to do? Why, we would suppose, if the wolf was within proper distance,

BOOK OF ABRAHAM

that he would kill him at once—kill him on the spot. It would have a tendency to place a terror on those who leave these parts, that may prove their salvation when they see the heads of thieves taken off, or shot down before the public." Journal of Discourses, Vol. 1, pages 72, 73.

President J. M. Grant.

President J. M. Grant said, Sept. 21, 1856: "I say there are men and women here that I would advise to go to the president immediately, and ask him to appoint a committee to attend to their case, and then let a place be selected, and let that committee shed their blood." Deseret News, Vol. 7, page 235.

President Heber C. Kimball.

President Heber C. Kimball said, July 19, 1854: "It is believed in the world that our females are all common women. Well, in one sense they are common—that is, they are like all other women, I suppose, but they are not unclean, for we wipe all unclean ones out of our midst; we not only wipe them from our streets, but we wipe them out of existence. And if the world wants to practice uncleanness, and bring their prostitutes here, if they do not repent and forsake their sins, we will wipe the evil out. We will not have them in this valley unless they repent, for so help me God, while I live I will lend my hand to wipe such persons out, and I know this people will." Deseret News, August 15, 1854, and Mill. Star, Vol. 16, pages 738-9.

Fanny Stenhouse.

Fanny Stenhouse: "There was the murder of the Aikin party—six persons—who were killed on their way to California. The same year a man named Yates was killed under atrocious circumstances; and Franklin McNeil, who had sued Brigham for false imprisonment and who was killed at his hotel door. There was Sergeant Pile, and there was Arnold and Drown. There was Price and William Bryan at Fairfield; there was Almon Babbitt, and Brassfield, and Dr. Robinson; there was also James Cowdy and his wife and child, and Margetts and his wife; and many another, too, to say nothing of that frightful murder at the Mountain Meadows." "Tell-It-All," page 319.

We could fill a volume with the history of the murders that have stained and scarred the Mormon Church, both in Missouri, Illinois, Utah and elsewhere, the history of which has made Mormonism a stench in the nostrils of civilization, and as one has said, has made Utah a land of assassination and a field of blood.

Mormonism Regards All Other Churches As Corrupt.

Joseph Smith claimed that in his first vision, which was in the spring of 1820, that after God had introduced Joseph to Christ, that Joseph asked Christ "Which of all the sects is right?" That Christ made the following answer to him: "I was answered that I must join none of them, for they were all wrong, and the personage who addressed me said that all their creeds were an abomination in his sight; that those professors were all corrupt; that they draw near me with their lips but their hearts are far from me, and they teach for doctrines the commandments of men having a form of godliness but they deny the power thereof." Church Hist., Vol. 1, pages 9, 10.

"Is it any wonder then, that we say of priests of modern days, that they are of Satan's own making, and are of their father the Devil? Nay, verily, nay, for no being but a scandalous sycophant and base hypocrite would say otherwise. We shall see all the preists who adhere to the sectarian religions of the day, with all their followers without one exception, receive their portion with the devil and his angels." Elders Journal, 59-60, August, 1838; La Rue, page 45.

"Respecting the Melchisedec Priesthood, the sectarian world never professed to have it, consequently they never could save anyone and would all be damned together. The sectarian world are going to hell by hundreds, by thousands and by millions." Mill. Star, Vol. 22, page 54; La Rue, page 45.

"They have taken away from the gospel of the Lamb many parts which are plain and most precious, and also many covenants of the Lord have been taken away—that they might blind the eyes and harden the hearts of the children of men."

The above is part of the preface of Smith's new Bible. The statement of the Lord to Smith showed that the churches had become corrupt and taken away much of the Bible to corrupt and deceive the people of the churches, and it was necessary for God to give Smith the plain and precious things which the wicked Christian churches had taken away from the Bible when they translated the Authorized Version.

In the first revelation published in the book known as the Doctrine and Covenants, Jesus Christ when speaking to Joseph Smith is reported to have said, speaking of the Mormon Church, as **"The only true and living Church** upon the face of the whole earth, with which I, the Lord, am well pleased." D. C. 1, 5.

"Behold, there is, save it be **two churches;** the one is the church of the Lamb of God, and the other is the church of the Devil. Wherefore, whoso belongeth not to the church of the Lamb of God belongeth to that great church, which is the mother of abominations; and she is the **whore** of all the earth." Book of Mormon, page 40; First Nephi, 3 ch., v. 220-223.

Orson Pratt.

Orson Pratt, the most eloquent Apostle, and the greatest writer of Mormonism, says: "Since the church with its authority and power has been caught away from the earth, the great Mother of Harlots, with all her descendants, has blasphemously assumed authority of administering some of the sacred ordinances of the gospel." Revelation Necessary by O. Pratt.

Apostle W. H. Kelley.

To the above may be added the statement made by Apostle W. H. Kelley, President of the Apostolic Quorum of the Reorganized Church. "The Priesthood having been caught up to heaven, no man on earth has authority to minister in gospel ordinances, and hence the necessity for new revelation." Presidency and Priesthood, page 224.

No Salvation Outside of The Book of Mormon and Mormonism

"I told the brethren that the Book of Mormon was the most correct of any book on earth, and the keystone to our religion; and a man would get nearer to God by abiding by its precepts than by any other book." J. Smith, in Mill. Star, Vol. 18, page 790; La Rue, page 62.

The Book of Mormon claims to be a divinely inspired record. It professes to be revealed to the present generation for the salvation of all who will receive it and **for the overthrow and damnation of all nations who reject it.** The nature of the message in the Book of Mormon is such that if true, no one can **possibly be saved and reject it."** Apostle Pratt, Divinity of Book of Mormon, No. 1, page 1; La Rue, page 81.

Brigham Young.

"Every spirit that confesses that Joseph Smith is a prophet, that he lived and died a prophet, and that the Book of Mormon is true, is of God, and every spirit that does not is of anti-Christ." Story of the Mormons, page 28; La Rue, page 81.

Reorganized Church.

"No book ever came before the race of mankind with such an august message as the Book of Mormon." Saints' Herald, Nov. 6, 1918, page 1082.

Orson Pratt.

"They (the Ministry) have dishonored the name of Christ by calling their powerless apostage filthy and most abominable churches, the church of Christ, the whole Romish, Greek and Protestant Ministry, from the Pope down through every grade of office, are as destitute of authority from God as the devil and his angels."

More revelation indispensable Necessary, page 19.

"All other churches are unauthorized of God. Their articles of religion, their creeds, their prayer books, their ordinations, their sacraments, their baptisms, their various forms of worship, their preaching and their religious assemblies are all an abomination in the sight of Heaven." Evidence of the Book of Mormon and Bible compared, page 61.

"We are commanded to accept the Book of Mormon and renounce all the wicked traditions of our fathers, as also the "Popish and Protestant ministry, together with all the churches which have been built up by them or that have sprung up from them as being entirely destitute of authority, they should turn away from all the priestcraft and abominations practiced by these apostate churches, falsely called Christians." The Bible Alone and Insufficient Guide, page 34.

"And as every creature in all the world, who would not believe the chosen eye witnesses of a risen Saviour were to be damned, so every living soul who rejects the testimony of the chosen eye witnesses of the ministry of the angel confirmatory of the Book of Mormon, **will be damned** for thus hath the Lord spoken." Evidence of the Book of Mormon and Bible compared, page 58.

"This generation has more than one thousand times the amount of evidence to demonstrate and forever establish the divine authenticity of the Book of Mormon than they have in favor of the Bible." Evidence of the Book of Mormon and Bible Compared, page 64.

"The Book of Mormon contains the everlasting gospel in all its fullness and it has been revealed to the inhabitants of our earth by an angel—let the nations know assuredly that the hour of God's judgment is come, and that they have **only one way of escape and that is by embracing the Book of Mormon.**" Prophetic Evidence in favor of the Book of Mormon, pages 82-84.

We have shown in this article from leading Mormons, from Joseph Smith down, that there is no salvation outside of the Mormon Church.

The Holy Scriptures Translated by Joseph Smith.

In a work published by the Reorganized Mormon Church, entitled "Three Bibles Compared," we are informed that it took a King and forty-seven scholars from 1604 to 1611, seven years to translate what is known as the King James translation, and that eighty-two scholars were employed fourteen years of the Old Testament, and ten years on the New Testament, when the Revised Version was given from 1870 to 1884.

These men had the wealth of the churches and the scholarship of the world behind them, while God commanded and directly inspired Joseph Smith, an illiterate young man of but twenty-eight years of age, surrounded with poverty and mobs, to translate the entire Bible of Old and New Testaments in three years. He commenced the work June, 1830, and finished it June, 1833.

The manuscript of this great work was preserved by the widow of Smith, and was given to her son, who, with I. L. Rogers and E. Robinson formed a committee of the Reorganized Mormon Church, to publish the New Bible. This was accomplished, and is now on sale by the Reorganized Church Publishing House.

The reader will find published in the Preface of the Mormon Bible the following, which in part disclosed the reason that Smith gave for his translation, "For behold they have taken away from the gospel of the Lamb **many parts which are plain and most precious and also many covenants of the Lord have been taken away,** and all this have they done that they might pervert the right way of the Lord, that they might blind the eyes and harden the hearts of the children of men, wherefore thou seest that after the book hath gone forth through the hands of the great and abominable church, there are many plain and precious things taken away from the book, which is the book of the Lamb of God, and after these plain and precious things were taken away it goeth forth unto all the nations of the Gentiles."

The above is taken from the Book of Mormon. The church referred to as "great and abominable" is considered the "Mother of Harlots and her daughters," or in other words, the church of Rome and the Protestant churches. They have taken away the plain and precious things in order to deceive the world, and now God has raised up Smith to bring back these plain and precious things so that the honest people may be saved and rescued from the "great whore of the earth," (Rome and Protestantism) and so has inspired Smith to give us the New Translation of the Bible.

The Lord further instructs Smith regarding this new Bible: "Thou shalt ask and my scriptures shall be given as I have appointed, and they shall be preserved in safety, and it is expedient that thou shouldst hold thy peace concerning them and not teach them until ye have received them in full, and I give unto you a commandment that then ye shall teach them unto all men, for they shall be taught to all nations, kindreds, tongues and people." D. C. 42, 15.

"Ye shall hasten to translate my scriptures—and all this for the salvation of Zion." D. C. 90, 12.

"The Scriptures shall be given even as they are in mine own bosom to the salvation of mine own elect." D. C. 34, 5.

Joseph was informed by the Lord that, "He should bring to light those parts of my scriptures which have been hidden because of iniquity." D. C. 6, 12.

Those who wish to read this marvellous work, the new Bible translated by Joseph Smith, by direct revelation, will discover that he has not translated a single word, that he had no manuscript of any kind, that he was an ignorant young man, is admitted. There is no evidence that he compared any originals with each other, nor could he have done so if the originals were before him. The claim is that it was all done by direct inspiration from the Almighty, but to call it a **Translation** is the height of impudence and nonsense.

Let us present Smith's own account describing the method of receiving revelations and translating: "But behold, I say unto you, **that you must study it out in your own mind. Then you must ask of Me if it be right? And if it is right I will cause that your bosom shall burn within you, therefore you shall feel that it is right.** Now if you had known this you could have translated." D.C. 9, 3-4.

Here is the secret of Smith's power to translate. He read the Bible, thought that such and such a change should be made, either by adding a few verses, or taking away a few verses. If he had the burning sensation in his bosom it was right, and so he cut and slashed away at the Word of God to his heart's content, and the result is the **Mormon Bible.**

We will take time to show one of thousands of changes that Smith has made by inspiration. When God inspired Smith to translate the Lord's prayer" in the Book of Mormon, he translated it exactly as it is found in the authorized version, Matt. 6, 13, **"and lead us not into temptation."** But when the same God inspired him to translate the Bible, he inspired him to translate it as follows, **"and suffer us not to be led into temptation"** Matt. 6, 14. We ask, Is it right in the authorized version, if so it is right in the Book of Mormon, but if right in the authorized version and Book of Mormon, Joseph's burning bosom business in the inspired translation of his new Bible, got him in wrong.

Closing this part of his marvellous work we now call attention to the changes he has made in the first twelve chapters of the Bible, this will be sufficient to show, as a fair sample of the entire translation, the monstrous work of Smith.

Christian Bible, First twelve chapters, Genesis, we find 319 verses.
Mormon Bible, First twelve chapters of Genesis, we find 454 verses. Joseph's burning bosom business just invented an extra 135 verses.
Christian Bible, Gen. 4th chapter has 26 verses.
Mormon Bible, Gen. 4th chapter has 13 verses.
Christian Bible, Gen. 7th chapter has 24 verses.
Mormon Bible, Gen. 7th chapter has 75 verses.

In one chapter the Mormon Bible has just half as many verses as is found in the Christian Bible, in the other chapter the Mormon Bible has more than three times as many verses as the Christian Bible. But why prolong the agony. The general reader will ere this conclude that Smith's burning bosom business was not the inspiration of God, but it was the imposition of a vile and impudent, false prophet, and that it is in line with his spurious revelations as recorded in his productions known as the Book of Abraham, Book of Mormon, Book of Commandments, Book of Doctrine and Covenants, and other so-called revelations which have dragged many thousands into the lying wonder of the latter days—Mormonism.

CHAPTER VII.

United States vs. Mormon Church

The Mormon Church has endeavoured, through her literature and pulpit to persuade the people that the trouble between the United States and the church was occasioned by the wickedness of the nation, as against the divinely commissioned people of the Lord, that the righteousness of the Saints was a standing rebuke to the corruption of the nation and hence the trouble, which resulted in the murder of many people, the driving of the Saints from their lands and possessions, and the assassination of their prophet, Joseph Smith.

We propose to open the pages of history with the hope that the real facts may be disclosed and the truth be known to all men.

Joseph Smith and his people make certain claims, and have endeavoured to put into operation the methods that will result in the destruction of the United States Government, and not only that Government, but every other nation now existing upon the earth, that upon the debris of all the nations of the earth, God inspired Joseph Smith and his people to establish a kingdom, to which Christ would come and reign therein forever.

Smith's First Vision.

Smith's first vision, said to have been given him when he was less than fifteen years of age, is as follows: God and Christ came down to have a talk with Smith in the woods at the rear of his father's farm. The Father begins the conversation by introducing his son, Christ, to Smith in these words, "This is my beloved son, hear him." It seems that the Father made the trip all the way from heaven just in order to have the great privilege of introducing Jesus to Joseph, for there is no evidence that He spake another word. Smith brushes aside all formalities and starts business at once by asking the all important question in a young farmer lad of fifteen winters, "Which of all the sects was right, and which I should join?" I was answered that I must join none of them for they were **all wrong, that all their creeds were an abomination in His sight, that those professors were all corrupt:** They drew near me with their lips, but their hearts are far from me, they teach for doctrine the commandments of men having a form of godliness, but they deny the power thereof."

He informs us that after some further chat, they left and he found himself lying on his back looking up into heaven. Church Hist., Vol. 1, page 10.

If this vision is to be relied upon the following must be conceded:
First—Smith was not to join any church.

Second—The churches are **all wrong.**
Third—All the creeds are abominable in the sight of God.
Fourth—Those professing to be Christians in those churches or presenting the creeds, **were all corrupt,** a great mass of hypocrites, denying the power of God and only giving him **lip** service while their hearts were far from God."

Just take this in for a moment: Men and women who have given their lives to promote Christianity, as they see it, they who have gone to the jungles of Africa, to the darkness of China and Japan, those who have braved the dangers of frontier life among the wild and savage tribes of America and the rest of the world, those who have preached the gospel as they understood it, were **all corrupt,** their teaching was an **abomination in the sight of God;** the mother who consecrated her children to Christ in the evening twilight while they knelt at her knee, she was just giving lip service while her heart was far from him, in other words, she was playing the hypocrite.

This sweeping condemnation and anathematization of every minister, layman, and church is characteristic of both Mormon literature and pulpit utterance from that day to this, and it is only when they desire to obtain favor that they withhold this cardinal principle of their faith.

Jesus Christ is supposed to have told Joseph Smith that he was commissioned to "lay the foundation of this church—the only **true and living Church upon the face of the whole earth with which I the Lord am well pleased."** Doc. and Cov., 1, 5.

This is the faith of the Mormon, or Latter Day Saint Church to this day, and every effort to cover this up is a manifestation of hypocrisy on their part, and it is this that has caused them much trouble with the people in every part of the world where they have attempted to establish a church.

They are taught that the church established by Smith is the Kingdom of God, and that the other churches are the kingdom of the Devil. Doc. and Cov., 3, 13, 87, 1-3.

Smith to Organize a Kingdom That Will Destroy All Other Nations.

They have taught that Joseph Smith was directed by the Lord to set up the Kingdom, or organize the church, and that it would never be destroyed, but that it should destroy all other churches and kingdoms and that the judgments of the Lord would come upon all churches and kingdoms, and that Smith and his people would triumph over all, and Christ would come to them and reign with them in the place called Independence, Missouri, but known in Smith's revelations as The City of Enoch, The New Jerusalem, and Zion. In support of this they present the following from the Bible and the revelations of Joseph Smith:

"And in the days of these kings shall the God of Heaven set up a kingdom which shall never be destroyed, and the kingdom shall not be left to other people, but it shall break in pieces and consume all these kingdoms and it shall stand forever." Dan. 2, 44.

"But the judgment shall set, and they shall take away his dominion, to consume and to destroy it unto the end, and the kingdom and the dominion and the greatness of the kingdom under the whole heavens shall be given to the people of the Saints of the Most High, whose kingdom is an everlasting kingdom, and all dominions shall serve and obey him." Dan. 8, 26-27.

Smith says that Christ told him how the destruction of these kingdoms will be accomplished. I cite but a few of the methods of destructions.

"Wherefore I, the Lord, will send forth flies upon the face of the earth, which shall take hold of the inhabitants thereof, and shall eat their flesh, and shall cause maggots to come in upon them, and their tongues shall be stayed that they shall not utter against Me, and their flesh shall fall off their bones, and their eyes from their sockets, and it shall come to pass that the beasts of the forests and the fowls of the air shall devour them up, and that great and abominable church, which is the whore of all the earth, shall be cast down by devouring fire." Doc. and Cov., 28, 5.

"But verily I say unto you, that I have decreed a decree which my people shall realize inasmuch as they hearken from this very hour, unto the counsel which I the Lord will give unto them. Behold, they shall begin to prevail against mine enemies from this very hour—and they shall never cease to prevail **until the Kingdoms of this world are subdued under my feet and the earth is given unto the saints to possess it forever and ever.**" Doc. and Cov., 100, 2.

Smith's revelations show, not only that he was to organize the only true church upon the earth, but the kingdom thus established would destroy all other churches and the kingdoms of this world would be humbled till they submitted to them and become the kingdoms of God, to be ruled over by his Saints, and in order to start this great work He commanded them first to sell their property and collect their wealth and all move to the little village of Kirtland in the State of Ohio, there a city would be built and a great temple erected.

"If thou lovest me thou shalt serve me and keep all my commandments, and behold **thou shalt consecrate all thy properties** that which thou hast unto me, **with a covenant and a deed which cannot be broken,** and they shall be laid before the bishop of my church." B. C., 44, 26; Doc. and Cov., 42, 8.

In a later edition of this book the word **"all"** is taken out, and the word **"of"** inserted, but I have a copy of the original revelation as first published. The change was made because many left the church rather than give all their property to the church, but after the change was made, the authorities became strong enough to again secure a revelation on the same matter and it says about the same thing, in fact the books agree on it:

"In answer to the question, O Lord, show unto thy servants how much thou requirest of the properties of thy people for a tithing? Verily, thus saith the Lord, **I require all their surplus property to put into**

the hands of the bishop of My church of Zion, for building of mine house, and for the laying the foundation of Zion, and for the priesthood and **for the debts of the Presidency** of my church—and this shall be a standing law unto them forever, saith the Lord."
Doc. and Cov. 106, 1; 42, 8, 9, 10; 101, 10-21; 51, 1-2; 72, 3.

So the people sold their property and travelled to their sacred mecca, Kirtland, Ohio. The little burg was surveyed into city lots, a temple was erected, in which Christ and several others from heaven talked to Smith and some others. This city was to dazzle the world, be the wonder of the earth, Smith and many others changed their names, Smith got three new names, viz.: Enoch, Gazelem and Baurak-Ale. He and his relatives and friends secured their inheritance and built their homes, and started a bank and run things with a high hand, till many lost hope in both God and man, as well as their property and left the church. Even William Smith, the prophet's brother denounced him and gave him a sound good thrashing, but being a Smith he was forgiven. But the trouble did not end here. Smith was tarred and feathered and finally left Kirtland on horseback, seeking for a more congenial clime. I shall not take time and space to record all this history, but shall give you the references and you may depend upon it every point stated here is taken from their own books. Doc. and Cov., Sections 91, 92, 93, 100, 77; Church Hist., Vol. 1, pages 240, 244; Vol. 1, pages 614, 624.

The next move to establish the Kingdom of God that was to break in pieces and destroy all other kingdoms, was made at the little town of Independence, Jackson County, in the State of Missouri. This place was dedicated to the Lord, the temple that Christ was to make His appearance in was to be built upon a certain lot, then a wild bush covered with trees. This was consecrated with great pomp. The Lord was to give the land unto His saints, for an everlasting inheritance, the wicked were to be driven out, the besom of God's wrath was to be poured out upon them, and here Zion was to shine in all its splendor. The pioneers who had secured the land from the government were told from time to time that they were to get out, or the judgments of the Lord would overtake them. Joseph Smith was directed by the Lord to write to the kings and presidents and rulers of all the nations, they were to come to Zion, send their wealth there and be good as directed by the revelations given through Smith or the time of judgment would soon be upon them, and the wrath of the Almighty would soon make an end of their wickedness and rebellion. Doc. and Cov. 57, 77, 83, 45, 72, 107.

David Whitmer.

David Whitmer, one of the three witnesses to the Book of Mormon, and one of the first six baptized into the new church, but who left the church in a few years never to return, informs us that Smith was a fallen prophet, that his revelations were false, that he has as much evidence that Joseph Smith had the revelation on polygamy, as he has to believe that George Washington ever lived. He declared that the revelations of Smith fell into the hands of the people of the world, and that the people of Missouri saw by those revelations that they were considered by the church as intruders upon the land of Zion, and that soon an effort would be made to drive them forth. They called a meeting of the citizens, and decided that it was either for them to drive the Mormons away, or the Mormons would soon be strong enough to drive them from their homes. The fight started; the Mormon printing press was destroyed, and some houses were torn down, and the Mormons driven out of their Zion. Now, while we do not agree with much suffering caused by the people as against helpless women and children, yet it must be admitted that the Mormons by living up to the pretended revelations and instructions of Smith were to blame. Whitmer's Address, 38, 54.

Smith Raised An Army.

Smith soon came out with revelations to fix up the trouble. God was going to vex the nation and cut off the wicked, and the Saints were to return and obtain their property. Doc. & Cov., 98, 12-23.

They would prevail against their enemies, and the kingdoms of the world would soon crumble and the Saints were to come in to their everlasting possessions, God's presence would be with them and when they **cursed their enemies, God would curse them too,** while Joseph was to organize the kingdom. Doc. & Cov., 100, 1-6; 102, 1-9.

Now let us permit the son of the prophet to tell us what his father was commanded to do. Joseph Smith, the prophet, raised an army to go to Missouri, they numbered several hundred and started from Kirtland, Ohio, gathering in number by the way. Their wagons were filled with food, clothing and munitions of war, they marched over one thousand miles, walking by the side of their wagons, filled with war material and food. "They provided themselves with fire-arms and all sorts of munitions of war." While they were marching Joseph had made provisions with his people in Missouri to erect a munition plant in which they made **swords, dirks, pistols, rifles and other arms."** During the long march, angels were often seen in their camp, they tell that their feet were blistered and their stockings wet with blood. The Lord protected them by sending large hail-stones upon their enemies, that made holes in their hats. In describing the hail-stones H. C. Kimball says they were as large as hens' eggs, and Lyman Wight says some of them were as large as turkey eggs. These hail-stones never touched the brethren of the Lord, though at times they hit the rifle stocks of the enemy and broke them. Now, these two witnesses were leading apostles of the Lord, so we should believe them. Joseph says that the water of a little river rose thirty feet in thirty minutes, and where the river was forty feet deep, the evening before it was only up to our ankles.

The Governor of the State of Missouri was called up. He advised the army to disband or there would be bloodshed, but Smith considered the Governor a coward, and commanded his army to march on, that they would not make terms "with land pirates and murderers," sweeping past Governor Dunklin, they soon ran up against the sheriff, of the county, Mr. Gillium. He tried to advise, but the army led by Smith went forward to conquer.

Joseph Smith was a real Napoleon. He chose twenty men for his life-guard, his brother Hyrum was captain, and George A. Smith was his armor bearer. The kingdom of God was to be established in a hurry and the United States would be remembered with pity and contempt.

Cholera hit the camp, sixty-eight fell before it, Smith being one of the smitten. Fourteen of the army died, they could not make coffins so they wrapped them in blankets. The people were discouraged and many left the church, but Joseph was ready with another revelation, and he told them the plague came because of disobedience. He said, "Ye are not willing to listen to my words, but have been in rebellion, that God had decreed that sickness should come upon them, and they should die like sheep with the rot." Then he sympathizingly said, "I am sorry, but I cannot help it." For a full account read Church Hist., Vol. 1, 454-487.

Now to conclude this part of the story, let us ask, Did God direct Smith to organize this army, erect munition factories to manufacture pistols, rifles, swords, dirk knives, and all kind of war munition? Did God tell Smith to drag those people over a thousand miles, send his angels, and floods and hail-stones like turkey eggs to break the guns of their enemies? Did God request those poor people to suffer all those deprivations and such sickness and death and then suffer them to make an ignominious failure, or was it the man Smith that caused all this trouble?

Just think of the impudence of Smith, after these people had suffered starvation, cold, sickness and death; after they had sold their property giving him the money; after they had followed him from their comfortable farms and city homes in the eastern countries, while some of them look upon the dead faces of those they loved in life, and amid their tears they laid them away without a coffin, for Smith to tell them this death and agony was caused by the Lord because they had rebelled against Smith in some little matters concerning camp life, and the wonder of it all was that many of the poor deluded people still followed him, but many apostatized and exposed Smith, so that hundreds left the church.

Many of them honestly believed that Smith was God's representative, in the establishing of the Kingdom of God that was to break in pieces the United States and all other governments and bring them into subjection to his reign and power, and because of their faith in his revelations, they went forth to conquer the world.

Smith's Army Destroy Towns.

Herewith I submit the history of the Mormon war as told by the Governor of the State of Missouri, under date of October 26, 1838: General John B. Clark, 1st. Division Missouri Militia.

Sir:—Application has been made to the Commander-in-Chief, by the citizens of Daviess County, in this state, for protection and to be restored to their homes and property, with intelligence that the Mormons with an armed force have expelled the inhabitants of that county from their homes, have pillaged and burned their dwellings, driven off their stock, and were destroying their crops, that they (the Mormons) have burned to ashes the towns of Gallatin and Millport in said county."

The letter continues to instruct the General to call out his soldiers and go forthwith to the seat of the trouble.

The next morning he wrote the same General as follows:

"Since the order of the morning to you, directing you to raise men, I have received information of the most appalling character which changes the whole face of things and places the Mormons in the attitude of open and avowed defiance of the laws, and of having made open war upon the people of the State. Your orders are, therefore, to hasten your operations with all possible speed. The Mormons must be treated as enemies, and must be exterminated or driven from the State, if necessary, for the public good. Their outrages are beyond all description." Church Hist., Vol. 2, pages 216-217.

I have given but a brief history of their conduct, but the reader will remember this comes not from a mob, or some excited bigot, but from the highest authority of the State of Missouri, the Governor, yet because the Mormons were whipped in the fight and driven from the State, they have told the world they were persecuted because they were Saints of the Lord, when the facts were, they were following the revelations of Smith, with the thought that they were doing their duty in driving the people from their homes in order that Zion would be built up. The people did not like the treatment, and refusing to be converted to Mormonism they appealed to the United States authorities, with the result that they were punished. Much more could be written, but we think that a discerning public will have discovered by this brief history, the cause of the trouble, and conclude the Mormons were the dupes of Smith.

Smith Foretells Destruction of United States.

After this terrible trouble in which many were killed on both sides Smith claimed the Lord directed him to go to Washington to see the President of the United States, and secure justice for himself and people. The President declined to submit to the persuasions of Smith and his comrades, whereupon Smith still undaunted, comes forth with the following:

"Now we shall endeavour to express our feeling and views concerning the President, as we have been eye witnesses of his majesty. He is a small man, sandy complexion, and ordinary features, with frowning brow and considerable body, but not well proportioned, as to his arm and legs and to use his own words, is "quite fat." On the whole we think he is without body or parts, as no one part seems to be proportioned to another, therefore, instead of saying body and parts, we say body and party, or partyism, if you please to call it, and in fine to come directly to the point, he is so much a fop or a fool (for he judged our cause before he knew it) we could find no place to put trust in him. For a general thing there is but little solidity and honorable deportment among those who are sent here to represent the people, but a great deal of pomposity and show." Church Hist., Vol. 2, page 397.

He wrote the above from Washington, and on his arrival home in the City of Nauvoo, he wrote the following of his judgment upon the people of the United States, and the men in office, and shows the Lord told him a little secret, the destruction of the United States; but let him speak:

"I arrived safely at Nauvoo, having witnessed many vexatious movements in government officers, whose sole object should be the peace and prosperity and happiness of the whole people, but instead of this, I discovered that popular clamour and personal aggrandizement were the ruling principles of those in authority, and my heart faints within me, when I see **by the visions of the Almighty the end of this nation,** if she continues to disregard the cries and petitions of her virtuous citizens, as she has done and is now doing. Church Hist., Vol. 2, page 419.

Missouri To Sink To Hell.

The above is in keeping with many other prophecies and visions, he claimed the Lord sent him. Here is another: When J. C. Calhoun, who aspired to be president of the United States, wrote to Smith, he replied: "Yet remember, if the Latter Day Saints are not restored to all their rights, that God will come out of His hiding place and vex this nation with a sore vexation, yea, the consuming wrath of an offended God shall smoke through the nation with as much distress and woe as Independence has blazed through with pleasure and delight. While I have power of body and mind, while water runs and grass grows, while virtue is lovely and vice hateful, and while a stone points out a sacred spot where a fragment of American liberty once was, I or my posterity will plead the cause of injured innocence until **Missouri** makes atonement for all her sins, or **sinks disgraced, degraded and damned to hell,** where the worm dieth not and the fire is not quenched. Church Hist., Vol. 2, pages 710-711.

The Mormons have never lost an opportunity to speak disparagingly of the United States and other governments, unless for cause, they, for the time being, wished to secure some favor.

The above visions, prophecies and curses upon the United States, have not injured that great country, she has prospered and become one of the greatest nations upon the earth, and Missouri has blossomed into one of the most magnificent of the Union. The nation never complied with Smith's demands, yet Missouri has not sunk disgraced to hell, strange!

Smith Ordained King.

Some time after that as Smith saw the curses promised failed to materialize, he thought he would try and run the nation himself. The Lord had made him Prophet, Seer, Translator and Revelator of the church, he secured the right to be sole trustee of all the church proper-

UNITED STATES vs. MORMON CHURCH

ties, some say he was crownd a king, as was one of his successors in office. This can hardly be denied as William Marks, the President of the High Council, and the man who ordained young Joseph, and was his Counsellor, says: "I was also witness of the introduction (secretly) of a kingly form of government, in which Joseph suffered himself to be ordained a king, to reign over the house of Israel forever." Saints' Herald, Vol. 51, Jan. 27, 1904, page 73. "Ye shall have no king." D. C. 38, 5.

The Lord had made him His sole mouthpiece to this generation; if any man would presume to go to law with him that man was cursed, so why not run the nation, so he was proclaimed by a great gathering of his people to be a candidate for the **Presidency of the United States.** He had a pull as Mayor of the city, and General of the Nauvoo Legion, and so the Elders and Apostles were sent out to electioneer for him, and he published a paper expressing his views, and asking for the vote of the people, coming out as an independent ticket. The people smiled and Smith and his dupes mounted the political stump, but that was all there was of it. For a more complete history of this nonsense, read Church Hist., Vol. 2, pages 713-726.

Smith Destroyed Printing Press.

This occurred in 1844, a few months after this, sworn evidence galore (which has been published many times and lately by the writer) was printed by many of Smith's former followers, including some of the leading men of the church, showing that Smith was guilty of crimes. He had been charged with having revelations on polygamy, and having many wives and concubines, and that he had insulted both young maidens and married women, and their husbands, fathers and brothers (strange as it may appear) did not seem to excuse the Prophet. When they complained they say their lives were in danger, by reason of his Danite Band, sworn to kill his enemies. Well, they published a paper, filling the first edition with their affidavits. This was too much for Smith. As Mayor he called the people together, and decided to destroy the property and they went at it and destroyed the press and threw the type and other materials into the streets. The proprietors fled for their lives. Smith in time was called to answer before the law, and while in jail he was shot to death by a number of people who broke into the jail.

His son tries to excuse his father of this dastardly attempt upon the liberty of the people, by saying: "In the evening of the day that the Expositor press and material was destroyed, a crowd gathered on Main Street and among them was the Mayor, **my father.** I heard my father's voice, measured and clear, "What ever you may think about it, you have this day made me do, in my official capacity as your officer, an act that I believe we shall all be sorry for and that will make us great trouble hereafter." Joseph the Prophet, page 746.

I am sorry that this son was weak enough to try to cover up his father's guilt. His apology only reveals another contemptible trait in his father's character. That father held the positions of Prophet, Seer, Revelator, Translator, sole trustee of all church property, God's mouthpiece to the church, the only man in the world who could give revelations for the government of the church, his word was law, none dare oppose it under the penalty of a curse, he was mayor of the city, general of the Nauvoo Legion of soldiers, yet having his base and wicked life bared before the world in that paper, his polygamy and infidelity, he had the press destroyed, and then was low and mean and cowardly enough to try and throw the blame on the poor dupes who had obeyed his command.

Soon after the printing establishment referred to was destroyed and the proprietors had fled from the city to save their lives, and Smith as his own son admits, tried to throw the blame for his dastardly act upon his followers, those interested travelled to the county seat and obtained a writ for his arrest, and with others Smith and his brother fled from the state. It is said that this affected some of their followers, and they were by some considered cowards, to escape from the state, in place of facing the courts. So they returned to Nauvoo, appeared before the judge, and were placed under bail to appear at the next term of the Circuit Court.

Smith Arrested on The Charge of Treason Against The State of Illinois.

The same day they were arrested on a charge of treason against the state of Illinois, and were committed to jail. Church Hist., Vol. 2, pages 737-744.

The people of the State knowing that Smith had men and money at his command, knowing that he had escaped from the State of Missouri when charged with treason and that he had escaped from the State of Ohio under several serious charges, and that many other times he had escaped from justice, concluded to take care of him this time, so the mob came, overpowered the jail guards, some entered the jail, while others remained outside to get him if he jumped from the open window, which he eventually did.

The mob fired several shots through the panel of the door, killing Hyrum Smith, and wounding John Taylor.

Now let us have a look at the other side of Joseph Smith. He was Prophet, Seer, Revelator, Translator, Sole Trustee of church property, President of the Church, God's sole mouthpiece to the church, General of the Nauvoo Legion, Mayor of the city, and had lately been crowned king. It is said that he was more like Christ than any man who ever lived, "that he did more for the salvation of men in this world than any man that ever lived in it, save Jesus only." One of their poetesses wrote of him as follows:

> "Great men have fall'n, and mighty men have died—
> Nations have mourn'd their favorites and their pride,
> But two so wise, so virtuous, great and good,
> Before on earth, at once, have never stood."

This was written by E. R. Snow on Joseph and Hyrum Smith. Miss

Snow swore she was one of Joseph Smith's wives. Her brother, an apostle under Smith, and who became President of the Utah Mormon church, told me he knew that his sister was a plural wife to Joseph Smith, and that he had taught him polygamy. He died confirming this statement.

A few days before his death Smith is reported to have said: "I am going like a lamb to the slaughter." This was to show that he would meet death like Jesus did, The Lamb of God. Isaiah 53, 7.

Let us see if he did die like Christ. They have published in their own history that he had a six shooter pistol concealed on his person, and when his brother was shot through the closed door "Joseph reached his pistol through the door, which was pushed a little ajar, and fired three of the barrels, the rest missed fire. **He killed two men and shot the arm of a third man."** His brethren boast of this act, and say: "In him was the spirit of dauntless bravery exemplified." Reorganized Church Journal of History, Oct. 1918, pages 399-416.

During the last hour of Smith's life, he gave the jail guard money to buy wine, pipes and tobacco." Joseph the Prophet, pages 522-523.

The facts show that Smith had been leading a life of hypocrisy and crime. Thousands of his faithful and most prominent followers had discovered his infamy, and left him, and from time to time exposed him. At the time of his death he was under arrest for **treason against the State,** and other charges were pending against him and his attempt to destroy all national governments and set up what he called the Kingdom of God, on earth, had failed. When in the midst of his wine, tobacco and murder he attempted to escape from the jail window, when he was shot dead.

I ask, was there anything in all this to show that he lived and died like Christ, Christ was the "Lily of the Valley," "the one altogether lovely." He was innocent of any crime. He was the personification of honor. The synonym of virtue and true manhood. He destroyed no printing press, debauched no maidens, never invaded the sacred precincts of other mens homes to destroy the womanhood of the country. Had no revelations permitting whoredoms, concubinage and polygamy. Nor did He spend His last hour with wine and tobacco while he murdered two men and spent His last moment trying to kill more. The effort made to compare Smith with the **"Holy One"** is the worst form of blasphemy. Words fail me to express my feelings on the matter so we draw the curtain over the dark picture.

The Reorganized Church Are Against The United States.

Since the death of Smith, his followers have continued their tirade of abuse and slander against the Government of the United States, and are still looking for the judgments of God to come upon that nation because of their treatment of the prophet and his kingdom. They at times make speeches and hoist "Old Glory," but they do that for a purpose as I have already shown and will continue to show.

I herewith submit part of an article written on the murder of Joseph

Smith, published in October, 1918, showing they still desire to educate their people along the same old lines against the United States. They may say it is but a re-print of that published years ago, that may be true, but if that is not their sentiments to-day, why republish it to the grand-children of those formerly concerned. Their faith in Joseph Smith, his prophecies of the United States and all other kingdoms and the final triumph of the Mormon kingdoms is unchanged."

"Shades of hell," we turn to you. Unroll the ponderous scroll of your grand secretary that chronicle of all the deeds of bloody crime, heartless villany and depravity that have marked the world's history from the death of righteous Abel, and see if they all afford a parallel with the crime of the last fifteen years, committed in a boasted age of civilization, religion and liberty.

Farewell to liberty, farewell to the rights of man, farewell to the institutions of a boasted republic, farewell to our glorious constitution, adieu to the blood of illustrious fathers, farewell to virtue, honesty, peace, tranquility and national happiness, farewell to the dulcet songs of freedom that were wont to animate the sons of Columbia, farewell to the **Stars and Stripes** of our national banner, that falsely tell the oppressed, as they float in the harbors of foreign climes that America is a land of liberty. These have passed away and become the things that were, and now are not. The bubble that contained them all floated for time upon the surface of a quiet sea, but the tempest has broken out in its fury. The bubble has burst and they have flown, **and soon the judgments of the Great God will wind up the scene, and spread the pall of darkness and desolation over the relics of a ruined world that blood will not be easy to wash out."** Journal of History, published by the Reorganized Church, Vol. 2, Oct. 1918, pages 425-426.

Hear the prophecy of one of the former apostles of the Mormon hierarchy:

The day will come when the United States government and all others will be uprooted and the kingdoms of this world will be united in one and the kingdom of our God (which means the Mormon hierarchy) "will govern the whole earth and have universal sway."

This certainly reveals a very clearly defined purpose. The leaders of the organization have never changed this definite purpose nor halted for one single day in their effort to accomplish that purpose. They have changed their methods of procedure as frequently as the exigency demanded but the one purpose has been ever before them. The court records of Salt Lake City reveal the persistent effort of the Mormons to rid themselves of the authority of our government. These records were printed and given to the public at the time of the Smoot investigation. After hearing the startling testimony of many witnesses Judge Anderson returned the following findings in reference to the claims of the Mormon Church:

1. "It claims to be the actual and veritable kingdom of God on earth; not in its fullness because Christ has not yet come to rule in per-

son; but for the present He rules through the priesthood of the church who are the vice-regents of God."

2. "This kingdom is both a temporal and spiritual kingdom and should rightfully control and is entitled to the highest allegiance of men in all their affairs."

3. "That this kingdom will overthrow the United States and all other governments after which Christ will return in person." Christian Statesman, page 84, Feb., 1920.

Having compiled this short history of the Mormon Church and Kingdom which shows from their own works that Smith was ordained a king, that said kingdom was to break in pieces all other kingdoms and stand forever. That Smith's revelations instructed him to organize an army to work destruction, defeat the United States and establish his headquarters in Missouri; that he and his people worked to that end till he was shot while in the act of committing murder, and that his people to date believe that their kingdom is yet to triumph in the destruction of the United States and all other kingdoms, as shown by Smith's prophecies. I leave the subject with you, asking that you ponder what my fate will be unless protected by the Almighty and his people. I thank God my eyes are opened and I feel called upon to let the world know something of the horrible thralldom from which I have been rescued. Thousands now feel that my sudden death would be a benediction to the Mormon church and that perhaps the time has come "That whosoever killeth you will think that he doeth God's service."

Having proved that both the original Mormon church and the Reorganized Mormon church both teach that God revealed to them that Zion was to be organized in Independence, Missouri, that was to be the only place of safety from pestilence and war, the place where Christ should come, it remains for me to prove that the present head of the Church, still believes and teaches that Zion must yet be established to make ready for the destruction of the United States, and coming of Christ. I submit his latest prophecy of the soon approach of the destruction of the United States, as prophecied by his grandfather, Joseph Smith.

"I wonder how long it will be till we have Zion, my concern has been intensified of late. Forces are at work which threaten our government and the men at Washington know this well, **discord and chaos are liable to break out over night** and the institutions upon which we lean for our safeguard **may crumble,** and our protection be weakened. I wish I could tell you some of the things I feel I **know;** and the great concern that has stirred me at times is, when that time of chaos comes will this people be prepared to furnish the place of safety God has intended that we should." F. M. Smith, Herald, March 3rd, 1920, page 193.

CHAPTER VIII.

The Book of Commandments

This book is the second sacred book published by the Mormons. It contains sixty-five revelations said to have been given direct by Jesus Christ to Joseph Smith. Some are given to the general church, but most of them to individuals. In one of the early ones Joseph Smith is made the Prophet, Seer, Revelator, Translator, Apostle and sole mouth-piece to the church, and the church is robbed of its liberty and thrown into slavery by the statement, "Thou shalt give heed unto all his words, and commandments, which he shall give unto you. For his words ye shall receive, as if from mine own mouth, in all patience and faith." Doc. and Cov. 19, 1-2, B. C. 22, 1-5.

"No one shall be appointed to receive revelations and commandments in this church excepting my servant Joseph Smith, Jr." Doc. and Cov., 27. 2.

This book was published by order of the church in Independence, Missouri, by W. W. Phelps and Company, in 1833. Many of the Mormons objected to the publication of these revelations, because they said, "If the world read those revelations, and the threats to destroy them or drive them from their lands, they will drive us away."

"The reason why the printing press was destroyed was because they published the Book of Commandments. It fell into the hands of the world, and the people of Jackson Co., Mo., saw from the revelations that they were considered by the church as intruders upon the land of Zion, and that they should be cut off and sent out of the land of Zion. The people seeing these things in the Book of Commandments became the more enraged, tore down the printing press and drove the church out of Jackson County." Whitmer's Address, page 54; D. C. 52, 9; 64, 7; 45, 15.

Elder Phelps was by revelation made printer to the church, and by revelation Cowdery was to assist him by copying and selecting, etc. that all things may be done right before me. Cowdery and John Whitmer were sent by revelation with the revelations to the printer. Doc. and Cov., 57, 5; 69, 1.

The Reorganized Church takes the position that the book was never completed, but this is absolutely false. Journal of Hist., Vol. 5, page 148.

That the said Reorganized Church is willing to misrepresent the facts about this, as other matters, may be proved by the following:

"After the book was completed the question of binding them was discussed, and it was decided to just put a paper cover on them, and

THE BOOK OF COMMANDMENTS

many of them were bound in leather by private persons. I had the copy of the complete book sent to me from the Elder to whom David Whitmer gave his complete book and the leather binding on the book was placed there by Whitmer's own hand." So stated the man to whom Whitmer gave the book, Elder Snider of Kansas City.

After the book was completed Smith wrote from Kirtland, saying: "Consign the box of the Book of Commandments to N. K. Whitney & Co., Kirtland, Ohio." Times and Seasons, Vol. 6, pages 800-801; La Rue, page 85.

That these books were completed and sent to Smith, care of Whitney, and that Smith received them is proved from the fact that Smith later wrote as follows: "The following errors we have found in the Commandments as printed." Times and Seasons, Vol. 6, pages 800-801.

That the Book of Commandments was completed and published and was quoted as an authority, is seen by the following: "It will be seen by reference to the Book of Commandments, page 135, that the Lord had said to the church," and also "But if any man will take the pains to read the one hundred and fifty-third page of the Book of Commandments, he will find there," etc. Church Hist., Vol. 1, pages 509, 510; Mill. Star, Vol. 15, page 823.

Whitmer says: "Early in the spring of 1833 at Independence, Mo., the revelations were printed in the Book of Commandments. Many of the Books were finished and distributed among the members of the church. When I objected to the revelations being published in a Book of Commandments, Brother Joseph prophesied as follows: "Any man who objects to having these revelations published shall have his part taken out of the tree of life, and out of the Holy City." "I prophesied that if they sent those revelations to Independence to be published in a book the people would come upon them and tear down the printing press, and the church would be driven out of the country." Whitmer's Address, pages 54-55.

The book was printed, the mob arose, the people were driven from the county and many of the books were destroyed and only a few left. But what shall we do with the Lord's revelation to Smith regarding this book which says:

"This is mine authority and my preface unto the Book of Commandments, which I have given them to publish unto you, Oh inhabitants of the earth. These commandments are of me. Search these commandments for they are true and faithful, and the prophecies and promises which are in them shall all be fulfilled." Church Hist., Vol. 1, page 228; B. C. page 1.

"This I know that in the year 1834, they say that some of the revelations **had to be changed**—so the Book of Doctrine and Covenants was printed in 1835." Whitmer's Address, page 56.

"When it became known that important changes had been made in the Book of Doctrine and Covenants, many left the church." Whitmer's Address, page 61.

"Joseph Smith took a copy of the Book of Commandments into the pulpit in Kirtland, Ohio, and declared that it was faulty." Saints' Herald, March 12th, 1887.

What shall we think of the leaders of the Reorganized Church who with all this evidence in their possession will wilfully misrepresent saying the Book of Commandments was never completed, and was not published?

We append some of the changes made, changes which alter the sense of the revelations and make additions that change the whole face of the church, both in organization and doctrine.

"If thou lovest Me thou shalt serve me and keep all my commandments, and behold **thou shalt consecrate all thy properties,** that which thou has t unto me, with a covenant and a deed which cannot be broken, and they shall be laid before the Bishop of my church and two of the Elders such as he shall appoint and set apart for that purpose, and it shall come to pass that the Bishop of my church after that he has received the properties of my church that it cannot be taken from the church, he shall appoint every man a steward over his own property, or that which he has received inasmuch as is sufficient for himself and family." B. C. page 75, chap. 44, 26.

"If thou loveth me thou shalt serve me and keep all my commandments, and behold thou wilt remember the poor, **and consecrate of thy properties** for their support, that which thou hast to impart unto them, with a covenant and a deed which cannot be broken, and inasmuch as ye impart of your substance unto the poor, ye will do it unto me, and they shall be laid before the bishop of my church and his counsellors, two of the Elders or High Priests, such as he shall or has appointed, and set apart for that purpose, and it shall come to pass after they are laid before the Bishop of my church and after that he has received these testimonies concerning the consecration of the properties of my church, agreeable to my commandments, every man shall be made accountable unto me, a steward over his own property, or that which he has received by consecration, inasmuch as is sufficient for himself and family." Doc. and Cov. 42, 8-9.

The reader will see many changes in this revelation, but the most important one is that in B. C. It says the man "shall consecrate **all his property,"** but in D. C. it says **"consecrate of thy property."**

Here is a splendid one that brought into prominence the crooked stick or witch hazel rod, with which Joseph Smith and his father before him professed to find water and gold, and which Cowdery is to do wonderful things.

"Oliver Cowdery, remember this is your gift. Now, this is not all, for you have another gift, which is the **gift of working with the rod,** behold there is no other power save God that can cause this rod of nature to work in your hands, for it is the work of God, and therefore, whatsoever you shall ask me to tell you by that means that will I grnat unto you, that you should know." B. C. page 16, Ch. 7, 3.

THE BOOK OF COMMANDMENTS

"Oliver Cowdery, remember this is your gift, now this is not all thy gift, for you have another gift which is the gift of **Aaron,** behold it has told you many things. Behold, there is no other power save the power of God that can cause this gift of Aaron to be with you, therefore, doubt not for it is the gift of God, and you shall hold it in your hands, and do marvellous works, and no power shall be able to take it away out of your hands for 'it is the work of God, and, therefore whatsoever you shall ask me to tell you by that means that will I grant unto you, and you shall have knowledge concerning it." D. C. 8, 3.

David Whitmer affirms that he was present in Fayette, N. Y. in 1830, when Smith gave the revelation entitled "The Articles and Covenants of the Church of Christ." This revelation appears in B. C. Ch. 24, and in D. C. Sec. 17. There are many changes in this revelation when you compare the revelation as found in B. C. and the same revelation as published in D. C. 17, chief among them are the additions of the two whole paragraphs numbered in D. C. as par. 16, 17. Not a word of those two paragraphs appearing in D. C. are found in the original revelation, and the worst of it is as stated by Whitmer and others, it changes the whole face of the church organization and places such officers as Presidency, High Council and High Priests, which are no where mentioned in all the revelations up to that date. Why, it is asked, did Joseph Smith make such wonderful changes in the revelations which God gave to the church.

We herewith append the extra two paragraphs as they appear in D. C.:

"16—No person is to be ordained to any office in this church where there is a regularly organized branch of the same, without the vote of that church; but the presiding Elders, travelling Bishops, High Counsellors, High Priests, and Elders, may have the privilege of ordaining, where there is no branch of the church, that a vote may be called."

"17.—Every president of the High Priesthood (or presiding elder), Bishop, High Counsellor, and High Priest is to be ordained by the direction of a High Council, or general conference." Doc. and Cov. 17, 16-17.

Here are eighty-nine words, added to a sacred revelation said to have been given by the lips of Jesus Christ, yet Smith and his comrades in crime deliberately make this change, which alters the whole face of the church organization, this to those who believe God gave the first revelation, is an unpardonable sin, and to those who refuse to believe that God had anything to do with the matter, fail to see how the faithful can respect Smith after seeing this indubitable evidence of his rascality.

Here is another change that is made to give Smith greater power, "And he (Joseph Smith) has a gift to translate the book, and I have commanded him that he shall pretend to no other gift, for I will grant him no other gift." B. C. Ch. 4, par. 2, page 9.

"And you (Joseph Smith) have a gift to translate the **plates,** and this is the **first gift** that I have bestowed upon you, and I have commanded that you should pretend to no other gift until it is finished." D. C. 5, 1.

The most remarkable thing in connection with the Smith revelations is, the Book of Commandments was published in 1833, and the Doctrine and Covenants in 1835, yet in neither of these books, the greatest revelation of all time, said to have been given to Smith in 1820, wherein God left heaven to introduce Christ to Joseph, and then lapsed into silence, and then Smith gave Christ the theological nut to crack "which of all the churches are right?" And Christ told him the churches were all wrong, the creeds all an abomination in his sight and all the professors corrupt, drawing near God with lip service while their hearts were far from him." Church Hist., Vol. 1, pages 9-10.

This was Smith's greatest revelation. Here was the foundation of his church mission as Prophet, Seer, Revelator. Here was the great denunciation of all the churches and the pronouncement of divine judgment upon all the hypocritical men and women who formed the Christianity of the world, yet not a word is said in his revelations as to this most wonderful and greatest manifestation of divine personality since the world began.

Moses was raised in the royal palace of the Kings of Egypt, associated with royalty all his life, yet when he was permitted to meet God, it is said that Mount was a flame of glory and filled with smoke, and the great mountain quaked greatly. If the people touched the mountain they were to die; the thunders roared; the lightning flashed. So great was the glory of the Lord that beamed upon the face of Moses, that he had to place a veil upon his face so that the people could look upon him. Read Exodus, Ch. 19, 20, 34.

But Smith the young farmer boy, unacquainted with men, had no trouble to stand in the presence of God and Christ, and chat with them both. It is true he tells us of both the great power of evil and good that was present during the vision, but the strangeness is that he never printed the story in the collection of revelations made in 1833 or 1835, but he waited for eighteen years to place that story in print, and now it is denied by the Reorganized Church in Child's History, page 1.

The Book of Doctrine and Covenants.

This is the third book published by the Mormons, the first was the Book of Mormon, 1830, the Book of Commandments, published in 1833, and the history shows that the church was changing its doctrine and organization to such a degree that it was necessary to change many of the revelations to fit the changes made, and so the Book of Commandments was set aside and the Book of Doctrine and Covenants was published in 1835.

David Whitmer says: "A few of the brethren knew about most of the important changes that had been put in the Doctrine and Covenants. In time it was generally found out and the result was some of the members left the church on account of it. The changes were made by a committee consisting of Joseph Smith, F. G. Williams and Sidney Rigdon." Whitmer's Address, page 61.

Before we attempt to show some of the hundreds of changes made in the revelations, we will let the Mormon prophets explain how they receive the revelations, which we are commanded to believe are spoken by Christ.

Joseph Smith gave the following revelation to Oliver Cowdery. This man Cowdery was promised that he should have power to translate. He tried and failed and hence the explanation:

"Behold you have not understood, you have supposed that I would give it unto you, **when you took no thought,** save it was to ask me, but behold, I say unto you, **that you must study it out in your mind, then you must ask me if it be right, and if it is right, I will cause that your bosom shall burn within you,** therefore you shall feel that it is right, but if it be not right, you shall have no such feelings, but you shall have a stupor of thought, that shall cause you to forget the thing which is wrong, therefore you cannot write that which is sacred save it be given you from me, Now if you had known this, you could have translated, nevertheless it is not expedient that you should translate now." D. C. 9: 3-4.

Here we have the method of Smith's translating and receiving revelations, surely as stated by Martin Harris, David Whitmer, Isaac Hale (his father-in-law) and Emma, his wife. He did not require to see the plates or any manuscript when translating, he just thought it out in his mind, and if he had a burning in his bosom the thing he thought was the inspiration of heaven, thus then we find how the Book of Mormon and Book of Abraham was translated, and how he received the revelations that are found in the Book of Commandments and Book of Doctrine and Covenants.

Joseph Smith, the son of the founder of Mormonism, who became the prophet, seer, revelator and mouthpiece of the Lord, to the Reorganized church, gave his experience as to how revelations were received:

"Revelations, as I understand it, are received in different ways, sometimes by **impression,** sometimes by the person becoming conscious of it, and sometimes by audible voice heard by the individual by whom the revelation is received and sometimes by a direct messenger, and sometimes by what we understand to be the direct intervention of the spirit. A man may be mistaken even though he be the president of the church as to the genuineness or authenticity of revelations claimed to have been received." Evidence in Temple Lot suit, pages 75-76.

It was strange to hear this man when under oath make the above statement when we had read the law of the church to be as follows:

"Wherefore, meaning the church, thou shalt give heed unto all his word and commandments which he shall give unto you—for his words ye shall receive as **if from Mine own mouth."** D. C. 19, 2.

"No one shall be appointed to receive revelations and commandments in this church excepting my servant Joseph Smith Jr., for he receiveth them even as Moses, thou shalt be obedient unto all things which I shall give unto him." D. C. 27, 2.

"And it shall be given thee in the very moment what thou shalt speak and write and they shall hear it, or I will send unto them a cursing instead of a blessing." D. C. 23, 3.

We will now present some of the thousands of changes that have been made in the revelations. I admit that if the Lord made these mistakes he should be permitted to correct them, but is it not blasphemy to attribute such mistakes to the Lord, Why not say Smith did the best he could, and when he improved in the art of revelating, that he made some corrections.

"Now for this cause, I know that man is nothing, which thing I never had supposed, but now mine eyes, mine own eyes, but not mine eyes for mines eyes could not have beheld." D. C. 22, 2, pub. 1901.

"Now for this cause I know that man is nothing, which thing I never had supposed, but now mine eyes (have beheld God) but not mine natural but my spiritual eyes, for mine natural eyes could not have beheld, for I should have withered and died in His presence." D. C. 22, 7, 1913.

The reader can see the awful grammar and the many changes made here. Was God guilty of such nonsense and then did He make the alterations? Are we to be cursed because we do not believe that these words fell from the lips of Jesus Christ, or that Smith did not receive revelations like Moses?

Now the readers might not be so critical had it not been that the Lord revealed the preface of the book, saying: "Behold this is mine authority and the authority of my servants, and **my preface unto the Book of my Commandments which I have given them to publish unto you, O inhabitants of the earth.** What I the Lord have spoken I have spoken, and I excuse not myself. The sword of the Lord is bathed in heaven, and it shall fall upon the inhabitants of the earth who refuse to give heed unto these prophecies and commandments." B. C. 1, 1833; D. C. 1, 1913.

From the above we learn that God gave the preface of the book, (not many books have their preface written by the Almighty), and further God makes no apologies and says: "I excuse not myself."

Now the cold facts are, the Doctrine and Covenants claim is that the revelations and commandments therein contained came direct from God, and the world will be cursed if they do not believe and obey them, while many who read it affirm that the revelations are a jumbled mass of bad grammar, poor spelling that they contradict themselves in many hundreds of places and that the very revelations which we will be cursed if we refuse to believe, have been altered in hundreds of cases, and whenever they have been republished, in many of them, most every paragraph has been changed in word and meaning. Sometimes hundreds of words have been added or taken from a single revelation. We affirm that having read several publications of these revelations, as made from 1832 to 1913, that they have been altered in thousands of places. To record the changes, would fill a large volume. If God will condemn a

THE BOOK OF COMMANDMENTS 133

person for not believing them as first published, then why should we believe them when changed in thousands of places?

We can only take time and space to briefly present a few cases in point.

Book of Commandments, Chap. 4, pub. 1833, compared with the same revelation published in Doctrine and Covenants Section 5, pub. 1913, is changed in every paragraph and in one paragraph the Lord, describing the abominations of the people, uses 144 words, when the same denouncement is made in the other edition there is 216 words used, the most abominable feature of the revelation is that Martin Harris is commanded to say **he saw the plates of the Book of Mormon** long before he claims to have seen them, if he refuses to so testify he is to be placed under condemnation, and the worst of it is that some of the very words which he is commanded to say, are found in his testimony as recorded in the Book of Mormon, more than a year after.

Turn to the Articles and Covenants of the Church of Christ. This revelation was published in a paper called the Morning and Evening Star, June 1832, the reader will find a paragraph of over one hundred words at the end of that revelation that is not found in the same revelation as published in the Book of Commandments, 1833, called chapter 24, Then let the reader turn to the Doctrine and Covenants of 1835 and other editions and he will find that the paragraph published in 1832 is not published in the revelation, and worse and more of it, he will find two whole paragraphs containing eigthty-nine words, published in this revelation that were not published in the Evening and Morning Star of June, 1832, nor were they published in the Book of Commandments of 1833. The two paragraphs added in another part of the revelation introduces a new system of church organization, thus changing the whole face of the church organization as taughtand understood by the membership from 1828 to 1830.

Some late writers have tried to make it appear that this section or chapter is not a revelation, but this is false as the following will prove. David Whitmer, the sixth man baptized into Mormonism and one of the three witnesses to the Book of Mormon, left the church in 1838. He testifies: "I was present when brother Joseph gave this revelation. Two paragraphs have been added to it having been thrust into the middle of it—as if God had made a mistake and left these high offices out of that revelation when it was first given." Whitmer's Address, pages 59-60.

"Of the date of the reception of this section, Joseph Smith states:

"In this manner did the Lord continue to give us instructions from time to time concerning the duties which now devolve upon us and among other things of the kind. We obtained from him the following by the spirit of prophecy and **revelation,** which not only gave us much information but also pointed out to us **the precise day upon which, according to His will and commandment, we should proceed to organize the Church** once again upon the earth." Times and Seasons, Vol. 3, pages 928-9; Lambert Objections, page 87; Ch. Hist., Vol. 1, page 67.

The reader will see the opening statement of this revelation starts out to command them to organize the church on April 6th and further we are therein informed that that was the date on which Christ came in the flesh, or was born, This is contradicted by most every historian. Christ is said to have been born in the spring A. D. 4. Smith's God was about four years out on that matter. Dict. of Bible, Wm. Smith Art. Jesus Christ.

We now invite your attention to Book of Commandments, Chapter 44, compare that with Doctrine and Covenants Section 42, claimed to be the same revelation given under date of Feb. 1831. There is a difference of nearly six paragraphs, hundreds of words, which changes the whole face of the revelation. Yet we are to be damned if we do not believe the original and I presume we will be damned if we believe the silly twaddle recorded in the present publication of that much-contradicted revelation.

Perhaps we would do injustice if we neglected to notice Chapter 28 of the Book of Commandments and compare Section 26 of the Doctrine and Covenants given Sept., 1830. Several hundred words are added to this revelation, several angels, excluding a visit from Peter, James and John who ordained Joseph Smith and Oliver Cowdery to the high priesthood, is told very nicely. The horror of it all is that after the edition has been made for over fifty years to this famous revelation, now to have the son of Joseph Smith, the president of the Reorganized church, come out flat footed and deny that Peter, James and John ever filled any such a mission, we cannot resist the temptation to make a paragraph of this statement and its contradiction.

"And also with Peter, James and John, whom I have sent unto you, **by whom I have ordained you and confirmed you to be Apostles and especial witnesses of my name.**" D. C. 26, 3.

"I was present with Joseph when the higher or Melchisedec Priesthood was conferred by the Holy Angel from on high. This priesthood was then conferred on each other by the will and commandment of God." Myth of the Manuscript Found, page 80. Statement of Oliver Cowdery.

"Mr. Smith testifies that Peter, James and John came to him in the capacity of ministering angels and by the laying on of hands ordained him an apostle." Apostle Orson Pratt, Divine Authority, page 4

Now hear young Joseph Smith, son of the original Joseph Smith and prophet, seer, and revelator of the church for over fifty years, give the frank lie to the statement of his father, the revelation of Section 26, the statement of Oliver Cowdery, and also Apostle Pratt and the combined testimony of the church for over eighty years.

"There is no historical evidence of such an event, nor is there any that Peter, James and John were present, either when the instruction was given to ordain or when the ordination actually took place. It is not safe then to write historically that Joseph Smith and Oliver Cowdery were ever ordained literally under the hands of Peter, James and John." Reorganized Church History, Vol. 1, pages 64-65.

If the revelation Smith, Cowdery, Pratt and all Mormonism for eighty years has to acknowledge this angelic ordination to be a false position as stated by young Joseph Smith, what credit can be given to Mormonism. We close the examination of the revelations given by old Joseph Smith, the first prophet, with one more glimpse just to show the autocracy of Smith, read B. C. ch. 45 and D. C. Sec. 43, revelations given Feb. 1831, and there we are informed Joseph Smith is the only one appointed by God to give revelations to the church, that if the church desires the mysteries of the kingdom revealed, they must provide Smith with food, and raiment and whatsoever thing he needeth to accomplish the work, but to the last he was game. He tells them that if God would deem him unworthy to speak through any more, that he would still have power to appoint his successor. Just think, suppose a young man loved a girl because of her virgin purity, but discovered that she was filthy and vile, he denounced her and left her because she had undervalued the virgin crown, and then said, now while you have forfeited your right to be my wife, **you still have the right to select the woman whom I shall marry.** With this we leave the first prophet Joseph, and give a brief examination of his son, the prophet of the Reorganized church.

Strange Statement Made in The Revelations of The Reorganized Church Prophets.

I confess that for years, before leaving Mormonism, I had grave doubts with regard to the revelations that were given by Joseph the second, there was nothing definite about them, too much guess work, too much "if" and "perhaps." They seemed to be a guess of a human being rather than a revelation from the divine, but we submit a brief examination of a few points for the consideration of the honest searcher for truth:

"Inasmuch as there has been much discussion in the past concerning the Sabbath of the Lord, the church is admonished that until further revelation is received, or the quorums of the church are assembled to decide concerning the law in the church articles and covenants, the saints are to observe the first day of the week commonly called the Lord's Day, as a day of rest, as a day of worship, as given in the covenants and commandments." D. and C. 119, 7.

It just seems to me that if the Lord had spoken he would have told them which was the right day. He would have settled the matter once and for all and not told them to wait for another revelation to settle it.

"The epistle is to be left without approval or disapproval by the conference, as the judgment of the quorum of twelve, until further experience shall have tested the matters therein stated." D. and C., 120, 1.

It just looks to me that if the Lord had condescended to speak on the position taken by the apostles that he would have confirmed their opinion or denounced it. Are we to believe that the Lord had not arrived at a proper conclusion regarding the matter, or will we say the man who presented the paper to the church was not settled in his mind? Or, if he was, there were strong men on each side of the controversy and he did not care to run up against them?

"The voice of the spirit is that E. C. Briggs be sustained for the present. J. W. Briggs and Z. H. Gurley are in your hands to approve or disapprove as wisdom may direct."

This E. C. Briggs was sustained for years. "For the present" sounds very indefinite, when we are asked to believe that the Lord said it. The other two men, one the most brilliant apostles of his time, the other the president of that august body, had denounced the body and soon after left the church and both believed to their death that Joseph Smith, the founder of the church, received the infamous revelations on polygamy and had many wives. Yet it looks like as if someone was afraid to say "put them out," or "keep them in," and so threw the burden upon poor weak man to decide the fate of these two stalwarts. But this milk and water policy did not keep these two brave men from giving to the world what they believe concerning the conduct of Joseph Smith.

"The one whom I had called to preside over the church (Joseph Smith) (R. C.) had not yet approved himself unto the scattered flock, and I gave this commandment (regarding money matters) (R. C.) unto the quorum next in authority in spiritual things, that the scattered ones, and those who had been made to suffer might have assurance that I would not suffer that he whom I had called should betray the confidence of the faithful, nor squander the moneys of the treasury for the purpose of self." D. C. 122, 5.

Does this look as if God was not sure that young Joseph would not go in the path another had walked in, and so the faithful would again be robbed by his squandering their money? So he ordered the Twelve to watch the money chest till the young prophet would prove himself. This seems like a good thing in one way, and it would not be a real bad move if the Lord, or the church, or someone would take a hand right now, so that the moneys of the faithful be not squandered. When we think of the hundreds of thousands that have been squandered of late years, and if the auditors report correctly and the Bishops spoke truthfully this year, while at general conference, I think it about time for the Lord to kindly give further instructions on this matter.

"My servant Thomas W. Smith is in my hand, and his bishopric shall be continued for a season. If he fully recover he will enter again into the work. If I take him unto myself another will be appointed in his stead when the quorum is filled." D. C. 122, 15.

The plot thickens. We are asked to believe that the Lord of heaven gave this revelation to his people. He advised that Apostle Smith be continued in office for a season. Fact is, the God who gave that revelation did not seem to know whether this very sick apostle would get better or not, but he wanted the people to permit him to hold office for a season till he had decided whether he would die or not. Was this the guess of a God or a man? "If" he fully recover he will enter into the work.

Did God not know that he would remain a helpless creature for a long time and never do any more apostolic work in this world? It appears not. But He gave the assurance that "if I take him to myself another would be appointed in his stead, when the quorum is filled."

"The quorum of twelve, my servants may choose and appoint one of their number to take the place of my servant Alexander H. Smith, and if they shall choose William H. Kelley from among them for this place it will be pleasing unto me. Nevertheless if directed by the Spirit of revelation and wisdom they may choose another." D. C. 124, 3.

Here we are asked to believe that the Lord will be pleased in the selection of one man, but he warns them what steps to take if the **spirit of revelation directs them to select another.** We had always thought that it was the Lord that bestowed the spirit of revelation. Surely this revelation should put to shame the poor, deluded sectarian world who know not God, and have not received of the spirit of revelation.

"The seer of the church has a vision in which he sees Frederick M. Smith and R. C. Evans sitting with the presidency (himself). When he beheld these men in that exalted station, he says: "I asked what was meant by the choosing of members of the presidency **so young in years.** I was informed that it was for the purpose that before the presidency should be invaded by death these younger men should be prepared by association to be of assistance to whomsoever should be chosen as the president upon the emergency which should occur." D. C. 126, 6, 8.

Not, one that I have talked to in all the years since that time has been able to explain this to me. Both the present prophet and his father admitted their inability to make it clear, for several reasons. Let us examine. First, why ask the question: why speak of those two men being so **young** in years to occupy that position? I was older than Joseph Smith was when he was called of God to do the marvellous work. Yes, dear reader, older than Joseph Smith, and (then) present prophet who saw the vision when he became the president of the church. Joseph 1st was not 25 years old when the church was organized. Joseph 2nd was not 28 years old when he was made president. R. C. Evans was over 40 years of age when he was called to the first presidency of the church. I was older than many others who had occupied that position. I had a thousand times more experience in church work than many of them, including both prophets. For I had been ordained and labored for years as a Priest, Elder, Seventy and an apostle. They had none of these offices before they were called to the important work. So, to many the very question seemed absurd. But worse and more of it. The reason for calling the two young men was that before death invaded the presidency that is, before the prophet Joseph should die, these younger men should be prepared by association to be of assistance to whomsoever should be chosen upon the emergency which should occur. If language is a science to convey ideas, then this means that these two young men would remain in the presidency, learning the ways of the prophet till death should call him away, and then these two younger men would be of assistance, or be the **counsellors** to the person who should be chosen by the Lord to be the next president. I have never talked to a man in the church but has considered that this position was the best light they could see this revelation in, and if that be correct it proves **that Frederick M. Smith is not the prophet of the Lord. It was not the Lord's wish that he should occupy in his father's place,** but that when death took his father away he would be counsellor with me to the incoming president. Now, if the Lord gave that revelation, what are we to think of one that came years late, calling Frederick M. Smith to be the president? Is it unfair to say that if this revelation is the word of the Lord, that the time came when poor old Joseph became stone blind, and almost totally deaf and agonizing under a complication of diseases that a strong two hundred and thirty pound man had an influence over this blind, deaf and now childish father to make arrangements for his son to take his father's place as president of the church.

There is another point in this vision that trouble the people. James Caffall, of the Apostles, was seen sitting with the evangelical ministers. This never came to pass. Caffall never believed the revelation but left the Twelve and died a disappointed man.

Section 127 contains a lengthy revelation concerning the building of a church sanitarium for sick folk. Joseph Luff, one of the most brilliant apostles of the church, had given some attention to the study of medicine, and the Lord is supposed to have said that he said Joseph Luff should "be associated with this sanatorium as a medical director and physician to the church and be put in charge—and this my servant Joseph Luff, may do and retain and exercise his apostleship."

I may say that in my many years of association with the prophet Joseph Smith, this was the first time that I had the courage to go to him and refuse to submit to the revelation that he said came from God. I compared the revelation as given by Jesus Christ in defining the commission of an apostle in the Bible, "Go ye into all the world and preach the gospel to every creature," and "They went forth and preached the gospel everywhere, the Lord working with them and confirming the word with signs following." Mark 15: 12, 20. And we are told "He gave them power to heal all manner of sickness and all manner of disease." Matt. 10.

Now, this modern prophet tells us the apostle could both go into all the world, preach the gospel and heal the sick, and stay at home and make pills to heal the sick in a sanatorium. I felt that the great gospel apostolic mission was degraded, and that this revelation was an evidence of humanity and at that time devoid of Divinity. This revelation was given April 14th, 1906.

Just three years later, April 18th, 1909, the Lord, we are asked to believe, had so changed his mind upon this matter that we hear Him say, through the same prophet: "My servant Joseph Luff cannot fulfill the duties of a member of the quorum of Twelve in actively looking after and caring for the missionary work in the field and discharge the duties

THE BOOK OF COMMANDMENTS 139

of his calling as a physician, ministering to the many seeking his advice and aid with safety to himself and others. It is wise, therefore, that the church release him from the responsibility of the active apostleship as a member of the quorum, that he may act unreservedly in his calling." D. C. 129, 2.

Shades of Latter Day Saintism.

Here is a clear backdown by the Lord or someone else and worse and more of it, the most eloquent apostle of the quorum is told to lay aside his holy apostleship in the sacred quorum of apostles, so that he can devote his time to the sanatorium. Bro. Luff has left the sanatorium and the doctor job, too.

"The voice of the spirit to me is: Under conditions which have occurred, it is no longer wise that my servant R. C. Evans be continued as counsellor in the presidency; therefore, it is expedient that he be released from this responsibility and another be chosen to the office. **He has been earnest and faithful in service and his reward is sure."** D. C. 129, 1.

The treatment I had received from some of the leading men, together with several other reasons, which I give in this paper, enabled me to conclude that it was best for me to tender my resignation as one of the first presidency, and I dictated it to R. C. Russell and he wrote it. I presented it to Joseph Smith. He wept and acknowledged that the treatment accorded me was enough to break the stoutest heart, but urged me not to insist on handing in my resignation. That we together would pray that the Lord would release me. I waited and prayed and lived a life of perplexity and sorrow, till this revelation came and I was then released. And immediately upon my release the prophet arose and told the conference that he had received direction from the Lord to present my name for ordination as Bishop. The presiding Bishop and others testified that they knew the Lord had so called me, and without one single objection, even from those who had hounded me all the time I was in the presidency, I was ordained a Bishop.

"Thus saith the voice of the spirit: in order that the quorum of Twelve may be placed in better condition to carry on the work of the ministry in various fields of occupation, it is expedient that Elders W. H. Kelley, I. N. White and J. W. Wight, be released from the active duties of the apostolic quorum on account of increasing infirmities of age and incapacity caused by illness of body, and stand with their associates among the high priests and patriarchs of the church for such special service as may be open to them, according to wisdom and the call of the spirit. To fill the vacancies caused by the release of these elders from the apostolic quorum, Elder James E. Kelley, William H. Aylor, Paul M. Hanson and James A. Gillen may be chosen as Apostles."

Two funny things appear here. The three men released lived and worked well. One has passed away, and other two still here and J. W. Wight has travelled extensively and done a great work up to date. While he was released because of illness of body and infirmities of age, he has been a hard worker in many parts of the United States and Canada up to this hour; and James E. Kelley was sick when he was called, and has occupied the hospitals and sanatoriums and been sick and a great expense to the church most of the time, and has passed away. The other men all working while he lay dying and two of them still living, and one of them very active. Did the God who gave that revelation know that Brother Wight was going to live and do the great work he has accomplished since his obituary notice was given by revelation, and did he know that James E. Kelley was to live in the sanatoriums for the sick and die without doing the work to which he called him? Though the Lord released W. H. Kelley and instructed that he was to work as a patriarch, he refused to be ordained a patriarch and died.

I submit the history of the revelation known as Section 117 of the Doctrine and Covenants, given under date of March 3rd, 1873.

It is alleged that Joseph Smith gave the revelation to President J. W. Briggs to submit to the quorum of the twelve, April 6th, 1873, accompanying the written revelation is a statement as follows:—

"I received the following as **there stood by me the sensible presence of the Holy Messenger,** filling my soul with light and peace."

Then followed the revelation just as published in the Doctrine and Covenants, with the exception of the paragraphs objected to. The revelation was presented to the quorum and they rejected it as being contrary to the law of God, as found in former revelations. They returned the revelation to Joseph Smith, and he is alleged to have written a letter to the Twelve, from which we quote the following:—

"Plano, Ill., April 8th, 1873. Brethren of the Twelve, I am privileged after a sleepless night, to offer for your consideration the following: 'Thus saith the spirit that portion of the revelation which is perplexing to you should be **"The Bishop of my church may also choose and appoint bishops agents until it shall be wisdom in Me to ordain other bishops in the districts and large branches of My church.** They being appointed and ordained in a similar manner that I commanded my servant, Newal K. Whitney should be an agent unto my disciples who tarried in Kirtland."

"**This explanation is unto you of the Twelve. Not unto the Church. Let the revelation be corrected.**" Joseph Smith, President of the church."

The part in the original revelation of March to which objection was made read in the original revelation as follows: **"The Bishop of My church may also ordain other bishops in the several districts and large branches of My church."**

I may add that I have a complete copy of the original revelation, as rejected by the Twelve, because it was contrary to the law and a flat contradiction to former revelations, and I have before me a copy of the letter alleged to have been written by the Prophet to the Twelve in which is found the confession of the false revelation, and the other revelation quietly given April 8th, in which the Lord, or the Prophet, took back the mistake and made the correction, after which the prophet of the Lord was weak enough to say: "This explanation is unto you of the Twelve, **not unto the church. Let the revelation be corrected."**

It is alleged that both revelations were written by Joseph Smith, both were given to Jason W. Briggs, the copies were made and certified to as being correct by one high in authority in the Reorganized church and given to me.

Comment—First we have the prophet claiming that the angel of the Lord stood by while the first revelation was given him, March 1st, 1873. Second, the twelve received the false revelation and rejected it, April 6th, 1873, and returned it to the prophet. Third, we have the prophet writing on April 8th, 1873 to the Twelve, after a sleepless night, and admitting the revelation was wrong and sending a correction. Fourth, when the correction was given, only part of the second revelation was accepted by the Twelve, and the rest set aside and never published. Fifth, when the two revelations were fixed up and parts of both objected to, the parts of both revelations were published as the one revelation under date of March 3rd, 1873, when according to the prophet's letters one was given March 1st, the other April 8th, and last of all, the letters alleged to have been written by the prophet seems to show acknowledged guilt, when he said: "This explanation is unto you of the Twelve, **not unto the Church. Let the revelation be corrected."**

Here was a false revelation, then a correction, think of it. God gave a revelation, He admitted it was wrong and then corrected it and He was afraid or ashamed for His people to know of the blunder, and so they were kept in ignorance and the whole blundering thing published under a false date, part given March 1st, part given April 8th, yet published under date of March 3rd.

They accuse me of loving Joseph. So I did. I looked upon him as God's mouthpiece to the church, His prophet and seer, but while I loved him, I am compelled to acknowledge that the Lord has opened my eyes. I have been made to see that in His effort to protect his father, and endorse his father's conduct, he too partook to some extent of the spirit that governed his father, and in his desire to be President of the church and prophet, seer and revelator, that he gave revelations that were contradictory and false.

Apostle Jason W. Briggs to whom these two revelations were sent, for the examination by the quorum of Twelve, stumbled at the thought that God made the mistake, and then corrected it, and that God was ashamed to tell the whole church about it, and so the Twelve were requested to keep the secret of the **Lord's** mistake to themselves and from the church according to the instructions of the Prophet. These matters troubled the Apostle and first president of the Reorganized church till, unable to bear up any longer he tendered his resignation and became like thousands before him, an outcast and an apostate from the church.

He left the original revelation and the letter above referred to where I was permitted to secure a certified copy of the original which is alleged to be in the hand-writing of the Prophet Joseph Smith.

The New Prophet, Seer, Revelator—God's Mouthpiece to the Church.

Having briefly examined the revelations perporting to come direct from Christ to the founder of Mormonism and his son, now let us look at the only attempt made by Frederick M. Smith, the grandson of the first prophet and son of the second prophet, who is now the prophet of the Reorganized church. He surely has made a mess of the prophet business already. But to the revelation:

"The voice of the spirit to me is that Bishop E. L. Kelley should be released from the responsibilities of Presiding Bishop, though he may act as travelling Bishop, counselling and advising on the law of temporalities in harmony with his successor and the Presidency. Let Benjamin R. McGuire be set apart and ordained presiding bishop of the church and two of the brethren be set apart as counsellors to him, **one to be selected by him and supported by the Conference, the other to be Bishop James F. Keir."**

The history of this revelation, as published in the Saints' Herald for April 19th, 1916, shows clearly that the new prophet had no faith in his first revelation himself. Space forbids the publication here of the entire proceedings, but the facts therein related are as follows:

Bishop Blakeslee was looked upon, according to a former revelation, as the coming Presiding Bishop, but he was holding back. If Smith believed his revelation, he would at once have proclaimed it. But did he? No, verily no. He tells the story himself. Let us see, he hides the revelation calling McGuire, telling but a few near friends about it. He makes arrangements to meet Bishop Blakeslee in Chicago. Blakeslee and his wife meet Smith and his wife, they have a nice time in the windy city. Smith tries his best to have Blakeslee accept the Presiding Bishop's office. Blakeslee gave a decided refusal on March 29th, about five o'clock in the afternoon. Had Blakeslee accepted the responsibility, the general church would doubtless never heard a word about the McGuire revelation. But when he made a positive refusal, Smith says: "Then came freedom to act. I am, therefore, now prepared to say—" Say what? "Why, that God had given him a revelation calling McGuire.

If Smith knew that God had given him a revelation calling McGuire to be the presiding Bishop, why spend time and money to go to Chicago to coax Blakeslee to accept the position. Why did he not rise in all the glory of the prophetic office and say: "The Lord has spoken, Bishop Kelley is to be released, and Benjamin R. McGuire is called to fill the sacred office.

There is another very great mistake in this blundering revelation in that it is in direct contradiction to two former revelations. A revelation through his grandfather says "the Bishop to choose two counsellors." D. C. 104, 32. Another revelation through his father, says: "The Bishop shall choose two counsellors." D. C. 117, 60.

Now, the new boss sets these two revelations aside. They had been the law under which the church had been governed through the years.

THE BOOK OF COMMANDMENTS 143

Was he afraid that when he gave McGuire the job he might make choice of two strong men whom Smith could not control? So he made the thing sure and the Bishop was told he might select one counsellor, but Bishop Keir was to be the other. The other counsellor is not yet selected. Why? Since writing the above, Smith's own brother has been made the other counsellor, so the prophet is safe.

If there was nothing else but this first attempt to play the role of Prophet, Seer, Revelator and God's sole mouthpiece to the church on the part of Fred M. Smith, it should be enough to convince all that God had nothing to do with his call to be a prophet.

In conclusion upon this subject permit me to say. It has been a great trial of my faith when from time to time I have heard some of the Twelve Apostles and other leading men of the church denounce the revelations of the Smiths in round terms. Robert G. Ingersol has never made the strong attack upon the revelations of the Bible that some of the Apostles in my hearing have made upon the revelations of the Smith prophets.

I was present when one of the revelations was presented for the endorsement of the Apostolic quorum. We struggled for days in the examination. Its publication was delayed for a time. One great Apostle said: "I have watched the revelations coming for more than twenty years. They have been weaker and weaker and weaker, and this one is the weakest of them all." This man still lives but has been deposed from the Apostolic quorum. Another Apostle rejected the instruction imparted to him in the revelation, was dropped from his office and never accepted the office to which the new revelation called him. He went down to death. Another Apostle said in my hearing: "If that **thing,** (the revelation) came from God, then I have never known anything about the spirit of God in all my ministry." Another suggested that we return it to the prophet and all unite to ask the Lord for **more light on the revelation,** when the former apostle sprang to his feet and with emotion said: **"Light,** more light, did you say? My God, man, if I were to ask the Lord anything about it I would not ask for **more light,** but for light, for that thing is the darkest thing that has ever beclouded the face of the church." The same Apostle speaking of the same revelation said to me: "Richard, I cannot believe a word of that revelation. I would be willing to walk to California on burning stones if the Lord would show me that he gave that message. All I ask is one ray of light, but all is midnight darkness. He also was soon disposed of by another revelation, that is was dropped from the quorum.

It is a significant fact that many of the most prominent and leading men of the church to whom these revelations were given have discovered Smith to be a false prophet, and they have left the church denouncing him as about everything that was vile. I may mention a few of the most prominent ones.

The Three Witnesses to the divine authenticity of the Book of Mormon, Oliver Cowdery, David Whitmer and Martin Harris, those who have occupied in the First Presidency, Sidney Rigdon, Frederick G.

Williams, John C. Bennett, William Law, Jason W. Briggs and R. C. Evans. I could enlarge the list with many of the Apostles, Bishops, High Priests, Seventies and Elders, and thousands of the membership. So I have but followed in the way of tens of thousands who were deceived and who, when they discovered the deception, did the only thing left for an honest person to do, that was to leave and denounce the lying wonder of the latter days.

CHAPTER IX.

The Order of Enoch

This Order is a mysterious affair, under which each member of the church is commanded to join, if he would secure salvation in the celestial splendours of the Kingdom of God; he must deed over to the President of the Order, who is the Presiding Bishop of the church, **all his property of every kind and character,** with a "deed and covenant that cannot be broken." This property whether it is real estate or money, bank notes, bonds, insurance, farm implements, or jewelry, cows, hens, household goods or clothing, **All** must be deeded over, and then the Bishop will give you a deed of what he considers shall be your **inheritance.** This is said to be a little home, which of all your property you may have deeded to them, is the only part you may claim if you should leave, or be expelled from the church.

In a word, as explained by the good Bishops, when you are born into this world, you arrive with absolutely nothing in your possession, but **life.** When you are born again into the Kingdom of God (which is the Mormon Church) you must start with absolutely nothing, but life. If you possess anything, it must be deeded over, that all starting on the same plane, may become stewards unto God, He being the proprietor of all, and it is clearly stated that if a member of the society dare to make claim that they own anything, no matter if you have deeded over millions, you are at once placed under **the curse,** which (according to the revelations through Joseph Smith, which will be quoted in this article) may be inflicted by those appointed to do the **cursing.**

After deeding **all your property** over, and you receive your inheritance, you go to work, but not for yourself, but the Order of Enoch, and you must make an inventory every year or month as required, and after taking out your living, the few or many dollars saved above bare living expenses, must be accounted for and handed over to the authorities of the **Order.**

The greatest blessing and honour you receive for all this deeding over to the Order, is that you receive a **New Name,** and an inheritance in Zion.

The history of this mysterious Order is a long, sad one. Many gave their all, got their new name, and finding out the wickedness of Mormonism, denounced it and fled for their lives to escape the curse. According to leading men who have left the church many failed to make their escape, and suffered the vengeance of the Destroying Angels, called the **Danites.**

The Organization of The Order of Enoch.

The Lord, through Joseph Smith, is supposed to command Bishop Edward Partridge, in May 1831, to organizer this Order. The person joining the Order is distinctly informed as follows: "When he shall appoint a man his portion give unto him a writing that shall secure unto him his portion, that he shall hold it, even this right and this inheritance in the church until he transgresses and is not accounted worthy to belong to the church. He shall not have power to claim that portion which he has consecrated unto the Bishop—therefore, he shall not retain the gift, but shall only have claim on that portion that is deeded unto him." Doc. and Cov., 51, 1.

A more extended description of this Order is given by revelation to Joseph Smith, from which we quote the following: "I give unto you, to prepare and organize yourselves by a bond or everlasting covenant that cannot be broken." The Order is called "Permanent and everlasting establishment and Order unto My church—to the **salvation of man and the Glory of God**—and if ye will that I give unto you a place in the **celestial world** ye must prepare yourselves by doing the things which I have commanded you and required of you." In this revelation Joseph Smith receives two new names. He is called **Enoch** and then **Gazelam.** Others also received their new name, Joseph secures other names later, to which reference will be made. Doc. and Cov. 77, 1-2.

Perhaps I may right here show the secrecy of this Order in granting new names to Smith and others and even to houses, factories and towns, all to cover up and deceive those who are not numbered with the elect.

Joseph Smith is called Baurak Ale, Enoch, Gazelam. Doc. and Cov., pages 195, 196, 270, 271, 274, 276, 282 and 283.

Newel K. Whitney is called Ahashdah. Doc. and Cov., pages 196, 243, 275.

Sidney Rigdon is called Baneemy. Doc. and Cov., page 283.

Martin Harris is called Mahemson. Doc. and Cov., page 274.

Oliver Cowdery is called Olihah. Doc. and Cov., pages 274-275.

Sidney Rigdon received another pretty name, Pelagoram. D. C. pages 196, 274.

Joseph Smith received a fourth name—Seth. Page 244.
John Johnson is called Sombre. D. C. pages 244, 274, 275.
The City of New York is called "Cainhannoch," D. C., page 279.
Kirtland is called "Shinehah." D. C. page 276.
For the word "**Print**" read Shinelah. D. C. page 277.
For the word "Printing" read Shinelane. D. C. page 278.
For "Shule" read Ashery. D. C. page 275.
The Kirtland Tannery was called "Tanhanes." D. C. page 274.
The Printing House was called "Lane-shine-house." D. C. page 274.
The store was called "Ozondah." D. C. page 274.
Dollars were referred to as "Talents." D. C. page 278.

Frederick G. Williams was called "Shederlaomach." D. C. page 235-274.

THE ORDER OF ENOCH

We will leave these mysterious names of the faithful while the reader ponders over the question, why all this secrecy in the Mormon Order of Enoch. Perhaps the full reasons may not be known till that which is done in secret will be revealed upon the housetop.

All Must Join the Order For Salvation—Those Who Fail Will Be Cursed, And All Property Must Be Deeded To The Order Without Reserve.

"Organize yourselves by a bond or everlasting covenant that cannot be broken. If ye will that I give you a place in the celestial kingdom." D. C. 77, 1, 2.

"Inasmuch as they have more than is needful for their necessities and their wants it shall be given unto my storehouse. Behold, this is what the Lord requires of every man in his stewardship, and behold **none are exempt from this law who belong to the Church of the Living God.**" D. C. 70, 2,-3.

"Therefore, verily I say unto you, it is expedient that my servants be bound together by a bond and a covenant that cannot be broken by transgression except **judgment shall immediately follow**—that every man may improve upon his talents, yea, even an hundred-fold to become the common property of the whole church." D. C. 81, 4.

"I give unto you counsel and a commandment concerning all the properties which belong to the Order, which I commanded to be organized, for the salvation of men. Therefore, inasmuch as some of my servants have not kept the commandment but have broken the covenant I have cursed them with a very sore and grievous curse, for I the Lord have decreed in my heart that inasmuch as any man belonging to the Order shall be found a transgressor, or in other words, shall break the covenant with which ye are bound **he shall be cursed in this life,** and shall be trodden down by whom I will." D. C. 101, 1.

In this same revelation Joseph Smith and many other leaders received their inheritances, and their new names figured largely, and as Smith had several names, his inheritance was a splendid one." D. C. 101, 3-8.

"Behold all these properties are mine or else your faith is vain, and ye are found hypocrites, and the covenants which ye have made unto me are broken, and if the properties are **Mine** then ye are stewards, otherwise ye are not stewards, and **all moneys** that you receive in your stewardship by improving upon the properties which I have appointed unto you **in houses or in lands or in cattle or in all things,** shall be cast into the treasury as fast as you receive moneys by hundreds or by fifties or by twenties or by tens, for it shall not be called his nor any part of it." D. C. 101, 10-12.

"If thou lovest me thou shalt serve me and keep all my commandments and behold thou shalt consecrate **all thy properties that thou hast with a deed that cannot be broken,** and it shall come to pass that the Bishop of my church after that he has received the properties of my church that it cannot be taken from the church, he shall appoint every man a steward over his own property, or that which he has received, inasmuch as is sufficient for himself and family."

The above revelation was given to Joseph Smith, Feb. 1831. It is found in the Book of Commandments, chapter 44, page 75, and caused many to leave the church, so in the Doc. and Cov. it is found as section 42, page 78, with some material changes. In place of reading "All thy properties," it is made to read "of thy properties." But this contradicts all the rest of the revelations, and when one of the Elders preaching a sermon published in Zion's Ensign for July 5th, 1917, quoting the original revelation, comments upon it as follows:

"It says here that they should consecrate **all** that they have, not a portion, not come up and consecrate something that you cannot use yourself, something that you can get along without, **but God requires that you shall give it all to him,** and then you are to receive back from the Bishop that which is necessary to support yourself and families, and then if he is able to make an increase, take that and bring forth a residue that in turn is to be given into the storehouse." Zion's Ensign, July 5, 1917.

The above is in keeping with what Joseph Smith wrote upon the subject: "A man is bound by the law of the church to consecrate to the Bishop before **he can be considered a legal heir to the Kingdom of Zion,** and this too without constraint, and unless he does this **he cannot be acknowledged before the Lord on the church books."** Reorganized Church Hist., Vol. 1, page 300.

The above is in keeping with all the revelations and church resolutions on the subject, and we quote one more which was given in answer to prayer: "Verily, thus saith the Lord, I require **all their surplus property** to be put into the hands of the Bishop of Zion, for the building of mine house, and for the laying the foundation of Zion, and for the priesthood, **and for the debts of the Presidency of my church."** Doc. and Cov. 106, 1.

This last revelation was given some time before Smith was killed, and the Order of Enoch received a rude shock at his death. While the Utah Mormon Church went to Salt Lake and continued to take the money from the people, the Reorganized Church was a little careful along money matters and for years young Joseph Smith had little to say regarding the Order of Enoch, indeed the Lord seemed to be a little doubtful of young Joseph and the money question, as would seem from the following revelation which the Lord is said to have given through the young prophet.

"When I said unto mine Apostles, 'The Twelve will take measures in connection with the Bishop, to execute the law of tithing and let them before God see to it that the temporal means so obtained is truly used for the purpose of the church, and not as a weapon of power in the hands of one man for the oppression of others, or for the purpose of self-aggrandizement by anyone, be he whomsoever he may be, **the one whom I had called to preside over the church had not yet approved himself unto the scattered flock,** and I gave this command unto the quorum

THE ORDER OF ENOCH 149

next in authority in spiritual things that the scattered ones and those who had been made to suffer, might have assurance that I would not suffer that **he whom I had called should betray the confidence of the faithful, nor squander the moneys of the treasury for the purpose of self."** D. C. 122, 5.

Two points are made apparent in this revelation. First, that the contention made in this paper is true, in that the leaders of the church in the past had robbed the people and taken the money for themselves, as all the history proves; and second, that the Lord was not sure at the time but what young Joseph Smith, the Prophet of the Reorganized Church, might follow in the wake of his father and the other leaders of the people of the old church. Be that as it may, the facts are the Prophet of the Reorganized Church had little to do with money matters for many years, and the Order of Enoch was almost a forgotten method of robbery, but in the weak and declining years of Joseph Smith, when he became almost stone deaf and was totally blind, the Order of Enoch was revived by revelation through him, but even then it was a poor, weak thing for years, but after the young, strong son of Joseph Smith took his father's place, the Order of Enoch sprang into prominence and at the last conference that I attended, April, 1918, I attended nine meetings of the Order of Bishops and one of the General Conference, in which all the priesthood discussed the Order of Enoch. The church is fast adopting all the terrors of the old order and there has been sent out by the Presiding Bishop many letters urging the people to comply with the law, and some are doing it. This is one last straw that compelled me to resign from the church. I opposed the action in the council of Bishops, and of course was reported to the young Prophet, I refused to make my inventory and hand over my property, nor would I teach others that they must do so, and of course I was not considered sound in the faith and was a poor Bishop.

In conclusion I submit part of a lengthy 'Questionaire' sent out to the membership of the church in all the world. Strange to say the Bishop did not send them to Toronto, nor to me, but I soon received one and when written to, to comply, I refused to do so.

You are requested to make a complete report of all things concerning yourself and every member of your family, the **physical defects of yourself, wife, daughters and sons** must be explained to the good Bishop. The name, sex, age, number of the family, what kind of work they do, what wages they earn; you must report what fuel, food, water, rent, fire-insurance and other kinds of insurance, taxes, clothing and doctor bills you have to pay yearly; you must tell what property you have, every lot and farm, whether it belongs to yourself or you got it in marriage from your wife, you must give size of lot or farm, tell of all city or country property in your possession, if country land, you must tell if it is timbered, fruit, grass, waste, cultivation; if rented, how much rental you receive; if city property, you must give location, size, value, and state, street improvements if any; you must give full account of money in bank, or in your pocket, mortgages, loans, interest on loans, stocks and bonds; you must give a complete account of how many shovels, rakes, hoes, plows and every other farm implement on the farm; you must tell how many hens, cows, horses, hogs and every other animal on the place; you are compelled to describe the size and number of houses and sheds, pig-stys and barns on each farm; you must tell about every wheel-barrow, wagon, auto, describe their value; you are to describe your jewelry, household goods, tell how many bedroom sets you have, chairs and tables and every other article you own must be described and valued.

This large sheet, of which I have but given a part, is sent to every member, and he with all these revelations about cursing and salvation depending upon your faithfulness or otherwise, is stirring up the people to fever heat.

If you can find a more complete document to take away a person's liberty, independence, manhood, or womanhood; if you know of any church demand made upon the privacy of husband, wife, son or daughter; if you have heard of any ancient or modern method of taking away human liberty than the revelations of the Mormon Church, concluding with this inventory issued by the Reorganized Church, I have failed to hear of, or find it, and therefore this part, with every other part of Mormonism I am compelled to denounce.

CHAPTER X.

A Brief Examination of Alleged Proofs That The Book of Mormon Is of Divine Authenticity

First—"It makes claim to have originated from the proper source—**God**."

Reply—So does the **Koran** of the Mohammedans, the **Tri-Pitikes** of the Buddhists, the **Five Kings** of the Chinese, the **Three Vedas** of the Hindus, the **Zendavesta** of the Persians, the **Eddas** of the Scandinavians.

Second—"It claims to be a proper message to mankind."

Reply—So does the revelations of Anni Lee, James J. Strang, who gave to the world **"The Book of the Law"** from gold plates which he found in the earth under a tree, he being directed there by an angel. This Strang claims to be the successor of Joseph Smith, that he was ordained by an angel like Smith, received plates out of the ground, like Smith. Both preached what they called the message of salvation, both taught and practised polygamy and both were killed by people whom they had outraged, yet both the Mormon Church in Utah, and the Reorganized Mormon Church ridicule the angel story and the Book of the Law as preached by James J. Strang.

Third—The object of the book is a proper one, as recorded on the title page of the book itself, **"The Convincing of the Jew and the Gentile that Jesus is the Christ."**

Reply—So far as convincing the **Gentiles that Jesus is the Christ,** what has Mormonism done in the matter? First the origin of the book has been exposed in many ways, as seen in most every book printed on the question, and is proved in this little work. The book has been altered and corrected in thousands of places since its first publication in 1830. The claims made for it have been proven groundless and the fruits of Mormonism is revealed in the Polygamy, Murder, Robbery and wholesale corruption of Mormonism, wherever it has had a home. See the history of the Mormons in Ohio, Missouri and many other places, till the Gentile world looks upon Mormonism as the lying wonder of the latter days.

So far as convincing the Jews is concerned, that people look upon the story as a huge joke. Personally we have been associated with the church for over forty years, we recall but one Jew that ever joined the church, and he left it. We also knew of one Jewish lady who married a Gentile and came into the church. The Book of Mormon has been on its mission for about ninety years, the Re-organized Church sent missionaries to Jerusalem some years ago, they saw the country, took pictures, held some meetings, baptized three or four, and the mission failed. One Jewish Rabbi coming to Toronto from Jerusalem told me that the man whom our Elders baptized in Jordan was dead drunk the next day, and is now dead. So in the first ninety years the object of the book has failed.

Fourth—The much circulated testimony of the Three Witnesses, that God commanded them to bear testimony to the divine authenticity of the book, and that he sent an Angel to show them the gold plates from which it is said to have been translated **all left the Church inside of eight years,** and have testified that Joseph Smith was a **liar, murderer polygamist, chief Danite.** One of them says Christ appeared to him and told him to leave the church. Another says an Angel appeared to him and told him to leave the church. Smith, in turn, called upon witnesses to prove in the courts that these Three Witnesses (who talked with God and Angels and handled the gold plates of the Book of Mormon) "were liars, counterfeiters and blacklegs of the blackest and deepest dye," For proof of all this, see other parts of this little work and read Whitmer's Address, page 4, 27, 28, 38; The True Origin of the Book of Mormon by Shook, pages 48-61; The Foundation of Mormonism by La Rue, pages 75, 76.

Question—If the Three Witnesses told the truth about Smith, who can believe that God, Christ, and Angels talked to Smith face to face, and that he received the Book of Mormon to convert the world? On the other hand, if Smith tells the truth about the Three Witnesses, who will believe that God and Angels talked to them? May it not be true "That birds of a feather flocked together," and that "when rogues fell out they told the truth about each other." We leave that part of the matter with the reader.

Fifth—The claim is made for the book that "it shall go forth unto the people unto the confounding of false doctrine and the laying down of contention." Book of Mormon, page 8.

Reply—The Mormons have not been able to establish peace, or set aside false doctrine, nor stop contentions, for we have the Mormon church itself divided into several warring sections, each denouncing the others. The Utah Mormons and several other factions claim that **polygamy is provided for in the Book of Mormon,** while others deny it. The great church that has become infamous through its practice of polygamy says that the Book of Mormon while condemning polygamy under certain conditions and at certain times, yet makes provisions for its introduction under other circumstances, and that Joseph Smith, when he introduced polygamy into the church, was acting according to the promise made in the Book of Mormon. They claim that the Reorganized Church is dishonest in quoting a part of a statement in which polygamy is condemned, when if they would quote the balance of the paragraph they would prove that God made provisions for the introduction of polygamy. Read Book of Mormon, page 116, Jacob 2, 6: **"For if I will, saith the Lord of Hosts, raise up seed unto Me, I will command My people, otherwise they shall hearken unto these things."** Nearly a half-

BRIEF EXAMINATION OF BOOK OF MORMON 153

million Mormons claim that through Joseph Smith God did command His people to practice polygamy, and the evidence is abundant that Smith had such a revelation.

Sixth—The claim is made that America was inhabited by great nations before Columbus discovered it, and that the Book of Mormon was the first book to give a history of these great nations and of their cities.

Reply—We have heard that for forty years, believing it, we taught it, but when the clearer vision came we learned of a host of works that had been published in America, England and elsewhere describing the ruined cities of Mexico, Central America, Peru and other parts of America. Let the reader consult any good work on American Antiquities (we have given elsewhere in this little book a list of more than twenty books of this kind, published before the Book of Mormon was in print), and a most significant fact may be stated here, that the celebrated Josiah Priest wrote a work on this subject, it was copyrighted by him, June 24th, 1824, in the office of R. R. Lansing, clerk of the district of Northern New York and printed in Rochester, New York, in 1824. Will the reader remember that **The Book of Mormon was copyrighted by Joseph Smith in the same office before the same man June 10th, 1829.** and printed in Palmyra, N. Y., just twenty miles away from Rochester, in 1830.

From the above it may be seen how easy it was for Spaulding, Rigdon or Smith to have copied the works referred to and from them make the historical part of the Book of Mormon.

Seventh—Joseph Smith's mother is a good witness against him, in that she proves beyond a doubt, that before Joseph obtained the plates, years before he translated them, he had acquired what might be considered a perfect knowledge of the cities and people of ancient America. Listen: "During our evening conversations, Joseph would occasionally give us some of the most amusing recitals that could be imagined, he would describe **the ancient inhabitants of this continent, their dress, mode of travelling, and the animals upon which they rode; their cities, their buildings with every particular; their mode of warfare, and also their religious worship. This he would do with as much ease seemingly as if he had spent his whole life with them."** Joseph Smith the Prophet and His Progenitors, by his mother, page 87.

Reply—This is evidently why Smith did not require the **Plates** to be in his hat when he translated, but they could lie covered up on the table or even be in the woods when he did the job, as testified by his wife and her father, who tells of his talking through his hat. See other part of this book where they so testify.

Smith evidently was well acquainted with the **"Plates,"** or Spaulding manuscripts, long before he received them from the angel (?). Yes, several years before.

Eighth—They claim that the Bible prophecies foretell the travellings of the Book of Mormon people from Palestine to America, and the coming forth of the Book of Mormon out of the ground—Isaiah, 29th chapter, and that it is the Stick of Ephriam. referred to in Ezekiel 37th chapter. Let us see.

Reply—A work was published in London, England, some time ago, by a Mohammedan, quoting and applying most of the same prophecies to the Ishmaelites, to the Arabs and to the Koran. Others apply the Stick of Ephriam to England. They have been twisted by many other cranks to suit their fancies.

These prophecies apply to the scattering of Israel over the old continent; they went to Spain, Italy, the Islands of the Mediterranean, into Morrocco, Congo, in West Africa, Northern Africa, into Egypt and Ethopia, China, India, and over Central and Western Asia.

Isaiah 18, 8: "Wandered through wilderness, gone over the sea." This refers to the dispersion of Moab, and says so plainly

Isaiah 11, 11-16: This shows that it refers to Israel in the Assyrian Empire.

Isaiah 1, 1: "The vision of Isaiah concerning Judah and Jerusalem." Not a word about Book of Mormon or America, but Judah and Jerusalem.

Isaiah 28, 14, 21: God will curse Jerusalem and perform his strange work.

Isaiah 29, 1-4: "Ariel," "Heaviness, Sorrow," "camp against," "lay siege," "To raised forts," **Ariel**—The city where David dwelt, one of the names given to the capital city of Moab, which means Lion of the Lord. It is the name given to Jerusalem, and sometimes to the temple there." Gardner Ch. Cyc., page 98.

2 Kings 25, 1-48, 11-21: Nebuchadnezzar took Jerusalem, laid siege, raised forts, famine, broken up, burned with fire, Judah carried away.

Jer. 39, 1-8: Nebuchadnezzar took Jerusalem, killed King Zedekiah and his family.

Jer. 52, 1-9: Nebuchadnezzar pitched against, raised forts, besieged.

Isaiah 29, 4: "Bought down, speak out of the ground," excavations give history of Jerusalem, thus making them speak out of the ground.

Isaiah 29, 7: "Those who fight against her be as dream of night vision." Babylon, Syria, Egypt, Assyria, all fought her and were destroyed later.

Isaiah 29, 9-10-11-12: The people were in deep sleep, their learned men in a stupor like a drunken man; they could not read the judgments coming any more than a man could read a sealed letter or a book. The margin says "sealed letter." Jeremiah says she came down wonderfully, Lam. 1, 9.

Isaiah 29, 11-12: Words of book delivered to learned, cannot read sealed book. Joseph Smith writing in Times and Seasons, Vol. 13, No. 13, May 2nd, 1838, says that Martin Harris made a certain statement regarding his visit to Prof. Anthon and Dr. Mitchell. This was Smith's statement, not Martin Harris'. It was written many years after it is said that Harris made the statement to Smith. Why not have Harris make his statement according to law, but we receive it from the pen of Smith many years after the visit.

Just think, Smith says, that Harris said that Prof. Anthon and Dr. Mitchell said: "I cannot read the words of the book for it is sealed."

Now let us take the statement found in Isaiah 29, 11, just as it reads: "And the vision of all is become unto you as the words of a book that is sealed, which **Men** deliver to **One** that is learned, saying: 'Read this I pray thee,' and he said: **'I Cannot for it is sealed.'** "

All Mormonism agrees with Apostle Kelley that neither Prof. Anthon nor Dr. Mitchell were able to read the characters presented. Presidency and Priesthood, page 205.

Joseph Smith informs us that he received the gold plates, the Urim and Thummim and the breast plate, the 22nd day of September, 1827. He soon found a friend, (Martin Harris) a farmer near by, who gave him fifty dollars to help him along. Joseph copied a number of the characters of the plates, and by means of the Urim and Thummim he translated some of them. In February, 1828, Mr. Harris secured the characters which Smith had drawn off the plates, and started with them to the city of New York. On his return home Smith says that Harris told him the following story:

"I went to the city of New York, and presented the characters which had been translated, with the translation thereof, to Prof. Anthon, a gentleman celebrated for his literary attainments. Prof. Anthon stated that the **translation was correct,** more so than any he had before seen translated from the **Egyptian.** I then showed him those which were not yet translated and he said that they were Egyptian, Chaldaec, Assyriac and Arabic, and he said they were the true characters. He gave me a certificate certifying to the people of Palmyra that they were **true characters and that the translation of such of them as had been translation was also correct.** I took the certificate and put it into my pocket, and was just leaving the house, when Mr. Anthon called me back, and asked me how the young man found out that there were gold plates in the place where he found them. I answered that an angel of God had revealed it unto him.

"He then said to me: "Let me see that certificate." I accordingly took it out of my pocket and gave it to him, when he took it and tore it to pieces, saying that there was no such thing now as ministering of angels and that if I would bring the plates to him, **he would translate them.** I informed him that part of the plates were sealed and that I was forbidden to bring them. He replied: "I cannot read a sealed book." I left him and went to Dr. Mitchell, who **sanctioned what Professor Anthon had said respecting both the characters and the translation."** Church Hist., Vol. 1, page 19.

Reply—Prof. Anthon denies the statement as made above in these words: "The whole story about my pronouncing the Mormonite inscriptions to be reformed Egyptian heiroglyphics is perfectly false." Ibid. page 21.

Were we to admit that Prof. Anthon made the statement and that Dr. Mitchell confirmed them as true, this in our judgment would destroy the very thing that Smith and Mormonism has tried to prove by quoting

Isaiah 29, 11-12, where the **learned man** was to have the words of the book delivered to him, and when requested to read he was to say **"I cannot for it is sealed."**

First: Prof. Anthon **did read it and pronounced the translation correct.**

Second: He declared they were translated from the Egyptian.

Third: He also was able, and did read the parts that were not translated by Smith, saying: "They were Egyptian, **Chaldeac, Assyriac and Arabic,** and said they were **true characters** which he could not have done unless he was able to read and translate.

Fourth: He offered to **translate the plates if Harris would bring them to him.**

Fifth: Harris had to **lie** when he made the excuse for not bringing the plates to him to be translated, because part of the plates were sealed, and he was forbidden to bring them. There is no evidence that he ever tried to bring them, or that he was forbidden to bring them, and worse or more of it, the seal has been broken and the plates that Smith translated were all ready for translation by Smith or anyone else able to do the job. Smith had to break the seal before he could translate the part he translated, so the part that Anthon would have translated was not at that time sealed.

According to Isaiah **"men"** two or more, were to deliver the words of the book to **"One"** that is learned, but Smith turned this upside down, and only **one** man did the delivering, **Harris,** and **Two** did the reading, Anthon and Mitchell, in place of **One.**

Smith added **eight verses to the twenty-ninth chapter of Isaiah in his new Bible. One verse containing more than a hundred words,** in order to have it fit in to the Book of Mormon, so it is not to be wondered at that he would make up this story about Harris going to Prof. Anthon and Dr. Mitchell. Surely it is the lying wonder of the latter days.

Joseph Smith has informed us that it was he who copied the characters of the plates, that Harris took to Prof. Anthon. Having discovered beyond a doubt that Smith was an imposter, some learned men have made an examination of these characters which Smith copied, and they have made a photograph of them and I have them, published in different books, showing that Smith in drawing the transcript employed different kinds and styles of **English** letters, changing a few of them to make the imposture less observable. I have a copy of the original paper received from David Whitmer and I agree with those already published, that those characters are **English letters and figures.** I can see the figures 1, 2, 3, 4, 5, 6, 7, 8, 9, 0, and many of the letters of the English alphabet, so we leave this clumsy fraud.

Ninth—Ezekiel 37, 15-22: We are told by the Mormons that these two sticks are books, one the Book of Mormon, the other the Bible. But let us examine—stick, rod, staff, sceptre; they were symbols of power, authority, not books.

Numbers 17: Take twelve rods, write name on it; Aaron's rod budded. He accepted.

Genesis 49, 10: The sceptre shall not depart from Judah.

Numbers 24, 17: A sceptre shall rise out of Israel.

The stick of Judah represented the Southern Kingdom, and the Stick of Ephriam represented the Northern Kingdom. The prophet was to show that these kingdoms were to be united again; nothing is said about the Book of Mormon and America, but "The stick whereon thou writest shall be in thy hand before their eyes." God in verse 22 says: He will take Israel and gather them together to their own land, and there would be no more two kingdoms but One Nation, and he would be their God.

Joseph Smith had a rod with which he searched for water and did wonders. He told Cowdery by revelation 'You have another gift, of working with the **Rod,** behold it has told you things, behold there is no other power save God that can cause this **Rod** of nature to work in your hands—whatsoever ye shall ask me to tell you by that means that will I grant unto you." Book of Commandments, Chap. 7, 3.

In Doctrine and Covenants 8, 3, the words are somewhat changed in this revelation, in place of calling it "The gift of working with the Rod," it says: "which is the gift of Aaron."

We have tried to be fair in our examination of this question, but without hesitation say that the so-called proofs for the Book of Mormon are not proofs, but glaring misrepresentations of the plain wording and historical statement of the Bible and the histories referred to.

CHAPTER XI.

Priesthood

Two Priesthoods in the Mormon Church, Melchisedec and Aaronic

"There are in the church two priesthoods, namely the Melchisedec and the Aaronic, why the first is called the Melchisedec priesthood is because Melchisedec was such a great high priest. Before his day it was called "The Holy Priesthood, after the order of the Son of God." The second priesthood is called the priesthood of Aaron because it was conferred upon Aaron and his seed throughout all their generations." D. C. 104, 1-8.

No Salvation Only Through The Mormon Priesthood

"Ye are mine apostles—even God's high priests,—I say unto you again that every soul who believeth on your words, and is baptized by water for the remission of sins, shall receive the Holy Ghost. They who believe not your words and are not baptized in water in my name, for the remission of their sins, shall be damned and shall not come into My Father's kingdom, and this revelation unto and commandment is in force from this very hour upon all the world." D. C. 83, 10-12.

"They are priests of the most high God after the order of Melchisedec, which was after the order of the only begotten Son, wherefore it is written they are **God's.**" D. C. 76, 5.

"Respecting the Melchisedec priesthood, the sectarian world never professed to have it, consequently they **never could save anyone,** and would all be damned together, the sectarian world are going to hell by hundreds and thousands and by millions." Jos. Smith, in Mill Star, Vol. 22, page 54.

The priesthood having been caught up to heaven, no man on earth has authority to minister in gospel ordinances and hence the necessity for new revelation." Apostle W. H. Kelley, Presidency and Priesthood, page 224.

"Behold, there is save it be **Two Churches,** the one is the Church of the Lamb of God, and the other is the Church of the Devil, wherefore, whoso belongeth not to the Church of the Lamb of God, belongeth to that great church, which is the mother of abominations, and she is the **whore of all the earth."** Book of Mormon, page 40; Nephi, Ch. 3, Vol. 220-223.

"In the first revelation published in the Book of Doctrine and Covenants Christ is said to have told Smith, when speaking of the Mormon church, as "The **only true and living Church upon the face of the whole earth** and with which, I the Lord, am well pleased." D.C. 1, 5.

"The nature of the message in the Book of Mormon as such, that if true **no one can possibly be saved and reject it.**" O. Pratt in La Rue, page 81.

The claim made is clear that no salvation can come to a soul on the earth unless they obey the Mormon faith, and be immersed by a priest of that church, as it is the only church that God is pleased with upon the earth, and as the priesthood was lost for more than twelve hundred years, no one of the many churches has authority of preisthood to administer the gospel ordinances save the men who received it from Joseph Smith, who it is claimed received the Aaronic priesthood by ordination under the hands of John the Baptist, and the Melchisedec priesthood under the ordination conferred upon him by three angels, named Peter, James and John.

We will examine the claims for these angelic ordinations in their order, and will show, first, that the claim made that the Aaronic priesthood was conferred upon Smith by the angel John the Baptist is false.

"While we (Joseph Smith and Oliver Cowdery), were praying in the woods, a messenger from heaven descended in a cloud of light and having laid his hands upon us, he ordained us saying unto us: "Upon you my fellow servants, in the name of Messiah, I confer the **Priesthood of Aaron,** which holds the keys of the ministering of Angels, and of the gospel of repentance and of baptism by immersion for the remission of sins" This messenger, said that his name was John, the same that is called John the Baptist in the New Testament. It was on the fifteenth day of May, 1829." Ch. Hist., Vol. 1, pages 34-35.

First, let me say, Oliver Cowdery one of those said to have been ordained by John the Baptist, left the Mormon church a few years after this ordination and said, when speaking of the visit of the angel John the Baptist: "The voice of John the Baptist did most mysteriously resemble the voice of Elder Sidney Rigdon." Shook's Origin of Book of Mormon, pages 49-54.

This is a mild way of saying that Rigdon was the John the Baptist who did the ordaining, but let us permit Smith to give the whole thing away.

"This second priesthood is called the Priesthood of Aaron, because it was conferred upon Aaron and his seed throughout all their generations—**"No man has a legal right to this office to hold the keys of this priesthood except he be a literal descendent of Aaron."** D. C. 104, page 8.

This is said to be a revelation from Christ, while we believe that Christ had nothing to do with it, yet admitting for the arguments sake that He gave this revelation, then it follows that **only the literal descendants of Aaron** can exercise in this priesthood, that being true, then it follows that John the Baptist, alias Sidney Rigdon, had no right to ordain Smith and Cowdery to that priesthood and the hundreds and thousands of Mormons who have been ordained as Priests, Teachers and Deacons, have acted under a counterfeit ordination and are not priests of God at all.

The Work of Aaronic Priests

The ceremony of the consecrations of the Aaronic priests is described in 28th and 29th chapters of Exodus, also in Lev. 8th and 9th chapters, as well as in Numbers 18th chapter. Moses washed them with water, Moses put oil on their heads till it ran down their whiskers, Moses killed a ram, and put the blood thereof on the right ear, the thumb of the right hand and upon the great toe of the right foot, thus did he perform with Aaron and his sons. Ex. 29, 20.

We learn further that Aaron and his sons were dressed with garments made to order by the Lord's instructions, consisting of linen drawers, with a close fitting cassock, also of linen, the white cossack was gathered around the body with a girdle of needle work, into which, as in the more gorgeous belt of the High Priest, blue, purple, and scarlet were intermingled with white, and worked in form of flowers. Ex. 28, 39-40. Upon their heads they were to wear caps or bonnets in the form of a cup-shaped flower, also of fine linen. In all their ministrations they were to be bare-footed, they were not to shave their heads. Ezek. 44, 20. They were to have gold bells attached to their garments to make a noise. "When he goeth in and cometh out, that he die not." Ex. 28, 34-35.

Then there was the killing and dressing of all these animals named bulls, goats, lambs, rams, calves, doves, with their blood sprinkled on the altar and on the clothing of the priests, and a full description as to what to do with fat, the rump, the inwards, the gall, the liver, the kidneys, the skin and the dung. Ex. 28, 29; Lev. 8 and 9th chapters.

The chief duties of these Aaronic priests were to watch over the fire on the altar of burnt offerings, and to keep it burning. Lev. 6, 12; 2 Chron. 13, 11. To feed the golden lamp with oil, Ex. 27, 20-21; Lev. 24, 2. To offer the offering, Ex. 29, 38-44, and several other duties recorded in the Bible.

When Joseph Smith was ordained to this Aaronic priesthood, did he wear these breeches, bonnets, bells and girdles, did he go bare-footed. Did John, alias Sidney, sprinkle his garments with the blood of rams, did he have blood put upon his ear, toe and thumb? Did he kill all these animals and look after their fat, kidneys, inwards, gall and dung? Nay, verily.

History informs us that the Aaronic priesthood starting with Aaron to offer bloody sacrifices became sensual, covetuous, tyranical, drunkards, adulterers, Isaiah 28, 7-8 and 56, 10-12; Jer. 5, 25-31; Lam. 4, 12-16; Zeph. 3, 4.

"In the scenes of the last tragedy of the Jewish history, the **order passes away** without honor, dying as a fool dieth—the destruction of Jerusalem deprived the order at one blow of all but an honorary distinction, their occupation was gone." Smith's Bible Dict. Art. Priest.

The history of the high priests, beginning with Aaron and ending with Phannias—they arranged themselves into three groups, those before

David, those from David to the captivity and those from the return of the Babylonish captivity, till the cessation of the office at the destruction of Jerusalem." Ibid. Art High Priest.

Aaronic Priesthood Abolished in Christ

The Mormon presumption that John the Baptist was an Aaronic Priest and that he therefore ordained Smith, is without support. There is nothing to prove that John the Baptist was an Aaronic priest, the Bible is silent as to when and where he was ordained or acted in that office, nowhere do we find anything about John killing rams, lambs, goats, bulls or doves. No where do we find that he wore the garments of a priest above described, but to the contrary, we are told that he denounced the works of the priests and that "he had his raiment of camel's hair, and a leathern girdle about his loins." Matt. 3, 1-17.

The truth is, John was called and inspired to preach the gospel and prepare the way of the Lord, not to kill rams and lambs, goats and bulls. The history of John condemns Smith's story and confirms the statement that he was a gospel preacher. Matt. 3, Mark 1, Luke 3; John 1.

To conclude this part of the article, let me show that the Law of Moses, with its sacrifices of bulls, goats, rams, lambs and doves, together with the Aaronic priesthood who was ordained for the purpose of offering those bloody sacrifices was abolished and done away, nailed to the cross and that when the law of sin and death was abolished there was a change in the priesthood, the gospel of the more abundant life was not to be ministered by the men called to kill sacrifices and take care of the fat, skin, rump, kidneys, inwards, gall and dung under the law, but that the Melchisedec priesthood, over which Christ presided forever, was to preach the gospel and administer in the ordinances of the Lord.

Rom. 10, 4: For Christ is the end of the Law.
Col. 2, 14: Took it out of the way, nailing it to the cross.
Rom. 3, 20: By deeds of law, no flesh justified.
Rom. 8, 2-3: Law of sin and death was weak.
Col. 2, 17: Law was a shadow of things to come.
Heb. 7, 19: The law made nothing perfect, but the bringing in of a better hope did.
Heb. 9, 9: Gifts and sacrifices could not have them perfect
Heb. 9, 10-16: Blood of bulls, goats, ashes of red heifer, imposed until reformation.
Heb. 10, 1-4: Not possible blood of bull take away sin, comers not perfect.
Heb. 10, 9: Take away the law, establish the gospel covenant.
Gal. 2, 16: No flesh justified by the law.
Gal. 2, 21: Righteous came not by the law.
Gal. 3, 13: Redeemed from the curse of the law.
Gal. 3, 19: Law added because of transgression.
Gal. 3, 24: Law only a school master to bring us to Christ.
Matt. 5, 17: Christ came to fulfill the law.

Heb. 7, 11: Law given under Levitical or Aaronic priesthood, need of Melchisedec priesthood.

Heb. 7, 12: For the **Priesthood being changed** there is made a **change of the law.**

Heb. 9, 9-16: Law had divers washings, Gospel one baptism, Eph. 3, 5; Kings 5, 14.

The Aaronic Priesthood Abolished and the Melchisedec Introduced

Heb. 7, 11-12: Priesthood changed from Aaronic to Melchisedec.

Heb. 5, 1-8: Christ called of God a High Priest after the order of Melchisedec.

Heb. 7, 1-6: Melchisedec priesthood without descent, abide continually.

Heb. 7, 11-28: Law and its Aaronic priesthood made nothing perfect, but gospel administered by the Melchisedec priesthood did.

Here we have a perfect statement that the Law of Moses and the Aaronic priesthood given to Aaron and his posterity to administer it, has failed, passed away, was abolished and ended with Christ, and that there being no further use for the shadows under bull and goats, rams and lambs, and the bloody work ending in sin and death, and added because of transgression, when abandoned, was set aside and the beautiful gospel of Jesus Christ, the Law of Life, the Law of the new birth, the Law of redemption, the power of God unto salvation, the perfect law of liberty, was introduced and the holy priesthood known as the Melchisedec priesthood was introduced, God calling Christ to that office, and Christ calling his brethren to act therein, was to continue to bless the sons of men, till under the perpetual benediction of that blessed saving power, every knee shall bow and tongue confess, that Jesus is the Christ to the glory of the Father.

So we must consider the wild ravings of Joseph Smith and his product, Mormonism, with its counterfeit Aaronic priesthood, to be the lying wonder of the Latter Days.

If he lied about the John the Baptist ordination story, as has been proven, even so did he lie about his wonderful story of Peter, James and John coming to ordain him to the Melchisedec priesthood, as exposed in another part of this little booklet, and so we dismiss Mormonism with its counterfeit priesthoods and all its other frauds and thank God that we have been permitted to see Christ and his Gospel ministry and perfect law of liberty, that is destined to break the fetters of priestcraft from every honest soul and bring them all to glorify God.

CHAPTER XII.

Nebuchadnezzar's Dream

This great king had a dream in the year B. C. 603, and died B. C. 567. In the dream the king saw a great image, the head was of gold, the breast and arms of silver, the belly and thighs of brass, the legs of iron, the feet part of iron and part of clay. For a complete description, read Daniel second chapter. The dream and the interpretation is therein recorded. **Nebuchadnezzar** was the **Head of Gold,** this was the kingdom of Babylon. **Cyrus** was the **Arms and Breasts of Silver,** representing the **Medes and Persians,** which destroyed the first monarchy in B. C. 538.

Alexandria was the **Belly and Thighs of Brass,** representing the **Grecian or Macedonian Kingdom which destroyed the other.** B. C. 330.

After his death his kingdom was divided: Egypt, Syria, Macedonia and Thrace. **Rome** was the fourth government, representing **the Legs and Feet of Iron and Clay.** This Empire was divided A. D. 395. Its extinction took place A. D. 479. The extent and duration of the dream was from B. C. 603 to A. D. 479, a period of 1082 years.

Daniel's Vision of Four Beasts Was Four Kingdoms—Dan., 7 Ch.

Daniel seen a **"Lion"**—Nebuchadnezzar—courage; **"Wings"**—rapid victories; **" Man's heart given it"**—Belshazzar was a coward. This was Babylonian kingdom. The second beast was a **" bear,"** This was Cyrus representing the Medes and Persians. **"Raised itself on one side"**—Victories all on one side; **"Three ribs in his mouth"**—Babylon, Lydia, Egypt conquered. **"Leopard"**—**Alexandria,** representing the Grecian or Macedonian kingdom. **" Wings"**—Rapid victories. **"Four wings and four heads"**—When Alexandria died his kingdom was divided into four parts, Egypt, Syria, Macedonia and Thrace. **"Fourth Beast"** was the Roman Empire, "dreadful and terrible, stamping residue with his feet. **"Iron teeth"**—Rome was cruel what she did not use she destroyed.

Mormonism will agree with all the above interpretation, but here we come to the parting of the ways. They say that the **ten horns** of this fourth beast represents **ten kingdoms,** as also that the **ten toes** of the image are ten kingdoms, and that we are living in the days of these ten Kingdoms, and that Smith has been inspired to set up the Kingdom of God in the days of these ten kingdoms. But, we will show that the dreams no where state the Toes or Horns represent Ten Kingdoms, but they say plainly, **in the days of these kings the God of heaven shall set up a Kingdom.**

Dan. 2, 44: In the days of these **Kings.**
Dan. 7, 24: The Ten Horns of this Kingdom are Ten Kings.

History clearly shows that the Fourth Government of antiquity was Rome, and her **Ten Kings were named as follows: Julius Caesar, Augustus, Tiberius, Caligula, Claudius, Nero Galba, Otho, Vitellious, Vespasian, Titus."** History Chronology by Osbon, page 110. Ency. Brit. Art. Rome.

The Eleventh King or Horn Was Domitian.

Dan. 7, 20-26: "Little Horn before whom three fell." His father and two brothers suffered at his hands. "Eyes like a man," sagacity—spying out for his own interest. He retired to his palace as if uninterested, yet caused the trouble that removed his father and brothers out of the way and soon placed himself on the throne. **"Mouth** speaking great things." He caused himself to be addressed under the title of "Lord and God," while wicked he professed great piety. See World's display, Vol. 2, page 22. Giesseler Eccl. Hist., Vol. 1, page 23, **"Made war with the saints, for a time and times and the dividing of time."** History shows that forty thousand Christians were killed by order of this monster. He placed John, the revelator, in a tank of boiling oil. His work of violence began upon the Christians in the early part of the year A. D. 93, and ended with his death which occurred September 14th, 96, figuring back **three years and a half** or 1260 days, brings us to March 93, the very period which Petavious fixes for the persecution of Domitian.

Rev. 11, 2 and 13, 5: Forty two months, is 1260 days, not years.
Rev. 11, 3: A thousand two hundred and three score days, not years.
Rev. 12, 6: A thousand two hundred and three score days, not years.
Rev. 12, 14: **For a time, times and half a time is 1260 days.**
Dan. 7: "A Time, times and the dividing of time.
Dan. 12, 7: Shall be for a time, times and a half.
Dan. 4, 32: Seven times shall pass over thee. This was seven years.

"The Ancients called a **year a time,** because it was the time of one apparent revolution of the sun around the ecliptic, the period occupied by the earth in making its revolution around the sun, called the astronomical equinoctial, natural, solar, tropical year." Webster Dict., Art. **Year.** Bishop Newton and many other scholars say that a **Time** means a year.

Newton on Prophecy, page 221, Osbons Daniel verified in History, page 115. From the above it is shown clearly that the pet theory that time, times and dividing of time and forty two months and a thousand two hundred three score days means **1260 Years when all history and the Bible shows it means days,** is a fallacy that should be abandoned by the real lover of truth. The history is complete that the Eleventh Horn or King of the Roman Empire persecuted the Christians as stated for three years and a half or 1,260 days. Dan. 7, 26: "They shall take away his dominion to consume and destroy it unto the end." Domitian was murdered, and the Senate issued a decree that his name should be

NEBUCHADNEZZAR'S DREAM

struck out of the Roman Annals, and obliterated from every public monument, thus was his dominion consumed unto the end. The Encyclopaedia Britannica says the last three years his behavior was that of a mad man.

We have proved that the dream of Nebuchadnezzar and the vision of Daniel had reference to the four great monarchial governments of antiquity. That the toes of the image and the horns of the fourth beast had reference to the ten kings of the Roman Empire, and the eleventh horn, to the Emperor Domitian.

We will now show that the fourth beast was not Papal Rome and the eleventh horn the Pope of the Roman Catholic church, as assumed by the Mormons and some others, but that the fourth beast was Civil Rome.

Rev. 13, 1: Saw a beast with seven heads and ten horns."

Rev. 17, 9: Seven heads are seven mountains.

The City of Rome was built on seven hills. Gibbons, D. F. R. E., Vol. 1, page 546.

Barnes, page 239-246-434, Smith's Bib. Dic. Art Rome, page 588, Newton, page 527.

It is common to apply these prophecies to Papal Rome, and the Popes. But it cannot be disputed that this refers to the civil power of Rome, and the Roman Government or fourth beast with its eleven horns, and the legs and feet of iron of the image together with its toes were destroyed. When the image is destroyed, the toes being part of the image were also destroyed. Who ever heard of a man dying and being destroyed and his toes living and having great power a thousand years after his death? Who ever heard of a beast being killed, destroyed, burned up, and yet its horns being alive and active? All know that when the body is destroyed, the members perish with it. How these toes and horns could be nourished into life and growth and power from the cinders and ashes exceeds the force of our ingenuity to explain.

Dan. 7, 11: The beast is destroyed and given to the burning flames.

Dan. 7, 26: Take away his dominion, consume and destroy it unto the end.

Dan. 2, 34-36: Smote image upon its feet, break them in pieces, no place was found for them.

The feet and toes belonged to the image, the horns to the beast. All were broken to pieces, destroyed, burned, consumed. No place found for them, in fact the dream and vision tell the same story and show the destruction of all by the stone kingdom set up in the days of these kings, or horns. The image or beast only existed 1,082 years, more than six hundred of that time had passed before Christ came, He was nearing the time of the feet and it was during the early period of Christianity that Rome lost her power.

Now the civil power was destroyed **before Papacy arose,** no credible authority will attempt to fix the date of Papacy, as a ruling power earlier than the beginning of the seventh century, and yet it is incontrovertible that the **Roman Empire was destroyed before the close of the fifth century.**

The Stone Kingdom Set Up By Christ.

Dan. 2, 34-35: Stone smote the image upon feet, break them in pieces.
Dan. 2, 44-45: Break in pieces and consume all these kingdoms, stand forever.
Ps. 108, 22: Stone disallowed of men chosen of God.
Isaiah 2, 2: Christ's Kingdom established upon the mountains.
Dan. 2, 35: Stone became great mountain and filled the whole earth.
Matt. 21, 42-45: The rejected stone will grind to powder.

The stone was to destroy the entire image, the iron age of Rome lies between the expulsion of Tarquin B. C. 509 and the usurpation of Julius Caesar, which occurred a little before the coming of Christ. The **Iron** strength began to yield, and the weakness of clay began to be manifest. The Stone broke it. It was during the early history of Christianity that Rome lost her power and soon after was destroyed as a nation, and the Kingdom of Christ destroyed her according to the dream.

Jesus was born, lived and died in the days of Imperial Rome, and set up His Kingdom—The Stone Kingdoms that broke in pieces Rome.

Matt. 2, 1: Now when Jesus was born in the days of Herod the King.
Josephus B. 18, C. 3, page 535: Now about this time Jesus was born.
Luke 3, 1-3: Jesus lived in the days of Herod, Tiberius, Caesar, Pilate.
Josephus B. 3, C. 3: Jesus lived. If it is lawful to call him a man.
Luke 2, 1: Caesar Augustus taxed the world, Jesus was born.
Josephus B. 18, C. 2, page 1: Caesar taxed the people, Pilate was there.
Matt. 22, 15-21: Render unto Caesar the things that are Caesar's.
Matt. 27, 1-27: Roman judge sentenced Jesus and Roman soldiers crucified him.
Matt. 27, 63-66: Roman Seal on tomb by order of Roman governor.
John 19, 1: Pilate scourged Him and Roman soldiers pierced His side.

We have elsewhere in this little book recorded the facts regarding Joseph Smith, claiming to receive command from God to organize the kingdom referred to that will break in pieces and consume all other kingdoms and stand forever, and that Christ inspired him to be crowned a King.

D. C. 1, 5: Start a church to save the nations.
D. C. 107, 1-3: Proclamation to kings and nations to come to Zion.
D. C. 102, 9: Kingdoms of the world to submit to and acknowledge Zion.
D. C. 101, 10: Kingdom built by Smith, Christ dwell in City.
D. C. 91, 1: Kirtland to be a city and stake of Zion.
D. C. 77, 1: City of Enoch, new name, Covenant binding.
D. C. 83, 1-2: New Jerusalem built in Missouri.

We will close this little chapter by recalling the prophecies of Smith showing that the United States will be destroyed, Missouri sink disgraced and damned to hell, as recorded in this book and quoted from their church history, Vol. 2, pages 419, 710-711.

I trust the reader will see that Christ will destroy all these evils, and that he set up his stone kingdom, and will carry it triumphant to the glory of the Father, till sin is done away, death swallowed up in victory, and the kingdoms and dominions of the earth shall know and love Him and crown Him King of Kings and Lord of Lords.

Bishop R. C. Evans Dragged Into Court.

The history of Mormonism reveals that when a person becomes convinced of the fraudulent character of Joseph Smith and his revelations, that that person must be destroyed. In the early days, "The Danites, or destroying Angels" were busy with dirk or pistol, but in more modern times, the weapons changed to cruel slander and base misrepresentation, from press and platform.

Having recorded, in this little work, that I followed my parents into the church, when in my childhood and with all the fervor of youth and vigor of manhood, I gave forty-two years to Mormonism, believing that God was the author of it. When my faith in Mormonism failed, and the Lord led me out of the darkness into the light, I tendered my resignation to the president of the church, and walked out of the church, not knowing that a soul on earth would follow me.

Through the years there had never been a charge presented against me, I had but two difficulties. The first was, when I refused to condone the conduct of a person when they were found in wickedness. The second was when some of the prominent leaders, through envy and jealousy sought to injure me. Through the years "the common people heard me gladly, and I preached to more people than any man in the church during my ministry.

When the Lord opened my eyes to the great deception of Mormonism I tendered my resignation and then the President of the church set his church hounds after me. Their three church papers were crowded with slander and tattle and misrepresentation. One paper of which the President was the editor, for two issues were doubled in size and every paragraph was about the bad man that had left the church.

We called for fair play and half the space to make reply. A petition was signed by the Secretary of more than five hundred people begging for space for me to reply, and in the event of a refusal, President Smith was challenged to meet me in public debate in the largest hall in Toronto, I to pay all expenses. They have not permitted me to write a word in one of those three papers, and Smith will not discuss Mormonism with me.

The next move was to drag me before the courts of the Land. They issued a writ against me, and after a delay of months, they admitted the writ was not able to secure conviction and they changed the writ. Then another delay of months. In the meantime they secured an American lawyer (who is a brother of President Smith, the son of Joseph Smith, who moved his family from Independence Mo., to Toronto, Ont. He was here several months working up the evidence against me and coaching his two other lawyers of the city. Then came High Priest Pitt and wife. They hired a house in Toronto for several months. Then came President Smith and wife. Then came R. C. Smith, his brother (the one that is called after me, in honor of the fact that I baptized his mother and solemnized the marriage between her and his father, The Prophet, Joseph Smith.) Then came five apostles, four bishops and a host of High Priests, patriarchs and other priestly dignitaries who have filled their pulpit and wrote to the papers, and visited the people to keep them from the wolf, and safe in the Mormon fold.

When the earth had been covered and they were ready, then came the trial, prophecies galore, in which God is supposed to have told them that I would be exposed in the trial and the world would know what kind of a man I really was, filled their homes and churches.

The trial came, chief Justice Falconbridge heard the case. Their three lawyers filled to the brim, did their best. They dragged from their witnesses every point which had been carefully studied. We were questioned for hours and the trial was on during the days of May 26, 27, 28, 29 and 30 and June 2-6 and 7.

In place of making the closing speech and ending the agony at once the written arguments did not reach the Judge till December 30, seven months more to prophecy defeat and destruction to the apostate, but it is said all things come to those who wait, and we waited till the learned judge handed down his judgments, which I herewith submit as reported in the Toronto papers.

Judgment For Evans On All Points of Suit—Suit Against Former Bishop of Church of Latter Day Saints Dismissed

Toronto Star, Jan. 14, 1920.

Chief Justice Falconbridge to-day delivered judgment in favor of Bishop R. C. Evans and others on all points in the suit of May and June, 1919.

Benjamin R. McGuire, Bishop of the Reorganized Church of Jesus Christ of Latter Day Saints, living at Independence, Missouri; Mary Wilson, president of the Ladies' Auxiliary of the Toronto branch of the Church; M. J. Crowley, president of the Zion Religio-Literary Society of the Church, Toronto; and Leslie Prentice, superintendent of the Toronto Sunday school, brought suit against Bishop R. C. Evans, minister of an independent church in Toronto; Lizzie Evans, president; Sara Crowley, secretary, and Bertha Gray, treasurer of the new Ladies' Auxiliary of the Independent Church; against Charles Gerrard, president; Ida Gerrard, secretary, and Pearl Bayliss, treasurer of the New Zion Religio-Literary Society; and against Ed. Barringham, superintendent, and Margaret Lewis, secretary of the new Sunday school.

Bishop R. C. Evans had been for many years bishop of the Reorganized Church of Jesus Christ of the Latter Day Saints' Church on Soho street, Toronto, and it was claimed that on June 3, 1918, he resigned and, with others, formed a new church.

The suit was for an accounting of all funds appropriated by the new Church.

Chief Justice Falconbridge, in his judgment says: "The case was argued before me on May 26, 27, 28, 29 and 30, and on June 2, 6 and 7, 1919.

"At the request of counsel I allowed written arguments to be put in, and most elaborate ones were handed to me on December 30.

"A judge cannot listen to witnesses for eight days without coming to a conclusion as to the merits of a case. I formed a strong opinion, but I was quite willing, with an open mind, to listen to further arguments.

"A very careful consideration of the arguments and authorities fails to remove the impression which I had in mind.

"It is unnecessary to go into particulars, the contentions of the parties being so fully set forth in writing.

"I find in favor of the defendants on all points, and dismiss the action with costs. There are some small figures to be readjusted, which counsel said they were willing to do. Fifteen days' stay."

G. Wilkie, of Hamilton, was solicitor for McGuire, and W. R. Smythe, K. C., for Bishop Evans.

Less than a month after rendering the above decision, this celebrated judge died. I herewith append one of the many glowing tributes those who knew him best paid him:

His friends and associates have paid many glowing tributes to his worth as a chief justice, and his sterling qualities as a friend and sportsman.

The following tribute comes from Wallace Nesbitt, K. C.: "As a judge, the late Sir Glenholme Falconbridge presided with great dignity and uniform courtesy, listening with sympathetic patience to argument and arriving at accurate conclusions, which he expressed in the tersest and most grammatical English. As a judge of fact, he was unrivalled since the death of Chief Justice Simons. Common sense, plus a very complete knowledge of the world, gave him an unerring instinct in detecting where the truth lay.

"His choice of English was refined and classic. His speech as chairman at the banquet given by the Toronto Club to the Duke of Wellington was only equaled, but not excelled, by the masterpirce of Sir Wilfrid Laurier at the Rideau Club on the occason of the dinner to the duke, when he used the beautiful imagery of Ruth in speaking of the duchess, the faithful companion of her consort.."

Yet the Mormon press reflected upon this great man, and their Elders from the platform accused him of being unfair and reflected upon him very unkindly and all because he gave the decision above quoted.

All that I care to say about the judgment is, that while I have spent many months under the ban of suspicion, while the tongue of slander was busy and the pen of envy was besmearing the pages with the most cruel misrepresentations ever published, yet to have one of the most prominent and learned judges that ever sat on the bench of the British Empire bring in the verdict, and make the observations that he made, is worth all my suffering and to those who love law and order, this should be a most complete answer to those who have tried to destroy me, and also a recommendation of my character.

Now that pen, voice, press, courts have done what they have, I know not what will be the next move, but my trust is in God, and to Him I leave the future.

I submit the following letter and set of propositions which I wrote and sent to President Smith, asking him to publish the same in his church papers and up to date he has neither published the letter nor replied to it in any honorable way.

The only satisfaction I have had is that many of the papers of Canada and the United States have published it, and the world knows that I stand ready to meet President Smith on the platform and make answer as to why I left Mormonism and to let the world know the facts.

An Open Challenge to President Frederick M. Smith

President F. M. Smith.
Dear Sir:

The Saints Herald for March 19th, 1919, pages 281-2 contains a letter purporting to have been written by one signing the name of T. W. Williams. For many reasons I decline to regard this person of many sides as being sincere, some of which I will submit to you, as reasons why I have, and shall continue to decline to appear on the same platform with him.

First—He was considered a strong Socialist, and he admits that he was secretary for that society in California for years. For reasons known to himself and others, he suddenly rushed from California to Canada to act as your representative in a tirade against me from press, platform and pulpit.

Second—The contradictory statements and misrepresentations made are so numerous that I would not consider for one moment holding a debate with him. The rules of logic demand that each disputant must mutually consider each other as standing on equal footing and desire for truth.

Third—This person now selected by you to defend Mormonism has denounced much of the faith of your church and for a time withdrew from active missionary work assailing through the press the cherished doctrines of the church, opposing the leading authorities in regard to Tithing, Gathering and other doctrines. He accused the leaders of not teaching the Law of God, and doing violence to the sacred law. He boldly accuses the leaders of teaching that which produces inequality, and affirms that they are in direct violation to the Law. He clearly proves that the revelations said to have been given to the church by God flatly contradict each other and affirms that the church is held up to "public shame and ridicule." That the leaders are robbing the people of their rights under the law of "common consent" and flings a shadow on the revelations of both your father and grandfather who are the acknowledged prophets of the church. He pleads with the leaders to correct the mistakes and not remain in darkness. (Herald, January 13th, 1909.)

Now for reasons known to himself and others, he is willing to abuse me because I believe and teach that the leaders of the church are guilty as charged by him. I do not think for a moment he has changed his opinion, but just his position, for reasons.

Fourth—He was present when I challenged you to meet me in debate in the largest hall in Canada, the night I tendered my resignation as a member of the church of the Latter Day Saints. He knows that I have printed one hundred and thirty thousand pamphlets in which I have challenged you to open discussion. He knows that I have in print declined to meet him in debate, giving my reasons, yet in order to secure cheap notoriety, he plays the coward and in most every speech cries aloud: "I challenge Mr. Evans to meet me." He knows he is perfectly safe in this. Were I to condescend to meet your importation from California, perhaps he would be willing to suffer for what he could make out of it, but what would be gained by such a debate? If defeated he would leave the country and you would say: "He never touched me," and you would request me to meet still another, all the while you would be having a good time at some summer or winter resort. No, sir; you must meet me, or there will be no debate on Mormonism, so far as I am concerned.

Fifth—You should be willing to defend Mormonism, and should not request some poor fellow, who is eating out of your hand, to make answer for you. You are the acknowledged President of the church, the successor of your Grandfather and Father, as Prophet, Seer, Revelator, and God's mouthpiece to the church. You are considered as the best educated man in the church. You are the one man above all others that should stand as the defender of the faith. If you cannot defend the revelations given to the church by your Grandfather, your Father and yourself, as the professed Prophets of the Almighty, and the sole mouthpiece of Christ to the church, you should not compel your importation from California to make the attempt for a consideration.

Sixth—As the inspired Prophet of the Lord, while in Toronto, you publicly made this statement: **"My Grandfather gave the law, my Father interpreted the law, and I am here to enforce the law."** If that be true, then you are the ONE MAN ON EARTH to defend that given by your Grandfather, interpreted by your Father, and enforced by you.

Seventh—I am ready to meet you for the above reasons, and further because you make claim to be God's Prophet, Seer, Revelator, and sole mouthpiece to the church, also President of the church. The world wants to hear from you. Let the world know what real Mormonism is. Tell them all about the corruption of the Bible, and how necessary it was that your Grandfather give them an inspired translation of the Bible, as printed and sold by your church. Tell them all about the "Golden Bible," known as the "Book of Mormon," with the wonderful "Peep Stone" and "Urim and Thummim," by which the Book of Mormon and the Book of Abraham were given to the world. Give them the history of the "Order of Enoch," organized by your Grandfather. Tell us all about how God changed His name from Joseph to Enoch, then to Baurak Ale, and then Gazelem. Lift the veil and tell the world the truth about the revelations on polygamy. Tell them about Christ soon coming to live with you folk in Independece, Missouri. Give a history of the Danites, a secret society organized to murder, if the testimony of leading Mormons be true. You folk admit such an order in Utah Mormonism. Was it organized in 1838, as stated by Whitmer and Cowdery?

While I wish I could forget Mormonism and spend the few remaining years of my life in preaching the true gospel of Christ, yet if it is necessary that I become a victim to be sacrificed upon the altar in order to draw you out, so that the world may know Mormonism, all I ask is fair play and half the time. So herewith I submit the following propositions for public debate to be held in the largest hall in Toronto, Ontario, time to be agreed upon later as we may arrange. I will not ask you to take your time or money to hire hall or advertise, I will do all that without one cent from you:

Propositions For Debate Between F. M. Smith and R. C. Evans

First—Resolved, That Joseph Smith, Prophet, Seer, and Revelator of the Latter Day Saint Church, taught, practiced and sanctioned polygamy, and that he affirmed that Jesus Christ gave him a revelation commanding his people to practice polygamy in order to be saved.

R. C. Eavns affirms. F. M. Smith denies.

Second—Resolved, That Jesus Christ commanded the church to "Give heed unto all his (Joseph Smith's) words and commandments," (saying) "For his words ye shall receive as if from mine own mouth."

F. M. Smith affirms. R. C. Evans denies.

Third—Resolved, That Jesus Christ commanded the church through Joseph Smith to organize the "Order of Enoch" and that it is the duty of the membership of the church to consecrate all their properties to the bishop of the church, as trustee of the Order "With a covenant and a deed which cannot be broken." This being essential to their salvation.

F. M. Smith affirms. R. C. Evans denies.

Fourth—Resolved, That all productions printed in the Doctrine and Covenants, accepted as revelations through Joseph Smith, your Grandfather, Joseph Smith, your father, F. M. Smith, yourself, are the words of Christ.

F. M. Smith affirms. R. C. Evans denies.

Fifth—Resolved, That Joseph was divinely inspired to translate a record inscribed on golden plates, given to him by an Angel of God, and that Joseph Smith was inspired by the Lord to publish to the world a correct translation of said record, known as the Book of Mormon, and that said book is the new and everlasting covenant, even the fullness of the everlasting gospel of Jesus Christ.

F. M. Smith affirms. R. C. Evans denies.

Now, Sir, I admit that God has blessed the honest people of the church when they preached and obeyed the first principles of the gospel, but that they have been deceived by the Mormon part, is beyond question. Many thousands of the church have thus concluded. It will avail you but little to tell the world that I once believed that Joseph Smith was a Prophet of God, that the Book of Mormon was divinely inspired. I admit that I taught and believed all that, and that my sermons defended the work of Smith. To quote my sermons of twenty or thirty years ago is not the question. Abraham, Moses, Paul, Luther, Knox and thousands of others were converted from error to see the light of God. Why denounce me because I have grown in grace and knowledge?

I ask in common justice that you publish this letter in both Herald and Ensign, where you permitted the other challenge to appear. Notwithstanding the many cruel and false statements that have been published in your papers, you have persistently refused me a reply, yet I shall continue to try to keep my heart from bitterness, and put forth every effort possible to love God and preach the gospel, and my earnest prayer is that you may yet see the light of the gospel, be rescued from the thraldom of Mormonism and be saved in the kingdom of God.

Yours sincerely,

R. C. Evans

51 Ozark Crescent, Toronto, Ontario, April 1st, 1919.

APPENDIX 1

Material Concerning Oliver Cowdery

Oliver Cowdery was one of the three witnesses to the Book of Mormon whose testimony is printed in each copy of the *Book of Mormon*. I have reproduced Oliver Cowdery's *Defence*, published in 1839, from a copy which was reprinted by Jerald Tanner from photographs of it which he got from Yale University Library. He pointed out that B. H. Roberts, a historian of the Church of Jesus Christ of Latter Day Saints, accepted it as authentic. (*A Comprehensive History of The Church*, Vol. I, p. 163) Cowdery's *Defence* is not a crystal clear renunciation of the *Book of Mormon* but it does indicate deep doubts and at least indicates that Smith may have deceived them.

A poem by J. H. Johnsons, in a Mormon publication, claims that Oliver (Cowdery) denied the *Book of Mormon*. (*Times and Seasons*, Vol. II, p. 482, 1841. This page is reprinted by Hal Hougey, *Oliver Cowdery and the Book of Mormon*, Concord, California Pacific Publishing Co., 1963, p. 21)

A Mormon in Utah, under oath, said: "That Oliver Cowdery, the immediate friend and associate of Joseph Smith, apostatized from the Mormon church." (R. N. Baskin, *Reminiscences of Early Utah*, 1914, p. 97. Baskin was not a Mormon. He was at one time Chief Justice of the Supreme Court of Utah.)

That Cowdery finally denied that Smith was a prophet of God and that the *Book of Mormon* was of divine origin is not only proved by the statement in *Times and Seasons* but also by the fact that he became a member of the Methodist Church. This would have been impossible for one who really believed the *Book of Mormon* or who believed that Smith at any time received any revelations from the Lord. I am not only reproducing material from the records of the Methodist Church at Tiffin, Ohio, but also the discussion concerning Cowdery by R. B. Neal. ("Did Oliver Cowdery Renounce Mormonism and Join the Methodist Church at Tiffin, Ohio?", *The Sword of Laban*, Pikeville, Ky. Issues of October, November, and December of 1909, and January and February–March, 1910.) I have tried to locate the documents and materials collected by Neal but have been unable to do so. If any reader knows of their whereabouts I would appreciate hearing from that reader.

I was corresponding with Charles A. Shook on the subject of Mormonism when he died February 21, 1939. His wife, Laura Shook, sent me his material on Mormonism; including personal copies of his own works on the subject which have some annotations by Shook. Among the papers was a typed copy of "The Overstreet Confession," at the end of which Shook had typed some information. The "Overstreet Confession" is not viewed by most students of Mormonism as being a reliable statement. Tanner, among others, has discussed it. However, Shook's comment, which I shall now quote, concerning Cowdery's funeral sermon does not depend for its validity on the "Overstreet Confession". Shook wrote, in a typescript of his which I have that: "Cowdery died March 3, 1850, near Richmond, Mo., and his funeral sermon was preached by the Rev. John Sexsmith, a minister of the M. P. Church at Cowdery's own request. Information furnished by the Rev. D. B. Turney, 1396 So. Hilton Street, Decatur, Illinois, May 11, 1917. On May 24, 1917, Turney informed me that the Confession of Overstreet was published and circulated in Utah in 1857 and that a copy of it was in the possession of R. E. Grant of Grand Rapids, Michigan, who loaned it to him to make his transcription. Rev. Sexsmith told Turney himself that he preached Cowdery's funeral sermon. Sexsmith died in 1890, a prominent minister of the U. P. Church."

Why would this have taken place if Cowdery had returned to the Mormon Church before his death? Furthermore, why did the Mormons publish only a very brief reference to Cowdery when he died if he had actually returned to their church?

Of course, the *Book of Mormon* is false regardless of what Cowdery did, but the evidence shows that Cowdery did become a member of the Methodist Church.

Whereas, the General Assembly of the State of Ohio, in accordance with a petition forwarded to that body, on the nineteenth day of January, in the year of our Lord one thousand, eight hundred and forty three, passed the following act to incorporate the several persons hereinafter, as the whole and foregas following, to wit:

"An Act to incorporate the Methodist Protestant Church of Tiffin, in the County of Seneca.

"Sec. 1. Be it enacted by the General Assembly of the State of Ohio, That John Sander, Joseph Walker, William Campbell, and William Patterson, their "associates and successors, be, and they are hereby created "a body politic and corporate, by the name and style "of the Methodist Protestant Church of Tiffin, in the "County of Seneca; and, as such, shall be entitled "to all the rights, privileges, and immunities granted "thereby, and be subject to all the restrictions of, the "was entitled" &c. not in relation to incorporated Religious Societies," passed March fifth, one thousand eight hundred and thirty six.

"Sec. 2. That said Corporators shall give at least ten days notice of the time and place of their first Meeting under this act, by posting up advertisements in three of the most public places in said town."

"Sec. 3. That private and individual property of the corporators shall be held responsible for the payment of the debts of said Church, after its corporate property shall have been exhausted."

"John Chaney,
"Speaker of the House of Representatives.
"James P. Farrin,
"Speaker of the Senate.

"January 17, 1848.

[See Volume 46, Ohio Local Laws, pages 31, 32, where the above Act may be found & confirmed—
And Whereas, the said Corporation, in pursuance and under "and according to, the foregoing Acts of

by the Chairman and Secretary.

Wm. Campbell Secretary.
January 6, 1854.

John Sanford Chairman.

[N.B. The act of March 5, 1836 referred to in the Charter of this Society recorded on page first, may be found in the Collated Statutes of 1841, Chapter 97, pages 760, 763, 764. C. Landry.]

Minutes of a Meeting of the Male Members of the Methodist Protestant Church of Tiffin, Seneca County, Ohio, held pursuant to adjournment. The Meeting came to order by appointing a Rev. Thomas C. Cheesman Chairman and Oliver Corday Secretary. On ascertaining, and it appearing that since then two thirds of the Male Members of said Society were present, it was, on motion

Resolved, That we accept the Charter for the Re-organization of said Society, passed by the General Assembly of the State of Ohio, January 19, 1843 and that be become, and shall are, organized under and in accordance with the provisions of the same.

On Motion it was further Resolved, that the Various Joseph Mather, William Campbell, John Springfield and Benjamin Nye, be, and they are hereby appointed and chosen Trustees of said Society for and during the term of one year, and until their successors are chosen and accept said office.

Resolved, That an annual meeting of the Male Members of this Society be held at this place, one year from this date, at half past 6 P.M. for the purpose of electing Trustees for said Society, unless previously called by a vote of two thirds of the Male members of this Society, to be held at another time.

Resolved That the Trustees appointed by this meeting, be authorized to call a special meeting of this as may be necessary for the well doing of the same.

Resolved, That the first meeting of the Trustees of this Society, elected by this meeting, be held at the Office of C. Cowley, on Tuesday the 22th inst. at half past 6 o'clock, P.M.

Resolved, that the proceedings of this meeting be signed by the Chairman and Secretary.

On Motion, the Meeting adjourned without day.

Charles Cowley Chairman.

Oliver Connelly Secretary.

January 18, 1844.

STATE OF OHIO
                        SS:
COUNTY OF TUSCARAWAS

        George G. Shurtz, being duly sworn according to law, says that he caused certain pages of a certain record book to be photostated and that the attached three photostat sheets are true copies of Pages 1, 3 and 4 of the Quarterly Conference Records of the Methodist Protestant Church of 1843 and 1844 of Tiffin, Seneca County, State of Ohio.

                                      George G. Shurtz

Sworn to before me and signed in my presence this the 30th day of June AD 1960.

                                    JOHN C. ROSS, Notary Public
                          (My commission expires Sept. 1, 1962)

                    *   *   *   *

Newcomerstown, Ohio
7/2/60

James D. Bales,
Searcy, Ark.

My Dear Mr. Bales: I went to Tiffin this week, which is about 150 miles from here and the Lady in whose home I was entertained had found the Record of the Conference of 1843-44.

She had sought everywhere for it and finally it was found in the Pastor's Study.

On Page 1 at the bottom you will find, a one line reference by O. Cowdery, and signed by him.

On Page 3 you will find Two lines of reference and signed O. Cowdery.

Down a few lines you will find the appointment of Oliver Cowdery as Secty. (And only a Member could hold this position)

On Page 4 Oliver Cowdery signs action of the Conference with his signature.

One thing I didn't get, but can and that is On the inside of the front cover of the Journal is a name; street and number and Independence Mo. and this signed Oliver Cowdery.

If you should see the Journal you will find no more than what I have found.

One thing is certain and that is that Oliver Cowdery united with the Methodist Protestant Church of Tiffin after his part in the founding of the Mormon Society.

And I notice another reference to Oliver Cowdery on Page 4 under the first resolution, "This Society elected by this meeting be held at the office of O. Cowdery.

I trust these things will assist you in what you are doing.

Sincerely,

Geo. G. Shurtz

**The Church
of
The Christian Brotherhood**

HEAD OFFICE: 162 ELM STREET
TORONTO, CANADA

Toronto, Dec 20th 1942

Rev James. D. Bales

Dear Sir

I was one of The Boys That was with Bishop R. C. Evans. at The Time of His Death.

And He Affirmed to The Last The Angels Message. Calling Him out from The L. D. S.

And one of The last Things He said Was. Remember Boys The Angels Message is true. And As God Lives The Angel Appeared to me in This Room.

Yours Very Truly
Elder W. B. Wilson

DEFENCE

IN A

Rehearsal of My Grounds

FOR

Separating Myself

FROM THE

LATTER DAY SAINTS

BY OLIVER COWDERY

Second Elder of The Church of Christ.

This Defence is not protected by a copyright, as I wish no man, to be confined alone to my permission in printing what is meant for the eyes and knowledge of the nations of the earth.

> "God doth not walk in crooked paths;
> Neither doth He turn to the right hand,
> Nor the left; neither doth He vary
> From that which He hath said."

DEAR PEOPLE OF GOD: — I offer you a "Defence" which I am grieved to make, but my opposers have put me to the necessity, and so far as my memory serves, I pledge my veracity for the correctness of the account.

I deny that I have ever conspired with any, or ever exerted any influence to destroy the reputation of the "First Elder," although evidence which is to be credited assures me that he has done everything he could to injure my standing, and his influence has been considerably exerted to destroy my reputation and, I fear, my life.

You will remember in the meantime, that those who seek to villify my character have been constantly encouraged by him. There was a time when I thought myself able to prove to the satisfaction of every man that the translator of the "Book of

Mormon," was worthy of the appellation of "a Seer" and a "Prophet of the Lord," and in which he held over me a mysterious power which even now I fail to fathom; but I fear I may have been deceived, and especially so fear since knowing that Satan has led his mind astray.

(1) When the Church of Christ was set up by revelation, he was called to be "First Elder," and I was called to be the "Second Elder," and whatever he had of Priesthood (about which I am beginning to doubt) also had I.

(2) But I certainly followed him too far when accepting, and reiterating, that none had authority from God to administer the ordinances of the Gospel, as I had then forgotten that John, the beloved disciple, was tarrying on earth and exempt from death.

I am well aware that a rehearsal of these things at this day will be unpleasant reading to the "First Elder"; yet so it is, and it is wisdom that it should be so. Without rehearsing too many things that have caused me to lose my faith in Bro. Joseph's seership, I regard his frequent prediction that he himself shall tarry on the earth till Christ shall come in glory, and that neither the rage of devils nor the malice of men shall ever cause him to fall by the hand of his enemies until he has seen Christ in the flesh at his final coming, as little short of a piece of blasphemy; and it may be classed with that revelation, that some among you will remember, which sent Bro. Page and me, so unwisely, to (3) Toronto, with a prediction from the Lord by "Urim and Thummim," that we would there find a man anxious to buy the "First Elder's copyright." I well remember we did not find him, and had to return surprised and disappointed. But so great was my faith, that, in going to Toronto, nothing but calmness pervaded my soul, every doubt was banished, and I as much expected that Bro. Page and I would fulfill the revelation as that we should live. And you may believe, without asking me to relate the particulars, that it would be no easy task to describe our desolation and grief.

Bro. Page and I did not think that God would have deceived us through "Urim and Thummim," exactly as came the "Book of Mormon"; and I well remember how hard I strove to drive away the foreboding, which seized me, that the "First Elder" had made tools of us, where we thought, in the simplicity of our hearts, that we were divinely commanded.

And what served to render the reflection past expression in its bitterness to me, was, that from his hand I received baptism, by the direction of the Angel of God, whose voice, as it has since struck me, did most mysteriously resemble the voice of Elder Sidney Rigdon, who, I am sure had no part in the transactions of that day. As the Angel was John the Baptist, which I doubt not and deny not. When I afterward first heard Elder Rigdon, whose voice is so strikingly similar, I felt that this "dear" brother was to be, in some sense, to me unknown, the herald of this church as the Great Baptist was of Christ.

(4) I never dreamed, however, that he would influence the "Prophet, Seer and Revelator to the Church of the Latter Day Saints," into the formation of a secret band at Far West, committed to depredations upon Gentiles and the actual assassination of apostates from the church, which was done in June last, and was only one of many wrong steps.

These are facts which I am rehearsing, and if they shall be called in question,

I am able to establish them by evidence which I can bring forward in abundance.

Still, although favored of God as a chosen witness to bear testimony to the divine authority of the Book of Mormon, and honored of the Lord in being permitted, without money and without price, to serve as scribe during the translation of the Book of Mormon. I have sometimes had seasons of skepticism, in which I did seriously wonder whether the Prophet and I were men in our sober senses, when he would be translating from plates, through "the Urim and Thummim," and the plates not be in sight at all.

But I believed both in "the Seer" and in the "Seer Stone," and what the First Elder announced as revelation from God, I accepted as such, and committed to paper with a glad mind and happy heart and swift pen; for I believed him to be the soul of honor and truth, a young man who would die before he would lie.

Man may deceive his fellow man, deception may follow deception, and the children of the wicked one may seduce the unstable, untaught in the ways of righteousness and peace, for I felt a solemn awe about me, being deep in the faith, that the "First Elder" was a Seer and Prophet of God, giving the truth unsullied through "Urim and Thummim," dictated by the will of the Lord, and that he was persecuted for the sake of the truth which he loved. Could I have been deceived in him?

I could rehearse a number of things to show either that I was then deceived, or that he has since fallen from the lofty place in which fond affection had deemed him secure.

I remembered his experience as he had related it to me, and lacking wisdom, I went to God in prayer. I said: "O Lord, how dark everything is! Let thy glory lighten it, and make bright the path for me. Show me my duty. Let me be led of thy Spirit."

Shall I relate what transpired? I had a message from the Most High, as from the midst of eternity; for the vail was parted and the Redeemer Himself, clothed in glory, stood before me. And He said:

"After reproving the Latter Day Saints for their corruption and blindness in permitting their President, Joseph Smith, Jr., to lead them forth into errors, where I led him not, nor commanded him, and saying unto them, 'Thus saith the Lord,' when I said it not unto him, thou shalt withdraw thyself from among them."

And I testify that Jesus, whose words I have been rehearsing, hath even so commanded me in an open vision.

The Lord revealed to me that the "First Elder" is leading the Saints astray, and ordered me to quit them after delivering the message which this "Defence" delivers. I shall ever remember this expression of the Saviour's grace with thanksgiving, and look upon his amazing goodness to me with wonder.

When I had sufficiently recovered my selfpossession to ask in regard to the errors into which Joseph Smith, Jr., was taking the Saints, the Redeemer instructed me plainly: "He hath given revelations from his own heart and from a defiled conscience as coming from my mouth and hath corrupted the covenant and altered words which I had spoken. He hath brought in high priests, apostles and other officers, which in these days, when the written Word sufficeth, are not in my church, and some of his deeds have brought shame to my heritage by the shedding of blood. He walketh in the vain imaginations of his heart, and my Spirit is holy and does not dwell in an unholy temple, nor are angels sent to reveal the great work of God to hypocrites."

I bowed my face in shame, and said: "Lord! I entreat thee, give me grace to bear thy message in print, where I fear to take it by word of mouth."

And he said, "The grace is given thee," and he vanished out of my sight.

Prepare your hearts, O ye Saints of the Most High, and come to understanding. The prophet hath erred and the people are gone astray through his error. God's word is open. We may read it. There is no "First Presidency" there, no "High Priesthood" save that of Christ himself, no Patriarch to the church, and wonderful to tell, the "First Elder" hath departed from God in giving us these things, and in changing the name of the church.

Oh, the misery, distress and evil attendant upon giving heed unto the "doctrines of men!" The gospel has been perverted and the Saints are wandering in darkness, while a full cup of suffering is poured upon them. A society has been organized among them to inflict death upon those who are deemed apostates, with the knowledge and sanction of the First Elder.

This, I confess, is a dark picture to spread before those whom I am to warn, but they will pardon my plainess when I assure them of the truth of what I have written.

Bearing this message to them is the hardest work of my life, although many have been the privations and fatigues whih have fallen to my lot to endure for the Gospel's sake since April 5th, 1829.

It is disgraceful to be led by a man who does not scruple to follow his own vain imagination, announcing his own schemes as revelations from the Lord.

And I fear he is led by a groundless hope, no better than the idle wind or the spider's web. Having cleared my soul by delivering the message, I do not deem it necessary to write further on the subject now.

Jesus has saved men in all ages and saves them now, and not by our Priesthood either. The "First Elder" errs as to that. The Lord has said, long since, and his word remains steadfast as the eternal hills, that to him who knocks it shall be opened, and whosoever will, may come and partake of the waters of life freely; but a curse will surely fall upon those who draw near to God with their mouths, and honor him with their lips, while their hearts are far from him.

I no longer believe that all the other churches are wrong.

Get right, O! ye people, get right with God, and may the Lord remove his judgments from you, preserve you in his kingdom from all evil, and crown you in Christ. Amen.

O. COWDERY.

March 3, 1839.

Cowdery's pamphlet was printed by Pressley's Job Office, Norton, Ohio, 1839. B. H. Roberts regarded it as authentic. (*A Comprehensive History of The Church,* Vol. I, p. 163.) Reprinted, from an original copy in Yale University Library, by Jerald Tanner, P. O. Box 1884, Salt Lake City, Utah.

The following is reprinted from *The Sword of Laban,*
Volume II, Numbers 3, 4, 5, 6, 7.
October 1909–March 1910.

DID OLIVER COWDERY RENOUNCE MORMONISM AND JOIN THE METHODIST PROTESTANT CHURCH AT TIFFIN, OHIO?

The importance of the issue presented and the value of the facts given in this article ought to and surely will win for it a place in every paper whose editor is in favor of suppressing error and of spreading truth.

Who Was Oliver Cowdery?

We permit this distinguished Mormon to introduce himself to our readers. Hear what he says:

I wrote with my own pen the entire "Book of Mormon" (save a few pages) as it fell from the lips of the Prophet Joseph Smith as he translated it by the gift and power of God, by means of Urim and Thummim, or, as it is called by that book, "Holy Interpreters." I beheld with my eyes and handled with my hands the gold plates from which it was translated. I also saw with my eyes and handled with my hands the Holy Interpreter. That book is true.

The Holy Priesthood is here. I was present with Joseph when an holy angel of God came down from Heaven, conferred on us or restored the lesser, or Aaronic Priesthood and said to us at the same time that it should remain upon earth while the earth stands. I was also present with Joseph when the higher, or Melchisedek Priesthood was conferred by the holy angel from on high. This priesthood was then conferred on each other by the will and commandment of God. This priesthood as was then declared is also to remain upon the earth until the last remnant of time.

Here's a sample of the revelations(?) he received:

Behold, thou art Oliver, and I have spoken unto thee because of thy desires; therefore treasure up these words in thy heart. Be faithful and diligent in keeping the commandments of God and I will encircle thee in the arms of my love. Behold, I am Jesus Christ, the Son of God. I am the same that came unto my own and my own received me not.

* * * * * * *

Behold the wounds which pierced my side, and also the prints of the nails in my hands and feet; be faithful, keep my commandments, and ye shall inherit the kingdom of heaven. Amen.

—Sec. 6, Book of D. and C.

Oliver Cowdery was the first person baptized into the Mormon Church. Joseph Smith, the Prophet, baptized him and he then baptized Joseph. He is one, and the main one, of the Three Witnesses whose names go out with every Book of Mormon to prove its divinity. He was nearer to Joseph Smith in this work of planting Mormonism than John, the beloved, was to the Savior when the Lord's Supper was instituted. He was the Second Elder, Joseph was the First Elder and both were equal in power in the Priesthoods.

He claimed that "Peter, James and John" ordained him and Joseph Smith to the Melchisedek Priesthood. Also that "the Angel John" (the Baptist) came down and ordained both him and Joseph to the Aaronic Priesthood, *laid his hands on their heads, saying:*

Upon you, my fellow servants, in the name of Messiah, I confer the Priesthood of Aaron, which holds the keys of the ministering angels, and of the gospel of repentance and of baptism by immersion for the remission of sins; and this shall never be taken again from the earth, until the sons of Levi do offer again an offering unto the Lord in righteousness.

—*Sec. 13, B. of D. and C.*

These young "Elders" of Mormonism who today travel up and down the earth with "grip" in hand preaching the "Gospel of Nephi," trace their authority to preach, to teach, to baptize, to "lay on hands" back to Oliver Cowdery, equally with Joseph Smith.

How important that they should be posted on the facts we hand out in this document. The right conclusion would *force* itself upon their minds. It is unthinkable that a man who saw Christ and to whom He talked, a man who had the hands of John the Baptist laid on him, telling him that baptism was by *"immersion"* and "for the remission of sins" should join a church that denies both statements. It is unthinkable that the man who nearly wrote the Book of Mormon, who said he saw an "Angel of God" with the "gold plates," and that when the angel showed him the "gold plates" the voice of God declared that Joseph Smith had correctly translated them in the "Book of Mormon," if he believed his own story, that he could join, live in and labor for years with a church that denied all such claims.

Every Mormon Elder and Editor denies that Oliver joined the M. P. Church at Tiffin, O. They have to deny it, and to maintain the denial, or lose their cause. When I first sent this affirmation into all their camps it caused consternation and created quite a commotion. The "Reorganized Church" sent out its best henchmen to persons and places I had mentioned in hopes of gathering information that would confute my statements.

Their "Church Historian," H. C. Smith, started an article on the rounds of Mormon papers, based upon his report. This article was to have been revised, put in tract form and scattered among the faithful. It "died a borning."

"The Saints' Herald," Lamoni, Ia., official organ of the "Reorganized Church," has an article of over eight pages reviewing my Tract. "The Evening and Morning

Star," Independence, Mo., official organ of the Hedrickite Mormon church, quotes largely from it with hearty approval. "Pilate" and "Herod" join hands to battle me over this, to them, a life or death issue.

The article winds up with the following flourish:

We submit the foregoing to the careful consideration of those who wish to know the truth; to those who are seeking for the opposite we have nothing to offer.

After I make manifest how their trusted men hunt for truth and juggle the facts they find, the public will conclude, and justly so, if Mormon papers refuse to publish this article, that the Editors and Elders are not honest, and brand them deeply as among those who are "seeking for the opposite of the truth."

All that class has to do is to read the Church Historian's article based upon Bishop Kelley's report.

The Saints' Herald says:

At our request, Bishop E. L. Kelley called at Tiffin, Ohio, on February 7 and 8, 1907, to look up the records on this point, and after examining all the records that he could find in the hands of the custodian of the records, Mr. C. J. Yingling, writes in a letter dated Independence, Missouri, February 11, 1907, as follows:

"Mr. C. J. Yingling, who had in charge the records of the Methodist church, thought before examination that it showed that Cowdery was a member of the church, but upon examination I discovered that it simply contained his work as an attorney, and pointed out the fact to Mr. Yingling, which he readily assented was the fact."

I promptly wrote to Mr. Yingling asking if the above statement was true. Here is the reply I received:

Tiffin, O., April 12, '07.

R. B. Neal,
    Grayson, Ky.

Dear Sir: Your favor of April 1st came duly to hand and contents noted. Mr. E. L. Kelley called to see me in February. He asked me if I knew anything about Oliver Cowdery. I showed him the minute book of the church. Mr. Kelley told me he was a lawyer. I did not know he was a Mormon. He seemed like a very nice gentleman. I enclose you a copy of all the minutes recorded in the Minute Book of the Methodist Protestant Church, of Tiffin, that contains anything about Mr. Cowdery, and all that Mr. Kelley saw. After Mr. Kelley had left Tiffin, I found something in Lang's history of Seneca county about Cowdery. I copied it and sent it to Mr. Kelley. I also enclose you a copy of the same. The copies of the minutes and what is in Lang's History is all I know about Oliver Cowdery, and all I showed Mr. Kelley.

The minutes of the church written up by Oliver Cowdery, January 18, 1844, should be conclusive evidence that Oliver Cowdery was a member of the Methodist Protestant Church. Every word of the minutes of the copies that I enclose was written by Oliver Cowdery except the names which I have underscored; the affixes, "Sec. and Treas." are in Oliver Cowdery's handwriting.

Yours respectfully,
C. J. YINGLING.

Comments.

Mr. Kelley did not reveal himself as a Mormon Bishop sent out by his church to gather facts for "the careful consideration of those who wish to know the truth."

This has a dishonest look. His concealing this fact that he was a Mormon on an honest hunt for facts prepares us to suspect a dishonest handling of facts found. The sequel confirms our suspicion. He wilfull and deliberately *misrepresents* Mr. Yingling.

Read the following

Deadly Parallel

Bishop Kelley.	*Mr. Yingling.*
Before reading the records Mr. Yingling thought that Cowdery was a member of the Church. After examination of the records he readily assented to my statement that Mr. Cowdery was not a member of the Church, but was simply acting as an attorney for it.	The minutes of the Church written up by Oliver Cowdery Jan. 11, 1844, should be conclusive evidence that Oliver Cowdery was a member of the Methodist Protestant Church.

Mr. Yingling not only denies that he assented to Kelley's statement that Cowdery was "simply acting as an *attorney* for the church" but he affirms that the church book "is conclusive evidence that Oliver Cowdery *was a member of the Methodist Protestant Church.*"

This first round gives a very black eye to Bishop Kelley as a fair handler of facts.

When we look at "the Minutes of the Church written up by Oliver Cowdery, Jan. 18, 1844," every candid man and woman will agree with Mr. Yingling that the evidence is conclusive that Apostle, Second Elder Oliver Cowdery, of the "Church of Jesus Christ of Latter-day Saints" renounced that church and joined the M. P. Church at Tiffin, O.

Here we rest until next issue.

Reprinted from *The Sword of Laban,* Volume II. Number 4

We continue with increasing interest this investigation. Mr. Yingling desiring to aid Bishop Kelley to find out "the whole truth and nothing else but the truth," in regard to Oliver Cowdery, referred him to the aged widow of Judge Lang, as one likely to know the facts in the case.

Kelley interviewed her and here's his report:

Mrs. W. Lang, the widow of Judge Lang, of Tiffin, was referred to as a witness who would know with reference to Cowdery's connection with the church. She was an aged lady, but of good memory, found at her residence and that of her niece, Miss Lang, at Tiffin, and upon inquiry with reference to Oliver Cowdery's connection with the Methodist church or any church society at Tiffin during his residence there. She stated that he was not a member of any church society there. She thought his wife might have attended the Methodist church and that the girl who lived with them, Adeline Fuller, did attend the Methodist church, but she was certain that Oliver Cowdery was never a member of the Methodist church at Tiffin. She said on the contrary he was a "Mormon."

I promptly wrote to Mrs. Judge Lang.

As death had claimed her, since her interview with Kelley, her son, Frank H. Lang, a prominent business man of Tiffin, replied. Here are extracts from his letter:

"Tiffin, O., May 15, 1907.

"R. B. Neal,

"Grayson, Ky.

"Dear Sir:

"I called upon Mr. Yingling and we together looked over the Church Records of January 18, 1844. * * * I will try and have a photograph taken of the page and send to you.

"Now, Mr. Neal, I wish you would send me a copy of Mr. Kelley's statement, or tract, in which he states his interview with my mother. Mr. Yingling had one but I do not like to ask him for it.

"Mr. Kelley has *undeniably misquoted my mother,* for I spoke to her about her conversation with Mr. Kelley within an hour after he had been there and she said that she told him that she did not know whether the Cowdery family were members of the Methodist church or not.

"He says that mother stated to him that she was positive they were not. He also misrepresented Mr. Yingling in his statement. And I am quite sure that he has also misrepresented Mrs. Joel W. Wilson in her statement. I may have to go to Toledo in a few days and if I do I will call on her."

We again call up the

Deadly Parallel

Bishop Kelley.

"Mrs. Lang told me that Oliver Cowdery was never a member of any Church Society at Tiffin. That she was certain that he was never a member of the Methodist Church at Tiffin, that on the contrary, he was a Mormon."

Frank H. Lang.

"Mr. Kelley has undeniably misquoted my mother, for I spoke to her about her conversation with Mr. Kelley within an hour after he had been there and she said she told Kelley that she did not know whether the Cowdery family were members of the Methodist Church or not."

This, the second round, blacks Kelley's other eye. Note what he says about Adeline Fuller, the girl who lived with the Cowdery family. We have her testimony and will present it at the right time. It presents another issue and we do not wish this one clouded by another just now.

I have before me an old letter written in 1881 by Mr. J. H. Gilbert, Palmyra, N. Y. He is the man who set the type and got out the first issue of the Book of Mormon.

Bishop Kelley interviewed him and made his report in this same Saints' Herald. Gilbert gets holds of a copy and his letter will have a bearing to put Mr. Kelley before the public in his true light. Gilbert says:

Kelley's report of the conversation with me is full of misrepresentations. The long paragraph in relation to Mr. Cobb and Lorenzo Saunders is a mixed mess of truth and falsehood. What he charges me with saying about Smith's and Tucker's book is all his own coining. Mr. Jackway tells me he did not tell Kelley that Joe and his father got drunk on cider, but on whiskey.

I do know that Kelly has misrepresented me in his report of my answers and statements, and I have no doubt he has misrepresented others also. What his object was I can not divine. He may think it will strengthen the faith of Mormons a little. Well, if people are fools enough to believe in it, let them; it is no worse than some other humbugs.

If you have any Mormon friends in your vicinity who have read Kelley's report in the Saints' Herald, you can say to them that he is a great falsifier, and I consider him the champion liar of America.

Yours truly,

J. H. GILBERT.

This was in 1881. In 1907, this same Bishop Kelley, twenty-six years older, is still hunting for truth (?) about Mormonism, and reporting the same old "Saints' Herald" and misrepresenting interviews in the same old way.

From what we have presented, and are about now to present, the public will conclude that Bishop Kelley still wears the belt as the "C. L. of A."

The Deadly Parallels above confirm his title to the belt, but they are weak documents for that purpose, compared to the way he *doctors* church records, to hand out to a public he thinks will never see the original copies.

How Kelley Handles Church Records.

We have type-written copies of the "records" he had on which to base his articles. We also have his article in print. This makes the task of comparison very easy.

Bishop Kelley says:

The first reference to the work of the First Methodist Protestant Church of Tiffin, contained in the record book, bears date of January 19, 1843. This was of a meeting called at that date of the male members of said church to form a society and obtain charter of such society. At the conclusion of the record of this meeting there is entered upon the record in the handwriting of Oliver Cowdery, which is marked in brackets, the following:

(See Vol. 41, Ohio Local Laws, pages 31 and 32, where the above act may be found. O. Cowdery.)

Kelley evidently designs to make *three* impressions upon the minds of his readers by the above comments.

1. That the "male members" of the church met to form some sort of *society* "for men only," separate from the church and to get a charter for it.

2. That this kind of work demanded the presence of a lawyer to advise, and that Cowdery, the great Mormon apostle, was there simply as an *attorney*.

3. That all that Cowdery wrote of the minutes of this meeting was the *appendix* contained in the brackets.

Here is a copy of the document he had before him:

Whereas, The General Assembly of the State of Ohio, in accordance with a petition previously presented to that body, on the Nineteenth day of January, in the year of our Lord, one thousand, eight hundred and forty-three, passed the following act to incorporate the several persons therein named, in the words and figures following, to-wit:

An act to incorporate the Methodist Protestant Church of Tiffin, in the county of Seneca.

Sec. (1). Be it enacted by the General Assembly of the State of Ohio, that John Souder, Joseph Walker, William Campbell and William Patterson, their associates and successors, be, and they are hereby created a body politic and corporate by the name and style of the Methodist Protestant Church, of Tiffin, in the County of Seneca and as such shall be entitled to all the rights, privileges and immunities granted by, and be subject to all the restrictions of, the act entitled "an act in relation to incorporated religious societies," passed March the fifth, one thousand eight hundred and thirty-six.

Sec. (2.) That said Corporators shall give at least ten days' notice of the time and place of their first meeting under this act, by posting up advertisements in three of the most public places in said Town.

Sec. (3.) The private and individual property of the corporators shall be held responsible for the payment of the debts of said Church, after the corporate property shall have been exhausted.

JOHN CHANEY,
Speaker of the House of Representatives.

JAMES J. FAREN,
Speaker of the Senate.

Jan. 19, 1843.

(See Volume 41, Ohio Local Laws, pages 31, 32, where the above Act may be found. O. Cowdery).

Comments.

Note 1. That the male members of the church met to accept an act of incorporation of their *church,* as a whole, both males and females, not to "form a society" in the modern use of that term either within or without the church.

This act of incorporation was their "charter" to create "a body politic and corporate by the name and style of the METHODIST PROTESTANT CHURCH OF TIFFIN, O."

2. The meeting was for male members. Members of the church, of course. Oliver Cowdery was present and just as sure as that he was a male he was a member of that church.

3. Oliver Cowdery wrote every word of the minutes of that page. Wrote the whole thing, appendix and all. Mr. Yingling says: "Every word of the minutes of the copies that I enclose was written by Cowdery, except the names I have underscored."

Mr. Cowdery was a ready writer and a good scribe. That is the reason Joseph Smith had him write the Book of Mormon. This the reason, now that he was a "male member" of the Methodist Church, that he was called upon to write so much. He wrote everything on that page and Bishop Kelley knew it. He saw the original page. His "attorney idea" demanded that he suppress the whole truth about Cowdery's hand-writing upon that page. In fact there is nothing here, or in any of these records, to indicate that Oliver Cowdery was even a lawyer, much less acting as an attorney for the church.

The way he handles the next "Record" is even more dishonorable than the way he handles this one. About that in our next issue.

Reprinted from *The Sword of Laban,* Volume II, Number 5

We resume our task of handling "Bishop Kelly" without gloves. In handling "Church Records" he makes an unsavory record that smells to the skies.

He continues his comments:

On January 6, 1844, the *society* was called together again with John Souders, chairman; William Campbell, secretary; but from the proceedings it seems they did not have sufficient to form a quorum, and their proceedings were not legal. At the conclusion of this record for January 6, 1844, there is inserted by O. Cowdery the following:

"'(The account of March 5, 1836, referred to in the charter of this society, recorded on page 1, may be found in the collated acts of 1841, chapter 97, pages 782, 783, 784. O. Cowdery.)"

Comments.

Note 1. He again says it was the *"society"* called together.

2. That Cowdery wrote the *conclusion* of the record. The implication is that that is all he wrote of the minutes. It would hurt the "attorney idea" to say that

he wrote the whole thing except the "names of the chairman and secretary." That he even wrote the "affixes," "chairman" and "secretary," to which they prefixed their names. Here is the document. Each reader can judge for himself as to Kelley's perversion of plain facts:

And whereas, the said corporators, in pursuance with, and according to, the foregoing act of incorporation, on the twenty-first day of December in the year of our Lord, one thousand, eight hundred and forty-three, at Tiffin, in said county of Seneca, posted up in three of the most public places therein, a notice in the records and figures following, to-wit:

"Notice:—A meeting of the Male members of the Methodist Protestant Church of Tiffin, Seneca county, Ohio, will be held on the 6th day of January next at their brick church in Tiffin, in said county, for the purpose of organizing under the act of incorporation of said Society, passed January 19, 1843. The meeting will be organized at 2 o'clock P. M. of said day.

"Joseph Walker,
"John Souder,
"W. M. Patterson,
"Wm. Campbell.

"Dec. 21, 1843

Whereupon, in pursuance of said notice, last aforesaid, to-wit: On the sixth day of January, A. D. 1844, a meeting was held accordingly, as will fully appear from the following minutes and records thereof:

"Minutes of a meeting of the male members of the Methodist Protestant Church of Tiffin, Seneca county, Ohio, held on the 6th day of January, A. D. 1844, at their brick church in said Tiffin, according to notice previously given.

"2 o'clock P. M. — The meeting came to order, John Souder was chosen chairman and William Campbell secretary. And it appearing that two-thirds of the Male Members of this society are not in attendance, on motion it is

Resolved, That this meeting do adjourn to meet again at this place on the 18th inst., at half past 6 o'clock P. M., for the purpose of fully carrying out the objects specified in the notice of Dec. 21st A. D. 1843, and such other business as the meeting may see proper to transact.

"Resolved, That the minutes of this meeting be signed by the Chairman and Secretary.

"John Souder, Chairman,
Wm. Campbell, Secretary."

"Jan. 6, 1844.

"(P.S. — The act of March 5th, 1836, referred to in the charter of this Society recorded on page first may be found in the Collated Statute of 1811, Chapter 97, Pages 782, 783, 784. O. Cowdery.)"

Comments.

1. He, Kelley, knew that it was a body corporate by the name and style of the

"Methodist Protestant Church of Tiffin, O." that was called together again. Yet he says it was the *"society."*

2. He knew that the notice was extended and limited to the "Male Members" of that church. Oliver Cowdery was present. ERGO he was a member of the church.

3. He knew that though Oliver Cowdery *was not* the secretary elect of that meeting that he wrote every word of the minutes except the name of the chairman and secretary. He even wrote the affixes "chairman" and "secretary."

How did he know it? He read the page; knew Cowdery's handwriting. He knew that Cowdery "inserted the conclusion" of the page, and he knew that he wrote the *whole page.* Why did he not say so?

He handles the third document still more recklessly. He writes:

January 18, 1844, the members of the society convened again, Rev. Thomas B. Cushman elected chairman and Oliver Cowdery secretary of the meeting. In this meeting the following named parties were elected trustees: John Souder, Joseph Walker, William Campbell and John Nye. The following resolutions were passed:

"Resolved, That the first meeting of the trustees of this society, elected by this meeting, be held in the office of O. Cowdery on Tuesday, the 23rd inst., at half past six o'clock, p.m.

"Resolved, That the proceedings of this meeting be signed by the chairman and secretary."

On motion adjourned the meeting without delay. Thomas B. Cushman, chairman; Oliver Cowdery, secretary. January 18, 1844.

Bishop Kelley then gravely draws the following conclusions:

This furnishes all the reference in the record to Oliver Cowdery. It will be seen from an examination of the facts that Oliver Cowdery acted as the attorney for these parties, hence the association of his name. It has been claimed that he was a trustee of the church, but the record does not so disclose, and had he been a trustee, that would not necessarily make him a member of the society, for neither the law of the church at the time nor the law of the land made it necessary for a party, in order to be a trustee of property, to be a member of the society.

This is the page we want photographed for a cut. It will convince every man who sees it, as it did Messrs. Yingling and Lang, that Oliver Cowdery *was a member* of the M. P. church at Tiffin, O.

A man who can even fancy that he sees a shadow of a fact in any of these records that indicates in the remotest degree, that Oliver Cowdery, the Mormon apostle, Second Elder in that church, holding the two priesthoods, the keys of Aaron and Melchisedek both, who believed, if he was still a Mormon, that the Methodists worshipped a false God, had no right to baptize and were bound, as the crow flies, for hades; that he was there simply as an attorney after Methodist money, and was elected and acted as secretary, is the man to send out to find the records that Cook and Peary left at the North Pole, or the grave of Moses, or an instance where Bishop Kelley ever fairly reported an interview or fairly represented a document.

I risk the statement, without the least fear of contradiction, that he never heard a man, woman or child at Tiffin, O., or anywhere else on this earth, say or claim that Oliver Cowdery was a "trustee" of the church at Tiffin, O. It is not likely that the great Mogul of Mormonism, an Elder, Bishop, Apostle and High Priest of the Mormon church would have accepted the position of "a trustee" of a small M. P. church property. Joseph Smith, Sidney Rigdon, Orson Pratt and others would have put the "Danites" on his track for such a prostitution of his position as that. Nor is it likely that a Methodist Protestant church, a church that battles "the bishop idea," would elect the next great Mormon to Joseph Smith a trustee of their property. It would be like putting a fox to guard a chicken coop and putting him on the inside.

(Concluded in January, 1910, issue.)

Reprinted from *The Sword of Laban,* Volume II, Number 6

We promised last month to conclude this series of articles in this paper. But such is the growing interest taken in them, and having "other proof" in hand, never before used, we will "make haste leisurely," knowing that "our friends the foe" will hear the statement with everything else but joy.

We now hand out

The Convincing Document:

Minutes of a meeting of the Male Members of the Methodist Protestant *Church* of Tiffin, Seneca County, Ohio, held pursuant to adjournment.

The meeting came to order by appointing Rev. Thomas Cushman Chairman, and *Oliver Cowdery Secretary.* On ascertaining and it appearing that more than two-thirds of the male *members* of said Society were present, it was on, motion,

Resolved, that we accept the Charter for the legal organization of said Society passed by the General Assembly of the State of Ohio January 19th, 1843, and that we become and now are organized under and in accordance with the provisions of the same.

On motion, it was further resolved that John Souder, Joseph Walker, William Campbell, John Shinefelt and Benjamin Nye be, and they are hereby appointed and chosen Trustees for said Society for and during the term of one year and until their successors are chosen and accept said office.

Resolved, That the annual meeting of the male members of this Society be held at this place one year from this date at half past 6 p.m. for the purpose of electing five Trustees for said society, unless previously called by a vote of two-thirds of the male members of this Society to be held at another time.

Resolved, That the Trustees appointed by this meeting be authorized to call a special meeting of this Society for the purpose of adopting such By-laws as may be necessary for the well being of the same.

Resolved, That the first meeting of the Trustees of this Society, elected by this meeting, be held at the office of O. Cowdery on Tuesday, the 23rd inst., at half past 6 o'clock p.m.

Resolved, That the proceedings of this meeting be signed by the Chairman and Secretary.

On motion the meeting adjourned without delay.

Thos. B. Cushman, Chairman.

Oliver Cowdery, Secretary.

Jan. 18, 1844.

Comments.

1. Kelley says: "The members of the Society convened again."

The record says: "The male members of the Methodist Protestant Church, Tiffin, O., met pursuant to adjournment."

2. Oliver Cowdery was there and was elected secretary and accepted and wrote and signed the minutes.

3. "As sure as the sun shines, grass grows and water flows," he was a member of that church.

4. The idea is absurd that a Mormon apostle, one who had the hands of John the Baptist placed upon his head and who was baptized by the Seer and Prophet of Mormonism, could be elected secretary by a M. P. Church board, or that he would accept if elected.

5. The only explanation is: *Cowdery has renounced Mormonism and embraced Methodism.* On no other ground can it be explained.

A photographic reproduction of this page ought to be scattered all over the earth. It is enough to convince even a "Digger Indian" that Oliver Cowdery joined the M. P. Church at Tiffin, O., and was an active and respected member of it.

Bishop Kelley, and those whom he serves, knows full well what that fact means. It sounds the doom of Mormonism. Hence his compromise with his conscience and his petty juggling of plainest facts.

Affirmative Proof.

I now present the positive and direct proof of my proposition. The first witness I introduce is Judge W. Lang, of Tiffin, O.

The Saints' Herald says:

Mr. Yingling also sent to Bishop Kelley a copy of what is contained in the history of Seneca Co., Ohio, on Oliver Cowdery, which is as follows, a transcript of which has been sent to us.

Then follows over a column of quoted matter. At the conclusion the Saints' Herald says:

We produce this extract because it was written by one who was intimately acquainted with Oliver Cowdery.

Neither Kelley nor the church historian were honest enough to tell the public that the writer was Judge W. Lang. He read law with Cowdery and was intimate with him from the time he moved to, and until he left, Tiffin. Judge Lang says in his article:

Cowdery entirely abandoned and broke away from all his connections with Mormonism.

I have two letters of Judge Lang's. I published one in full in Tract No. 9, entitled "Oliver Cowdery's Defence." He says in it:

In the second year of his (Cowdery's) residence here (Tiffin, O.,) he and the family attached themselves to the Methodist Protestant church, where they held fellowship to the time they left for Elkhorn, Wis.

This certainly ought to end the controversy. But I have more evidence and equally as good.

My next witness is Judge W. H. Gibson, of Tiffin, O. He was a personal friend of Cowdery. They traveled together, practiced law in the same courts, as well as lived in the same city.

I have two of his letters written in August, 1882. He says:

Oliver Cowdery was an able lawyer, a fine orator, a ready debater and led a blameless life while living in this city. *He united with the Methodist Protestant Church and was a consistent member.*

* * * * * * *

Members of his church inform me that in all his intercourse with the members, he never alluded to Mormonism.

Judge Lang was a student with Oliver Cowdery and is a most reliable gentleman.

In his letter of August 8, Judge Gibson says:

I have just conversed with a very old and esteemed citizen, G. J. Keen, who besides being a personal and political friend of Oliver Cowdery belonged to the same church.

There is nothing ambiguous about these statements. If we can find out what church Mr. Keen belonged to we can locate Cowdery's membership.

I have two letters of Mrs. Adeline M. Bernard (nee Fuller), "the girl who lived with the Cowderys."

In her letter of March 4, 1881, she was loth to give information along certain lines because, she says: "Mr. Cowdery adopted me as his own child."

In spite of this feeling she states some things that the public has a right to know. They will come out in good time, but just now it is not in order to divert attention from the main issue before us. In her letter of October 3, 1881, she says:

I know that Mr. Cowdery joined the Methodist Protestant Church. He joined the church in 1841, and you can write to Judge W. Lang, of Tiffin, O., and he will search the church records and send you transcript of his (Oliver Cowdery's) membership.

While the above proof *proves,* we have some still stronger for our next issue.

Reprinted from *The Sword of Laban,* Volume II, Number 7

Here's the promised "stronger proof," for it *proves the proof,* thus making certainty doubly sure.

Our readers have the records in full. Kelley's have them so mutilated that the writer, Oliver Cowdery, himself, could not recognize them.

In conclusion, I "clinch every nail" of this proof with extracts from an affidavit made by G. J. Keen, to whom Judge Gibson refers in complimentary terms and stated that he and Cowdery belonged to the same church. This affidavit is given in full in tract No. 9 of the anti-Mormon series. I quote only the points that bear directly upon our issue. He states:

Mr. Cowdery opened a law office in Tiffin, and soon effected a partnership with Joel W. Wilson.

In a few years Mr. Cowdery expressed a desire to associate himself with a Methodist Protestant church of this city.

Rev. John Souder and myself were appointed a committee to wait on Mr. Cowdery and confer with him respecting his connection with Mormonism and the Book of Mormon.

We accordingly waited on Mr. Cowdery at his residence in Tiffin, and there learned his connection, from him, and his full and final renunciation thereof.

We then inquired of him if he had any objection to making a public recantation.

He replied that he had objections; that, in the first place, it could do no good: that he had known several to do so and they always regretted it. And, in the second place, it would have a tendency to draw public attention, invite criticism and bring him into contempt.

"But," said he, "nevertheless, if the church require it I will submit to it, but I authorize and desire you and the church to publish and make known my recantation."

We did not demand it, but submitted his name to the church, and he was unanimously admitted a member thereof.

At that time he arose and addressed the audience present, admitted his error and implored forgiveness, and said he was sorry and ashamed of his connection with Mormonism.

He continued his membership while he resided in Tiffin, and became superintendent of the Sabbath school, and led an exemplary life while he resided with us.

I have lived in this city upwards of fifty-three years, was auditor of this county, was elected to that office in 1840.

I am now in my eighty-third year, and well remember the facts above related.

(Signed.)
                                                                G. J. Keen.

Sworn before me and subscribed in my presence, this 14th day of April, A. D. 1885.

                                                        Frank L. Emich,
                                                Notary Public in Seneca, O.

G. J. Keen, Esq., is one of our oldest citizens, is a respectable man, and is very highly esteemed.

(Signed.)
                                                        O. T. Lock, Postmaster.

This locks the argument and establishes the fact forever that Oliver Cowdery was a member, and a good member, of the Methodist Protestant Church at Tiffin, O.

Only Joseph Smith, the Prophet and Seer, could have hit Mormonism a deadlier blow by renouncing it and becoming an active and honored member of a Methodist church.

This act speaks louder against the "high-falutin' " claims of Mormonism about angels, gold plates, etc., than all his words do for it. It is a coffin nail for the ism, for Cowdery's testimony has done, and is doing more to build it up than any other man's, excepting possibly Joseph Smith's.

Aid me in putting this tract on "the wings of the wind" and sounding out the fact to all the earth that Oliver Cowdery renounced Mormonism and embraced Methodism.

The proposition is established and it sounds the knell of the ism.

ADDENDA.

The following correspondence is self-explaining and confirmatory. It proves the proof.

Grayson, Ky., 5-18, 1907.

Frank H. Lang, Tiffin, O.

Dear Sir:—I submit to you the original of a letter purporting to be from your father, Judge Wm. Lang. I published this letter in full in my anti-Mormon tract No. 9, entitled "Oliver Cowdery's Defence." You have a copy of the tract. I ask you three questions with a view of handing out your answer to the public.

"1. Is the letter correctly published in the tract?"

"2. Was the original written by your father?"

"3. Do you know that he was in a position to know that what he states about Oliver Cowdery joining the Methodist church at Tiffin, and living for years a consistent member, was a fact?"

Yours truly,
R. B. Neal.

Tiffin, O., May 30, 1907.

R. B. Neal, Grayson, Ky.

Esteemed Sir:—Pardon my delay in answering your letter. Sickness in the family the cause.

In answer to your question No. 1, I would say that father's letter is correctly published in your Tract No. 9.

No. 2. That the letter is unquestionably written by father. He wrote a peculiar hand, easy to read but hard to counterfeit. I recognized it at a glance.

No. 3. I know that my father was Oliver Cowdery's confidential friend. Father read law with him and was in touch with him in every phase of life, both public and private. And if father said that Cowdery joined the Methodist church you can rely upon it as being the truth. Any one knowing father would vouch for his veracity.

The church records here plainly show that he was a member of the Methodist church, and not only a member, but an officer of the church. The records will verify my father's statement.

Very truly yours,
Frank H. Lang.

We submit the foregoing to a careful consideration of Bishop Kelley and the historian of the "Reorganized Church." If they are among those "who wish to know the truth" and desire their readers also "to know the truth," they will read and publish these articles in "The Saints' Herald." If they refuse, our reading public will brand them as among those "who are seeking for the opposite of truth" and trying to deceive the public. (R. B. Neal, Pikeville, Ky.)

DATE DUE			
DEC 0 1 1980			
FEB 1 8 1982			
APR 2 3 1984			
MAY 1 1 1984			
APR 1 3 1986			
MAR 0 8 1991			
GAYLORD			PRINTED IN U.S.A.